The African
in Latin America

D1327077

BORZOI BOOKS ON LATIN AMERICA

General Editor

JOHN WOMACK, JR.

Harvard University

THE AFRICAN
IN LATIN AMERICA

Edited with an Introduction by

Ann M. Pescatello

ALFRED A. KNOPF   New York

THIS IS A BORZOI BOOK
PUBLISHED BY ALFRED A. KNOPF, INC.

Library of Congress Cataloging in Publication Data

Pescatello, Ann, comp.
  The African in Latin America.

  (Borzoi books on Latin America)
  Bibliography: p.
  1. Slavery in Latin America—Addresses, essays, lectures.
2. Negroes in Latin America—Addresses, essays, lectures. 3.
Slave-trade—Addresses, essays, lectures. I. Title.
HT1052.5.P47 1975   301.44′93′098   74-28588
  ISBN 0-394-47547-X
  ISBN 0-394-31674-6 pbk.

63642

In memoriam

Aos escravôs (To the slaves)

In praise

As mães negras e suas filhos (To black mothers

and their children)

ACKNOWLEDGMENTS

This book is an introduction to my multivolume, mono-graphic, comparative study of land and labor systems in the Iberian Empire.

I am grateful to Professor Lewis Hanke for suggesting, and Professor John Womack for encouraging a Borzoi publication on the African in Latin America. I am particularly appreciative of my students at Washington University, who, in seminars devoted to study of the black experience and slavery, helped me to refine the structure and contents of the book, offered acute suggestions and constructive criticism, and in other ways contributed to the volume's final make-up. I am indebted, too, to John Murrin, who, in our "Comparative Colonial Experience in the Americas" seminar, aided in the process of narrowing down the selections. Special thanks are also due to Charles Boxer, David Davidson, Richard Graham, Mary Karasch, Franklin Knight, James Lockhart, Stuart Schwartz, Stanley Stein, Frederick Bowser and Milton Vanger for their suggestions.

Jim Wilson made preliminary translations from certain selections—some of which do not appear here. Charlotte Peskind deserves special thanks for the secretarial services she provided. Bonnie C. Wade was of much help in gathering material and in offering editorial suggestions.

I am grateful to have been able to avail myself of the facilities and personnel of the libraries at Brown University, Boston University, Yale University, Harvard University, UCLA, Berkeley, and the Library of Congress, as well as archival, library, and museum collections in Latin America, Africa, Europe, and North America. I am further indebted to numerous authors and publishers who gave permission to translate and reprint their works.

Throughout it all Knopf editors Arthur Strimling and David Follmer have been bulwarks of aid and succor—to them my gratitude. Deborah Drier of Alfred A. Knopf was a thoughtful advisor and of enormous help in putting together the final version. I must add a special note of thanks again to John Womack, who as general editor of the Borzoi series, examined diligently each draft, always made valuable suggestions, and otherwise contributed his considerable talents to this final product. To all others who lent their help and support but who cannot be mentioned for lack of space, many thanks. And, of course, to Clem who helps, who understands, and who cares!

A. M. P.

CONTENTS

Contents

COLONIAL
LATIN AMERICA

Colonial boundaries
Modern national boundaries

ATLANTIC OCEAN

GULF OF MEXICO   Havana
CUBA
MEXICO *VICEROYALTY OF NEW SPAIN*
Guadalajara
Veracruz
Mexico
City   *CARIBBEAN SEA*

Cartagena   Valencia   Caracas
Porto Bello   Orinoco R.
PANAMA Panama   VENEZUELA
       City   GUIANA
VICEROYALTY OF NEW GRANADA   Bogotá
Separated from Viceroyalty of Peru in 1717, 1739   COLOMBIA

Quito   Belém
ECUADOR   PARÁ
                        Amazon R.   MARANHÃO

                    SOUTH AMERICA
                                BRAZIL   Recife
                                               PERNAMBUCO
VICEROYALTY OF PERU   MATO   ALAGOAS
                        GROSSO   Salvador
              PERU   Cuzco   BAHIA
         Lima   BOLIVIA
                     (ALTO PERÚ)   Santa Cruz   Goiás
         Arequipa   La Paz   de la Sierra
                     Sucre   MINAS
                     Potosí (Chuquisaca)   GERAIS
PACIFIC OCEAN   RIO DE JANEIRO
                               São Paulo
                        PARAGUAY Santos   Rio de Janeiro
                        EL GRAN   SÃO PAULO São Sebastião
                        CHACO Asunción
AUDIENCIA OF CHILE   PARANÁ
Retained by Viceroyalty of Peru, 1776 RIO GRANDE
                        ARGENTINA   DE SUL Porto Alegre
                        Córdoba
         Valparaíso   URUGUAY
         Santiago   Mendoza   (BANDA ORIENTAL)
                    Rosario   Montevideo
         Concepción Buenos Aires Río de
                                   la Plata
                    VICEROYALTY OF LA PLATA
                    Separated from Viceroyalty of Peru, 1776

0   500   1000
       Miles

Adapted from Leslie Bethell, *The Abolition of the Brazilian Slave
Trade* (Cambridge: Cambridge University Press, 1970), pp. xiv, xv;
Charles Gibson, *Spain in America* (New York: Harper Torchbooks,
1966), p. 96; Magnus Mörner, *Race Mixture in the History of Latin
America* (Boston: Little, Brown, 1967), frontispiece.

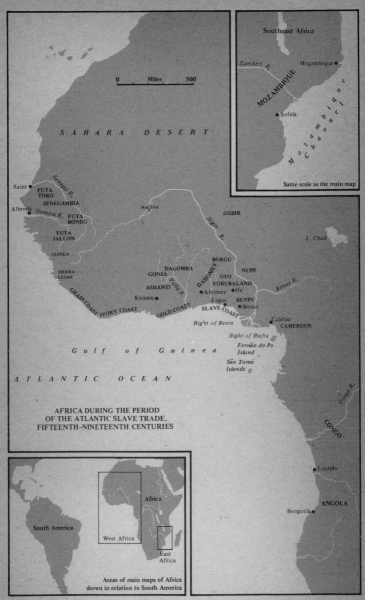

AFRICA DURING THE PERIOD
OF THE ATLANTIC SLAVE TRADE,
FIFTEENTH–NINETEENTH CENTURIES

Adapted from Charles R. Boxer, *Four Centuries of Portuguese Expansion: 1415–1825* (Los Angeles and Berkeley: University of California Press, 1969), end map; Robert I. Rotberg, *A Political History of Tropical Africa* (New York: Harcourt, Brace & World, 1965), pp. 79, 98, 107, 137, and 159.

The African
in Latin America

INTRODUCTION

The entrance of Africans into the Americas begins one
of the most vital yet depressing chapters in the history of
three continents. The story of black men and women in
an alien environment is one of both human endurance
and the survival of cultures. The African brought with
him to Latin America a rich heritage of art and religion,
advanced agricultural methods, technology, and sophisti-
cated political and social organizations.[1] With this, however, came another tradition, one in which servitude was
the expedient device for obtaining manpower in labor-
deficient economies.

Slavery is a memory that most peoples of African ancestry in America hold in common; prejudice and discrimination are the injuries that the descendants of slaves
have endured. The purpose of *The African in Latin
America* is to enable the reader to gain a fuller understanding of the experience of Africans in the New World
and of the contributions they have made to Latin American culture. The volume concludes with the abolition of
slavery in Brazil in 1888, with the formal end in Latin
America of a variegated system of labor exploitation. To
have included the post-1888 experience of Afro-Latinos
would have taxed the conceptual and structural framework of the book.

[1] For a detailed discussion of early relations between European,
Middle-Eastern, and African groups, see Robert Rotberg, *A Political
History of Tropical Africa* (New York: Harcourt, Brace & World,
1965), pp. 13–94.

Although this volume does not attempt explicit comparisons of slavery and race relations in the Americas, the selections address major issues that have emerged in recent literature and can serve as guidelines for comparative studies. Among the topics treated are legal and religious theories supporting slavery, the maintenance of the slave system, patterns of labor, the rearing of slave children, and the position of women in a slave society. Also discussed are slave "revolts," the treatment of runaways, manumission, and the position of the free colored in Latin American society.

The prevailing theory on slavery has been that conditions of slavery and race relations in the New World were not uniform and that variations were due primarily to the laws, institutions, and values brought here by European colonizers. In Chapter I Frank Tannenbaum argues that thesis, while David Davis offers a counter-thesis based on his analysis of American economies, racial attitudes, and social structures.

In Chapter II the numbers, proveniences, destination, and carriage of Africans to the New World are elaborated in Philip Curtin's selection on the Atlantic trade. In addition, a collection of narratives by Europeans, Americans, and Africans details the actual buying and selling of human cargo for slavery.

Chapters III, IV, V, and VI are addressed to two major analytical categories: treatment of the black and mulatto, and manumission. In Chapters III and IV the conditions of life among blacks and mulattoes, slaves and freedmen are discussed and compared. Chapters V and VI describe the pathways to freedom: those taken violently by the black man, and those given legally by the white man.

An African Heritage

Early African history is the record of small groups of state-forming conquerors merging with more numerous, conquered populations. With the formation of states from the eleventh century on, slavery and slave trading had developed to meet the demands of an expanding foreign trade. A "slave economy" was established by at least the fourteenth century in western and central Sudan, and by the fifteenth century it had spread to the Senegal and Lower Guinea coasts. Once Europeans entered the trading arena, West African rulers and merchants "reacted to the demand with economic reasoning and used it to strengthen streams of economic and political development that were already current before the Atlantic slave trade began."[2]

The area from Senegal to Sierra Leone was the dominant slave-exporting region during the fifteenth century. An area of small states, its population was divided into groups with differing degrees of power and wealth, a significant fact in light of increasing warfare there and the consequent despoilation of the masses.[3] In the sixteenth century Europeans acquired labor supplies from the Senegambia-Guinea-Bissau-Sierra Leone areas and from regions south of the mouth of the Congo River. The Wolof Empire, which had dominated the region between Senegal and Gambia, eventually disintegrated into several separate kingdoms. This resulted in protracted warfare, which provided an abundance of prisoners of war for sale as slaves.[4]

In the areas around the Congo, African political feuds and penetration by the Portuguese also influenced the

[2] J. D. Fage, "Slavery and the Slave Trade in the Context of West African History," *Journal of African History*, 10 (1969), 393–404. Fage also concludes that whereas in East and Central Africa the slave trade could be extremely destructive to society, in West Africa it was part of a sustained process of development.

[3] Basil Davidson, *A History of West Africa* (New York: Anchor Books, 1966), pp. 62–63.

[4] D. P. Gamble, *The Wolof of Senegambia* (London: International African Institute, 1957), p. 173. The Wolof, while prominent in sixteenth-century Latin America, were never again numerous in the trade.

course of slavery.[5] Under Portuguese influence São Tomé
became the slave entrepôt for the entire Lower Guinea
coast and also for the Congo, where struggles between
African chiefs for political succession and economic control had provided another supply of prisoners of war.[6]
By the last quarter of the sixteenth century, the "kingdom of Kongo" was little more than a giant slave warehouse. Mulatto offspring of Africans and Portuguese
served as agents in its slave trade, establishing a pattern
that endured until the 1640s. During this period the
Portuguese province of Angola also increased in importance as a source of human labor. The first three centuries of Angolan history (ca. 1550–1850) were, in fact,
a patchwork of small wars, expeditions, and commerce
in human beings.[7]

Coeval with increasing European involvement in
African commercial activities were the massive political,
technological, and social changes occurring within West
Africa, all of which had a profound impact on slavery
in America. By the early seventeenth century West Africa
was an organization of highly developed states and empires.[8] Professional armies guarded its lucrative trade
routes, causing frequent and destructive wars and thus
swelling markets with prisoners of war. Troubles with
political and commercial alliances along long-distance

[5] For an excellent though slightly dated survey of Portuguese
involvement in Africa, see James Duffy, *Portuguese Africa* (Cambridge, Mass.: Harvard University Press, 1961). See also Duffy,
Portugal in Africa (Baltimore: Penguin Books, 1963); and Ronald
Chilcote, *Portuguese Africa* (Englewood Cliffs, N.J.: Prentice-Hall,
1967).

[6] L. da Paivo Manso, *História do Congo: Documentos* (Lisbon:
n.p., 1877), p. 54.

[7] Jan Vansina, *Kingdoms of the Savanna* (Madison: University of
Wisconsin Press, 1968), pp. 53, 138–139. This is an excellent study
based on archeology, linguistics, and the oral tradition in Central
Africa before European occupation. For a full-scale discussion of the
Congolese and Angolan milieus, see *passim*.

[8] Davidson, *A History of West Africa*, pp. 150–161, 162–189
passim.

trade routes and in the western Sudan also affected trade, as did new commercial links forged between West African and European polities. With the arrival of European ships, Africans, particularly along the Guinea coast, could now purchase commodities from traders directly at shore. The source of supply for goods was thereby shifted from North Africa to West Africa, eliminating costly middlemen along the land routes.

This new local economic partnership changed throughout the seventeenth century from one of transactions in raw materials and manufactures to overseas trade in prisoners of war. From the 1450s until the 1650s African slaves either "were persons who had lost their civic rights, in the state that sold them, by sentence of the courts, or they were citizens of another state who had lost their rights through capture in war,"[9] a situation similar to that of medieval Europe. The shift to reliance on slaves as the chief commodity for trade occurred partly because of the distintegration of old empires in Africa and partly because European-African commercial opportunities increased with the extension southward to the coast of old trade routes.

The South Atlantic System

The Atlantic slave trade, already underway, changed and acquired momentum during the second quarter of the seventeenth century. Old patterns of servitude and traditional sources of supply persisted in Africa, on the one hand because of the changes that had occurred in Afro-European relations, on the other because plantation systems had already taken root in America. European colonists succeeded in obtaining millions of African

[9] Basil Davidson, "Slaves or Captives? Some Notes on Fantasy and Fact," in *Key Issues in the Afro-American Experience,* vol. 1, eds. Nathan I. Huggins, Martin Kilson, and Daniel M. Fox (New York: Harcourt Brace Jovanovich, 1971), pp. 54–73.

workers because "in the master-servant organization which operated in many states and societies . . . Western African chiefs and kings regularly turned war captives and certain classes of law breakers into slaves."[10] This servitude is best characterized as one in which certain peoples had fewer rights and more obligations relative to the general populace.

By the late seventeenth century expanding trade had engendered new coastal markets and power centers, controlled by Africans acting as middlemen between European sea merchants and African inland merchants. Prosperous city-states developed in the Niger Delta and along the Dahomey coast, while in the Guinea-Gold Coast-Senegal-Gambia area commerce underwent tremendous expansion. The eighteenth century also witnessed the proliferation of slaving along the western coast of Senegambia to Angola, and from central Africa around the Cape of Good Hope to Mozambique.[11] The acquisition of firearms, the reinforcement of slavery as an institution in Africa itself, European encouragement of hostilities between African peoples, and the development of slave-trading organizations among Africans and Europeans, all assured the continued growth of slavery.[12] Some states, such as Ashanti and Dahomey, emerged solely in response to the demand for slaves. These states depended on European guns to maintain armies for con-

[10] Davidson, *A History of West Africa*, p. 215.

[11] Philip D. Curtin, *The Atlantic Slave Trade: A Census* (Madison: University of Wisconsin Press, 1969), pp. 127–128, 130. See also Edward A. Alpers, "Trade, State and Society Among the Yao in the Nineteenth Century," *Journal of African History*, 10 (1969), 409.

[12] Karl Polanyi, *Dahomey and the Slave Trade* (Seattle: University of Washington Press, 1968), pp. 22, 117; and Colin Newbury, *The Western Slave Coast and Its Rulers* (Oxford: Oxford University Press, 1961), pp. 17–29 *passim*. Also see G. I. Jones, *The Trading States of the Oil Rivers* (London: Oxford University Press, 1963); and M. H. Kingsley, *West African Studies* (London: Macmillan and Co., 1899), p. 535.

tinuous warfare and slave raiding.[13] This important chapter in African history is one of almost continuous warfare, of the growth of complex states that depended on war and indigenous socioreligious institutions (such as the Ibo oracle) to support their slave-based economy.[14]

The South Atlantic system, established by the beginning of the seventeenth century, was based on a plantation system of export agriculture. It's primary commercial crop was sugar. This required massive supplies of labor that the Africans were called upon to provide.[15] Slave-trading operations had three phases: the slave was captured in Africa, he or she was transported to an African coastal trading point and attractively displayed to European buyers, and then he or she was shipped to America. The growth of plantation slavery in the Americas had coincided with a revolution in European maritime technology, which gave Europe a naval hegemony almost everywhere in the world. With this also came a sharp change in transport costs: ships could carry more cargo, more swiftly and over longer distances, for less money.[16]

[13] A Norman Klein, "West African Unfree Labor Before and After the Rise of the Atlantic Slave Trade," in *Slavery in the New World,* eds. Eugene D. Genovese and Laura Foner (Englewood Cliffs, N.J.: Prentice-Hall, 1970), pp. 87–93. Also see J. D. Fage, *Introduction to the History of West Africa* (Cambridge: Cambridge University Press, 1962), p. 97.

[14] Curtin, *The Atlantic Slave Trade,* p. 240. Other pertinent sources include S. J. Ottenberg, "Ibo Oracles and Inter-Group Relations," *Southwestern Journal of Anthropology,* 14 (Autumn 1958), 295–314; K. Onwuka Dike, *Trade and Politics in the Niger Delta, 1830–1885* (Oxford: Oxford University Press, 1956); Michael Crowder, *A Short History of Nigeria* (New York: Praeger, 1966), pp. 59, 87, 110; Pierre Verger, *Les Afro-Américains* (Dakar: IFAN, 1952), pp. 11–104; and J. F. de Almeida Prado, "Les Relations de Bahia (Brésil) avec le Dahomey," *Revue d'Histoire des Colonies,* 41 (1954), 167–226. For a full discussion of changing socioeconomic patterns along the slave coast, see Newbury, *The Western Slave Coast and Its Rulers.*

[15] Philip D. Curtin, "Epidemiology and the Slave Trade," *Political Science Quarterly,* 83 (June 1968), 190–216.

[16] See Carlo M. Cipolla, *Guns, Sails, and Empires: Technological Innovation and the Early Phases of European Expansion, 1400–1700* (New York: Pantheon, 1966). See also J. H. Parry, *The Age of Reconnaissance* (London: Weidenfeld and Nicolson, 1963).

American planters generally preferred male workers to female; the feeling was that the economic value of women slaves was greatly reduced by the eventuality of motherhood. Curtin states that slavers normally imported two men for each woman. Since birth rates depend directly on the number of women of child-bearing age in a population, this meant an automatic reduction of 30 percent in potential birth rate among slaves. Also, since planters regarded female slaves essentially as labor units, they did not encourage their female slaves to bear children, and the women themselves used abortive and contraceptive techniques. The key, then, to the continuation of the Atlantic slave trade was the failure on the part of American slaveowners to foster a self-sustaining slave population.[17]

The Atlantic slave trade represented the greatest involuntary migration in Western history. Not only was it of demographic importance to Africa and the Americas, but it also was at the core of an economic system in which Africa supplied the labor, Europe the entrepreneurial expertise, North America the food and transport, and South America the precious metals and other raw materials.

The African's Latin America

From the beginning of Iberian colonization, Africans were present in various capacities in the viceroyalties of Peru, New Spain, and especially Brazil. They made up part of the military establishment; they were miners, domestics, farmers, shepherds, cowboys, and urban workers, as well as plantation field hands. Naturally, their life styles differed from situation to situation.

But the most common experience for the African in

---

[17] Philip D. Curtin, "The Slave Trade and the Atlantic Basin: Intercontinental Perspectives," in *Key Issues in the Afro-American Experience*, vol. 1, eds. Huggins, Kilson, and Fox, pp. 74–95.

Latin America was slavery. Slavery in the broadest sense indicated a relationship in which one human being held another human being in bondage. Most cultures had similar concepts and laws regarding slaves and the institution of slavery. In fact, it has been theorized that "slavery is more than solely a means of controlling the labor of others. It was one of man's most important institutions and it has been part of the institutional system of myriad societies."[18] It was not until the advent of modern technology that practices markedly changed.

Differences in systems of slavery reflected not only economic developments and the emergent capitalism of American nations, but also the effectiveness of the mother country's control over her colonies.[19] One of the distinguishing features of slavery in the New World is that it was imposed by foreign powers. The plantation system that provided Europe with so much wealth relied on an alien and immobile labor supply. The linkage of American slavery to the growth of capitalism and to world market systems generated in the American colonies a culture fundamentally different from that of Europe and a slave environment different from any other in history.

There were many means by which slaves did resist their bondage. Escapes, resistance movements, rebellions, and insurrections were relatively common. Legally, the slave could gain freedom through *coartación* or manumission.

Not all scholars feel that slavery is totally responsible for present-day racial problems in Latin America. For example, Magnus Mörner has suggested that answers to such problems are more likely to be found in conditions that developed after abolition.[20] Carl Degler has theorized that recognition and acceptance of the mulatto as a

---

[18] Sidney Mintz, "Review of Stanley Elkins' *Slavery*," *American Anthropologist* 63 (June 1961), 579.

[19] *Ibid.*, pp. 579–587 *passim*.

[20] Magnus Mörner, "The History of Race Relations in Latin America: Some Comments on the State of Research," *Latin American Research Review*, 1 (Summer 1966), 17–44.

member of a special intermediary racial stratum has permitted the assimilation, acceptance, and rise of members of the black race into Brazilian society and that the contrasting failure to recognize the mulatto in the United States is the reason for major differences in race relations in those two nations.[21]

Whatever the cast of the African's experience, however, his culture has benefited all non-Africans in a myriad of ways, and his history is an integral part of the history of the Americas. This is part of his story.

[21] Carl Degler, *Neither Black Nor White: Slavery and Race Relations in Brazil and the United States* (New York: Macmillan, 1971).

I

Africans and Iberians: Theories of Slavery and Race Relations

A RENAISSANCE COMMENTARY

"One of the marvelous things that God used in the composition of man, is color: which undoubtedly cannot be considered without great admiration in beholding one to be white and another black, being utterly contrary colors." —*Francisco López de Gómara.**

There are two major schools of thought regarding the slave, slavery, and race relations in Latin America. The first is almost exclusively concerned with tradition and cultural continuity, while the second dwells on the material foundations of, and especially class relations in, particular slave societies. The earlier theory was expostulated by Frank Tannenbaum in *Slave and Citizen*, a work that initiated the comparative study of American slavery. Tannenbaum's work has greatly influenced historical thinking on slavery in colonial Latin America. A main tenet of his thesis is that Africans under the Iberian rule benefited from an ancient body of law, *Las Siete Partidas*, which held that a slave was, nevertheless, a human being with legal and moral rights. Catholic doctrine asserted that master and slave were equal in God's sight, that all human beings were brothers in Christ. Tannenbaum wove these laws and doctrines of Catholicism into a strong argument that slavery in the Catholic-dominated colonies of

---

*Translated from *La Crónica de la Nueva Espana.*

South America was much less oppressive than it was in the Protestant-dominated colonies of North America. Its harshness, according to Tannenbaum, was further alleviated by easier means of manumission. The argument was adopted by Stanley Elkins in *Slavery*, a classic analysis of the slave system in the United States.

For two decades the Tannenbaum-Elkins thesis remained the premier historiographic argument regarding Afro-American slavery. Within the last decade, however, the Tannenbaum thesis has been challenged by a more materialistic theory that holds that although a society may idealize behavior in its law, baser human passions will drive a wedge between theory and reality. In other words, greed and prejudice cannot be obliterated through legislation.

The outlines of this argument were sketched by Eric Williams in *Capitalism and Slavery*, but lay dormant until the 1960s when several scholars proceeded to analyze slavery in terms of its economics: capital investment, rates of profit, and, in general, the effects of these factors on treatment of Africans.[1] Historians, sociologists, and anthropologists such as Marvin Harris, Magnus Mörner, Eugene Genovese, Sidney Mintz, Arnold Sio, and David Brion Davis have continued to challenge the position that Latin Americans were more humane to their slaves than were Anglo-Americans.[2] They, too, suggest that scholars will better find the answers they seek regarding race relations by investigating the economic and social underpinnings of slave societies.

The Tannenbaum thesis and an opposing argument are presented in the following selections.

[1] Eric Williams, *Capitalism and Slavery* (Chapel Hill: University of North Carolina Press, 1944).

[2] See Marvin Harris, *Patterns of Race in the Americas* (New York: Walker and Co., 1964), still the only study that provides a total alternative to the Tannenbaum thesis. Other works of importance include: Magnus Mörner, *Race Mixture in the History of Latin America* (Boston: Little, Brown, 1967); Eugene Genovese, *The Political Economy of Slavery* (New York: Vintage Books, 1965); Sidney Mintz, "Review of Stanley M. Elkins' *Slavery*," *American Anthropologist*, 43 (June 1961), 579–587; Arnold A. Sio, "Interpretations of Slavery: The Slave Status in the Americas," *Comparative Studies in Society and History*, 7 (1965), 289–308.

1

FRANK TANNENBAUM

SLAVE OR CITIZEN:
A PROBLEM OF SEMANTICS?

*The late Frank Tannenbaum was Professor of Latin
American History at Columbia University.[1] A spe-
cialist in problems of social history, he wrote ex-
tensively on labor, prison reforms, and race relations.
By far the most influential of all his works was the
slim volume that compared the positions of black
men in the United States and Latin America. "Man
as a moral being proved the most important influence
both in the treatment of the slave and in the final
abolition of slavery," stated Tannenbaum in* Slave
and Citizen. *In the following selection from that
famous work, he explains why he believes Latin
American slavery to be more benign than its Anglo-
Saxon counterpart.*

The Negro slave arriving in the Iberian Peninsula in
the middle of the fifteenth century found a propitious en-

From *Slave and Citizen*, by Frank Tannenbaum, pp. 43–56, 62–63,
88–89 *passim.* Copyright 1946 by Alfred A. Knopf, Inc. Reprinted
by permission of the publisher.

[1] For a discussion of Tannenbaum's life and work, see Stanley R.
Ross, "Frank Tannenbaum (1893–1969)," *Hispanic American Historical Review*, 50 (May 1970), 345–348.

vironment. The setting, legal as well as moral, that made this easy transition possible was due to the fact that the people of the Iberian Peninsula were not strangers to slavery. . . . At the end of the fifteenth century there were numerous slaves in Portugal and Spain, and especially in Andalusia, among them not only Negroes, but Moors, Jews, and apparently Spaniards as well. . . . By the middle of the sixteenth century Algarves was almost entirely populated by Negroes, and they outnumbered the whites in Lisbon. . . . But the mere survival of slavery in itself is perhaps less important than the persistence of a long tradition of slave law that had come down through the Justinian Code. The great codification of Spanish traditional law, which in itself summarizes the Mediterranean legal *mores* of many centuries, was elaborated by Alfonso the Wise between the years 1263 and 1265. In this code there is inherent belief in the equality of men under the law of nature, and slavery therefore is something against both nature and reason. But the doctrine of the equality of human nature had long before been asserted by Cicero. According to him, there is "no resemblance in nature so great as that between man and man, there is no equality so complete." Reason is common to all men, and all are equal in their capacity for learning. Under guidance, every race of men is capable of attaining virtue. This doctrine of the equality of man is applied to the idea of slavery by Seneca. . . . "A slave can be just, brave, magnanimous." Slavery is the result of misfortune, and hateful to all men. But, after all, slavery affects only the body, which may belong to the master; the mind "cannot be given into slavery." The soul of the slave remains free.

. . . These theories of the equality of man were in the background when the New Testament and the Christian fathers came upon the scene and proclaimed that all men are equal in the sight of God. The conception of the identity of human nature over all the world is like that in Cicero and Seneca. And when St. Paul touches upon the subject of slavery, it is to the effect that in the sight of God "there is neither bond nor free." . . . These underlying doctrines become part of the theory of the later church fathers, and take the form of saying that God made not slaves and free men, but all men free. . . .

This belief that equality among men is natural and reasonable is, therefore, both pagan and Christian, and stems from the Stoics and from the Christian fathers. The conception that man is free and equal, especially equal in the sight of God, made slavery as such a mundane and somewhat immaterial matter. The master had, in fact, no greater moral status than the slave, and spiritually the slave might be a better man than his master. *Las Siete Partidas* was framed within this Christian doctrine, and the slave had a body of law, protective of him as a human being, which was already there when the Negro arrived and had been elaborated long before he came upon the scene. And when he did come, the Spaniard may not have known him as a Negro, but the Spanish law and *mores* knew him as a slave and made him the beneficiary of the ancient legal heritage. This law provided, among other matters, for the following:

The slave might marry a free person if the slave status was known to the other party. Slaves could marry against the will of their master if they continued serving him as before. Once married, they could not be sold apart, except under conditions permitting them to live as man and wife. If the slave married a free person with the knowledge of his master, and the master did not announce the fact of the existing slave status, then the slave by that mere fact became free. If married slaves owned by separate masters could not live together because of distance, the church should persuade one or the other to sell his slave. If neither of the masters could be persuaded, the church was to buy one of them so that the married slaves could live together. The children followed the status of their mother, and the child of a free mother remained free even if she later became a slave. In spite of his full powers over his slave, the master might neither kill nor injure him unless authorized by the judge, nor abuse him against reason or nature, nor starve him to death. But if the master did any of these things, the slave could complain to the judge, and if the complaint were verified, the judge must sell him, giving the price to the owner, and the slave might never be returned to the original master. Any Jewish or Moorish slave became free upon turning Christian, and even if the master himself later became a Christian, he recovered no rights over his former slave.

Las Siete Partidas goes into considerable detail in defining the conditions under which manumission could occur. A master might manumit his slave in the church or outside of it; before a judge or other person, by testament or by letter; but he must do this by himself, in person. If one of the owners of a slave wished to free him, then the other must accept a just price fixed by the local judge. A slave became free against his master's will by denouncing a forced rape against a virgin, by denouncing a maker of false money, by discovering disloyalty against the King, by denouncing the murderer of his master. The slave could become free if he became a cleric with the consent of his master, or in certain cases without his consent, providing another slave in his place. And if the former slave became a bishop, he had to put up two slaves, each valued at the price that he himself was worth, while still a slave. A Christian slave living among the Moors might return to live among the Christians as a free man.

The slave could appeal to the courts

1. if he had been freed by will and testament, and the document maliciously hidden; under these circumstances he could appeal against anyone holding him;

2. if the slave had money from another and entrusted it to someone for the purpose of being bought from his master and given his liberty, and if then this person refused to carry out the trust, by refusing either to buy him or to free him if he had bought him; and

3. if he had been bought with the understanding that he would be freed on the receipt of the purchase price from the slave, and refused either to accept the money or to release him after accepting it. He could appeal to the courts for defense of the property of his master in his master's absence, and the King's slaves could appeal to the courts in defense of the King's property, or of their own persons—a special privilege permitted the King's slaves in honor of their master.

. . . A man considering himself free, but demanded for a slave, might have a representative to defend him; a man held a slave, but claiming to be free, might argue his own case, but not have a representative, and he must be permitted to argue and reason his case; the slave's relatives might plead for him, and even a stranger could do so, for "all the laws of the world aid toward freedom." Slaves could be witnesses, even against their masters, in accusations for treason against the King; in cases of murder of either master or mistress by either spouse; or in cases against the mistress for adultery; when one of the two owners of a slave was accused of killing the other; or in case of suspicion that the prospective heirs had killed the master of another slave. A slave who became the heir of his master, in part or in totality, automatically became free. If a father appointed a slave as the guardian of his children, the slave by that fact became free; and if he was the slave of more than one person and became an heir of one of his masters, the other must accept a price in reason for that part of the slave which belonged to him. He who killed his slave intentionally must suffer the penalty for homicide, and if the slave died as a result of punishment without intention to kill, then the master must suffer five years' exile.

Spanish law, custom, and tradition were transferred to America and came to govern the position of the Negro slave. It is interesting to note that a large body of new law was developed for the treatment of the Indians in America, whereas the Negro's position was covered by isolated *cedulas* dealing with special problems. It was not until 1789 that a formal code dealing with the Negro slave was promulgated. But this new code, as recognized by the preamble itself, is merely a summary of the ancient and traditional law. . . .

This body of law, containing the legal tradition of the Spanish people and also influenced by the Catholic doctrine of the equality of all men in the sight of God, was biased in favor of freedom and opened the gates to manumission when slavery was transferred to the New World. The law in Spanish and Portuguese America facilitated manumission, the tax-gatherer did not oppose it, and the church ranked it among the works singularly agreeable to God. A hundred social devices narrowed the gap between bondage and liberty, encouraged the master to release his slave, and the bondsman to achieve freedom on his own account. . . . [S]lavery under both law and custom had . . . become a contractual arrangement between the master and his bondsman . . . a mere matter of an available sum of money for redemption . . . a matter of financial competence on the part of the slave, and by that fact lost a great part of the degrading imputation that attached to slavery where it was looked upon as evidence of moral or biological inferiority. Slavery could be wiped out by a fixed purchase price, and therefore the taint of slavery proved neither very deep nor indelible. . . .

In addition to making freedom something obtainable for money, which the slave had the right to acquire and possess, the state made manumission possible for a number of other reasons. . . . These many provisions favoring manumission were strongly influenced by the church. Without interfering with the institution of slavery where the domestic law accepted it, the church early condemned the slave trade and prohibited Catholics from taking part in it. The prohibition was not effective, though it in some measure may have influenced the Spaniards to a rather limited participation in the trade as such. The grounds of the condemnation were that innocent and free persons were illegally and by force captured and sold into slavery, that rapine, cruelty, and war were stimulated in the search for human beings to be sold at a profit. . . .

. . . But the church did not interfere with the customary institution where it derived from known practices   a given community, such as born slaves, slaves taker just war, or those who had sold themselves or had   d condemned by a legitimate court.

The presumption against the slave trade was that it forced people into slavery outside the law and against their will. More important in the long run than the condemnation of the slave trade proved the church's insistence that slave and master were equal in the sight of God. Whatever the formal relations between slave and master, they must both recognize their relationship to each other as moral human beings and as brothers in Christ. The master had an obligation to protect the spiritual integrity of the slave, to teach him the Christian religion, to help him achieve the privileges of the sacraments, to guide him into living a good life, and to protect him from mortal sin. The slave had a right to become a Christian, to be baptized, and to be considered a member of the Christian community. Baptism was considered his entrance into the community, and until he was sufficiently instructed to be able to receive it, he was looked upon as out of the community and as something less than human. . . . Under the influence of the law and religion, the social milieu in the Spanish and Portuguese colonies made easy room for the Negroes passing from slavery to freedom. The older

Mediterranean tradition of the defense of the slave, combined with the effect of Latin-American experience, had prepared an environment into which the Negro freed from slavery could fit without visible handicap. Slavery itself carried no taint. It was a misfortune that had befallen a human being, and was in itself sufficiently oppressive. The law and religion both frowned upon any attempts to convert this into a means of further oppression.

2

DAVID BRION DAVIS

SLAVERY: THE CONTINUING CONTRADICTION

Critical of the juridical thesis, David Davis delineates numerous flaws in Tannenbaum's argument. Davis points out that throughout the Americas the institution of slavery and the treatment of slaves was much the same. He suggests that differences in the present status of blacks in North and South America are probably a result of earlier attitudes toward racial intermingling and laws regarding manumission.

David Brion Davis is Professor of History at Yale University and the author of several books and articles on United States history and traditions of thought in Western culture.

There would seem to be some basis for questioning two assumptions which have been widely accepted by modern historians.

The first is that Negro slavery in the British colonies and Southern United States was of a nearly uniform

Reprinted from David Brion Davis: *The Problem of Slavery in Western Culture,* pp. 224–225, 224n–225n, 227–229, 234–237, 241, 243, 262–264, 273, 282, 284–287 *passim.* Copyright © 1966 by Cornell University. Used by permission of Cornell University Press.

severity, the slave being legally deprived of all rights of person, property, and family, and subjected to the will of his owner and the police power of the state, which barred his way to education, free movement, or emancipation. The second assumption is that the French, and especially the Spanish and Portuguese, were far more liberal in their treatment of slaves, whom they considered as human beings who had merely lost a portion of their external freedom. Untainted by racial prejudice and free from the pressures of a fluid, capitalistic economy, these easygoing colonists are supposed to have protected the human rights of the slave and to have facilitated his manumission. Some historians have simply held that slavery in North America was much harsher than that in Latin America, but Stanley M. Elkins has argued more persuasively that the great contrast was not in the bondsman's physical well-being but in the recognition of his basic humanity. As a methodological device, this distinction has obvious merit, since a master might look upon his slaves as subhuman animals and still provide them with comfortable maintenance. On the other hand, it would be unrealistic to draw too sharp a line between moral status and physical treatment. It is difficult to see how a society could have much respect for the value of slaves as human personalities if it sanctioned their torture and mutilation, the selling of their small children, the unmitigated exploitation of their labor, and the drastic shortening of their lives through overwork and inadequate nourishment. While a few isolated instances of sadistic cruelty would reveal little about the legal or moral status of slaves, we should not exclude physical treatment when it is part of a pattern of systematic oppression which is fully sanctioned by the laws and customs of a society. We shall find, however, that there is other evidence than physical treatment for challenging the assumption that Latin Americans were more sensitive than Anglo-Americans to the essential humanity of their slaves. . . .

. . . My aim is simply to show that the importance of

. . . national and cultural differences has been exaggerated, and that all American slave-holding colonies shared certain central assumptions and problems. I do not believe that the modern historian can escape what Elkins terms the moral "coercions" of the great nineteenth-century controversies by portraying both American slavery and anti-slavery as the pathological results of "the dynamics of unopposed capitalism." It should be noted that Elkins borrowed much of his conceptual framework from Frank Tannenbaum . . . Though Tannenbaum was one of the first historians to emphasize the importance of Negro slavery in the overall development of the Americas, it seems to me that his comparison of Latin and Anglo-

of Latin America, refused to recognize the slave as a moral personality. But this is an error, . . . Second, he ignores the fact that the "classical" view of slavery, as embodied in Latin culture, drew as much from Plato and Aristotle as from Cicero and Seneca. Nineteenth-century Brazilian reformers, such as José Bonifácio, found it necessary to counter their opponents' use of classical authorities by arguing that Greeks and Romans had been ignorant of divine religion, and that, in any event, slavery in antiquity had not been so severe as that in Brazil, where racial and cultural differences deprived the bondsman of opportunities for equality. . . . As in Roman and North American law, the slave in Latin America was conceived at once as a chattel or instrument, and as a man with a soul. Third, Tannenbaum seems to think of Negro slavery in Latin America as a relatively unchanging institution, and assumes that certain humane laws of the late eighteenth and nineteenth centuries were typical of bondage in all Latin America throughout its long history. Even more questionable is his assumption that the admirable laws of European governments were obeyed by colonial slave-holders. . . .

. . . Any comparison must consider Negro slavery as a

system of forced labor, of social organization, and of class and racial discipline. . . .

There is little reason to doubt that slavery in Latin America, compared with that in North America, was less subject to the pressures of competitive capitalism and was closer to a system of patriarchal rights and semifeudalistic services. But after granting this, we must recognize the inadequacy of thinking in terms of idealized models of patriarchal and capitalistic societies. Presumably, an exploitive, capitalistic form of servitude could not exist within a patriarchal society. The lord of a manor, unlike the entrepreneur who might play the role of lord of a manor, would be incapable of treating men as mere units of labor in a speculative enterprise. But neither would he think of exploring new lands, discovering gold mines, or developing new plantations for the production of sugar and coffee. It is perhaps significant that accounts of Latin American slavery often picture the relaxed life on sugar plantations after their decline in economic importance, and ignore conditions that prevailed during the Brazilian sugar boom of the seventeenth century, the mining boom of the early eighteenth century, and the coffee boom of the nineteenth century. Similarly, Southern apologists tended to overlook the human effects of high-pressure agriculture in the Southwest, and focus their attention on the easy-going and semipatriarchal societies of tidewater Maryland and Virginia. Eugene D. Genovese has recently suggested that while the North American slave system was stimulated and exploited by the capitalist world market, it retained many precapitalistic features, such as a lack of innovation, restricted markets, and low productivity of labor, and actually gravitated toward an uneconomical paternalism that was basically antithetical to capitalistic values.[1]

[1] A re-analysis and reassessment of all these factors is undertaken by Genovese in his superb new seminal study, *Roll, Jordan, Roll* and by Robert Fogel and Stanley Engerman in their landmark cliometric study, *Time on the Cross.* See the Bibliographic Essay.— Ed.

Although a particular instance of oppression or well-being can always be dismissed as an exception, it is important to know what range of variation a system permitted. If an exploitive, capitalistic form of servitude was at times common in Brazil and Spanish America, and if North Americans conformed at times to a paternalistic model and openly acknowledged the humanity of their slaves, it may be that differences between slavery in Latin America and the United States were no greater than regional or temporal differences within the countries themselves. And such a conclusion would lead us to suspect that Negro bondage was a single phenomenon, or *Gestalt*, whose variations were less significant than underlying patterns of unity. . . .

Much has been made of the fact that the Spanish model law, *las Siete Partidas*, recognized freedom as man's natural state, and granted the slave certain legal protections. But the argument loses some of its point when we learn that the same principles were accepted in North American law, and that *las Siete Partidas* not only made the person and possessions of the bondsman totally subject to his master's will, but even gave owners the right to kill their slaves in certain circumstances. Some of the early Spanish and Portuguese legislation protecting Indians has erroneously been thought to have extended to Negroes as well. In actuality, the first laws pertaining to Negroes in such colonies as Chile, Panama, and New Granada were designed to prohibit them from carrying arms, from moving about at night, and above all, from fraternizing with Indians. It is true that in the late seventeenth and early eighteenth centuries the Portuguese crown issued edicts intended to prevent the gross mistreatment of Negro slaves. But . . . Brazilian law was a chaotic tangle of Manueline and Filipine codes, encrusted by numerous decrees which often contradicted one another, and which were interpreted by lawyers and magistrates notorious for their dishonesty. . . .

In theory, of course, the Portuguese or Spanish slave

possessed an immortal soul that entitled him to respect as a human personality. But though perfunctorily baptized in Angola or on the Guinea coast, he was appraised and sold like any merchandise upon his arrival in America. Often slaves were herded in mass, stark naked, into large warehouses where they were examined and marketed like animals. As late as the mid-nineteenth century the spread of disease among newly arrived Negroes who were crowded into the warehouses of Rio de Janeiro brought widespread fears of epidemic. The Spanish, who ordinarily sold horses and cows individually, purchased Negroes in lots, or *piezas de Indias*, which were sorted according to age and size. There is abundant evidence that Brazili   ¬ were little troubled by the separation of Negro famili

Obviou.   ¬h depended on regional differences in economy and social tradition. . . . [R]ecent studies of the extreme southern provinces of Brazil reveal a picture of harsh chattel slavery and racial prejudice which stands in marked contrast to the familiar images of benign servitude in the north. During the last third of the eighteenth century the southern states developed a capitalistic economy which was initially stimulated by the export of wheat but which came to rely heavily on the production of jerked beef. Whether engaged in agriculture, stock raising, or the processing of meat or leather, the slaveholding capitalists were bent on maximizing production for commercial profit. Because the economy rested on slave labor and because physical labor was largely associated with the African race, Negroes and mulattoes were regarded as mere instruments of production, wholly lacking in human personality. . . .

Conditions were undoubtedly better in the cities, where protective laws were more often enforced and where Negroes had at least a chance of acquiring money that could purchase freedom. . . .

There is evidence that, beginning in the late eighteenth century, Negro bondage became milder and better regulated in certain parts of Latin America. In such areas as New Granada the very survival of the institution was jeopardized by the revolutionary example of Saint Domingue, the outbreak of rebellions and continuing raids by fugitive *cimarrons*, the uncertainty of the African trade in the face of war and British humanitarianism, and the unsettling effects of war on markets and credit. The tumultuous period from the French Revolution to the Spanish American wars for independence brought abrupt changes in economic and political interests which often favored the Negro slave. But even Cuba, which had a long tradition of encouraging manumissions, was the scene of gross cruelty and heavy slave mortality through much of the nineteenth century; and critics of the regime, . . . were either silenced or banished from the island. . . .

With the exception of legal barriers to manumission . . . the salient traits of North American slavery were to be found among the Spanish and Portuguese. Notwithstanding variations within every colony as a result of environment, economic conditions, social institutions, and the personality of owners, the Negro was everywhere a mobile and transferable possession whose labor and well-being were controlled by another man. Any comparison of slavery in North and South America should take account of the fact that Brazil alone had an area and variety comparable to all British America, and that the privileged artisans, porters, and domestic servants of colonial Brazilian cities can be compared only with their counterparts in New York and Philadelphia. Similarly, conditions in nineteenth-century Alabama and Mississippi must be held against those in the interior coffee-growing areas of south-central Brazil. Given the lack of detailed statistical information, we can only conclude that the subject is too complex and the evidence too contradictory for us to assume that the treatment of slaves was substantially better in Latin America than in the British colonies taken as a whole. . . . It is an incontestable fact that slaves in Latin America had more opportunities for manumission than did those in the

British colonies or the United States. This acceptance of individual emancipation, coupled with a growing tolerance of racial diversity, probably helped Latin Americans to avoid the tragic hatreds, the malignant fears, and the unjust discriminations that followed the abolition of slavery in North America. When one looks at the striking contrast between American and Brazilian experience in the late nineteenth century and the twentieth century, it is only natural to presume that attitudes toward race and freedom were always so sharply differentiated. On the other hand, it is theoretically possible that the divergence had less to do with the character of slavery in the two countries than ⁻ith economic and social structures which defined the relations between colored freedmen and the dominant white society. . . .

The strongest evidence for a radical and fundamental difference regarding manumission is the restrictive legislation of the British West Indies and mainland colonies. From the late seventeenth century to the time of the American Revolution, virtually every British colony enacted laws which in some way limited the master's power to free his slaves. . . . Despite a tendency to liberalize these restrictions in the period immediately after the American Revolution, slaveholding states showed an unmistakable trend toward limiting the number of manumissions. By the mid-nineteenth century the American master who wished to free his slaves was forced to rely on legal ingenuity and subterfuge. And while the Code Noir placed no restrictions on emancipation, the French colonies followed a similar pattern of development. . . . In both British and French colonies the chief motives behind such restrictions were the beliefs that free Negroes were an unassimilable element, and that they contributed to crime, prostitution, public disorder, and above all, discontent among the slaves.

Since the Spanish and Portuguese colonies were generally free from such legal restraints, and at times even encouraged the manumission of slaves, it would appear that national attitudes toward race and the capacity for freedom were radically different even in colonial times. . . .

What differences there were in national attitudes toward manumission can partly be attributed to changing views on racial intermixture. White men had sexual intercourse with Negro bondwomen throughout the Americas. But such relations were naturally more common and acceptable in regions where there were relatively few white women. In colonial Brazil, the French West Indies, and even Barbados and Jamaica, planters and administrators met the need for female companionship, as well as for sexual gratification, by living openly with Negro mistresses who were often accorded many of the privileges of legitimate wives. The governors of the Spanish provinces, being forbidden to marry, had no compunctions about living with slave mistresses, and accordingly set an example for men of less exalted rank in Louisiana as well as South America. . . .

. . . In many societies . . . a stigma of slavish origin had been fastened on freedmen and their descendants, even when slavery was not racial in character. This was true, in fact, even among the West Africans. It would appear that racial differences reinforced this common tendency to attach some of the burdens and disabilities of slavery to the free offspring of slaves. In any event, . . . racial discrimination was coextensive with American Negro slavery, and . . . divergence between British and Latin America in the treatment of the colored race was a slow and gradual phenomenon, and not the result of original differences in their systems of slavery and caste.

Even a relative acceptance of racial blending did not mean an absence of racial prejudice. In time, racial prejudice was probably eroded in certain colonies by the militancy of mulattoes and quadroons, who resented and struggled against the restraints which attached to their condition, but who could take pride in their white blood, which placed them in a position above the Negro. . . . In southern Brazil . . . a racial ideology and unfavorable stereotypes of the Negro persisted well into the twentieth century.

Such prejudice was also strongly pronounced in the French West Indies, where it was official policy to regard slavery as an ineffaceable stain that contaminated a slave's entire posterity. . . .

We cannot begin to consider why legal discriminations increased in the United States and gradually disappeared in the West Indies and Latin America. It is surely of the utmost significance that free Negroes in the Southern United States were subjected to the harshest restrictions at precisely the time when Jamaica and Barbados were removing legal disabilities from their free colored populations. In the British West Indies, as well as in Brazil, free Negroes had achieved legal equality before the enactment of general emancipation. This progress may not have hastened the énd of slavery, but it certainly had a profound effect on the consequences of abolition. . . . [T]he important point is that the disabilities suffered by freedmen and their descendants were roughly similar in most American colonies before the Age of Revolution. . . .

The grim and overriding fact is that in every colony free Negroes and mulattoes suffered from legal and social discrimination, and were at once condemned for idleness and prevented from enjoying economic opportunity, accused of being disorderly and deprived of equal justice. Variations in detail and terminology are less impressive when we learn, for example, that even in colonial Brazil free mulattoes were often legally associated with slaves. This uniform discrimination must have been related to a fairly uniform conception of slavery as a state of absolute subjection and degradation. Like sovereignty, which more than liberty was its polar opposite, slavery could be circumscribed and its limits set by law and custom.

II

The Atlantic Slave Trade

THE CURSE OF AN AFRICAN ALAFIN

"My curse be on you for your disloyalty and disobedience, so let your children disobey you. If ye send them on an errand, let them never return to bring you word again. To all the points I shot my arrows will ye be carried as slaves. My curse will carry you to the sea and beyond the seas, slaves will rule over you, and ye their masters will become slave."—Oyo Alafin, Awole, 1796*

The Atlantic slave trade is a classic example of man's inhumanity to man, of commercial transactions based entirely on the estimated value of a pound of flesh. Even sadder, perhaps, it reveals that greed can turn brother against brother and that exploitation of humans for gain knows no national, racial, or religious boundaries.

Trade in human beings had flourished in Africa itself for at least five centuries before the first Africans were carried overseas into slavery in Europe in 1444. Portugal, a nation of expert seamen, was the first European country

---

*Cited in Samuel Johnson, *The History of the Yorubas* (Lagos: C. M. S. Bookshop, 1937), p. 192.

to undertake voyages along the African coast for purposes of trade. She developed a thriving African commerce, which included slaves as a commodity, and also made occasional raids along the coast with the intention of colonization. Church aid was invoked to support her claims against other European rivals, and she moved to gain a monopoly on trade in Africa.

At first Spain accepted her exclusion from the African slave trade, but once the New World was opened to colonization and trusted servants were required, Spain, too, sent Africans overseas. To regulate the carriage of Africans to America the Spanish crown issued business firms licenses, or *asientos*. The first such license, issued in 1510, marked the beginning of the traffic in African slaves between Europe and America.

Factors such as royal pressure and Hispanic humanism kept Spain from becoming a major shipper of slaves, and in most of her later slaving activities in America, she licensed her trade out to Portugal or to other slave-trading European nations. Contrary to popular belief, the Portuguese themselves never enjoyed a monopoly of the slave trade. By the middle of the seventeenth century the Protestant nations of Europe, asserting their political hegemony over sea and land routes, challenged Iberian control. England, France, and Holland developed and supported national trading companies and enforced laws that required their colonies to conduct trade exclusively with their own merchants and shippers. As a result, these countries, and to a lesser extent the Scandinavian and Germanic duchies, remained preeminent as shippers and merchants of human livestock.

The following selections include a detailed quantitative analysis of the trade in Africans and several personal narratives, African and European, on the actual process of transporting slaves from Africa to American plantations.

3

PHILIP D. CURTIN

THE ATLANTIC SLAVE TRADE

*The selection that follows is from the first compre-
hensive demographic and historical analysis of the
Atlantic slave trade. It supersedes all other accounts
available on the subject.*

*Philip Curtin is Professor of History at the Uni-
versity of Wisconsin and the author of numerous
books and articles concerning African and Afro-
American history.*

The slave trade was a commercial system to recruit
forced workers in one society and transport them to
another with a vastly different culture. Both Africans and
Europeans participated in the trade, and both societies
were deeply influenced by it. . . . The institutions of the
slave trade were common to the Atlantic community as a
whole . . . Contrary to the parochial view of history that
most North Americans pick up in school, the United States
was only a marginal recipient of slaves from Africa. The
real center of the trade was tropical America, with almost
90 per cent going to the Atlantic fringe from Brazil
through the Guianas to the Caribbean coast and islands.

From Philip D. Curtin, *The Atlantic Slave Trade: A Census*
(Madison: University of Wisconsin Press; © 1969 by the Regents
of the University of Wisconsin), pp. xv–xvi, 15, 21–23, 30–31, 44–47,
49, 88–89, 208–209, 223, 226, 228–231, 241–243, 258–260, 265–266,
268.

. . . [It] is equally clear that more Africans than Europeans arrived in the Americas between, say, 1492 and 1770. . . .

The Hispanic nations of the Iberian peninsula were the first to begin the slave trade, and the last to quit. In the fifteenth and sixteenth centuries, the Spanish and Portuguese carried the rudimentary institutions of the South Atlantic System from the Mediterranean to the Atlantic Islands, then to Santo Domingo and Brazil. In the seventeeth and eighteenth centuries, the Dutch, English, and French dominated the slave trade, but, in the nineteenth century, Brazil and Cuba accounted for the vast majority of slaves imported—and by that time the northern powers had made their own slave trade effectively illegal. The long duration of this trade to Brazil and Spanish America greatly complicates the problem of estimating the total imports, and the earliest phases provide very uncertain evidence.

. . . During most of the long centuries of the slave trade, Spain carried few slaves under her own flag. After trying unsuccessfully in the sixteenth century to break the Portuguese hold on the Africa trade, she reverted to a system of licenses or *asientos*, issued mainly to foreign firms. An asiento gave the foreign shipper permission to infringe the Spanish national monopoly over the trade of the American viceroyalties, in return for an obligation to carry a stipulated number of slaves to specified destinations over the period of the contract. One source for calculating imports into Spanish America is therefore the series of asientos, which appear to be completely recorded from 1595 to 1773, even though all asientos were not equally precise in the terms they laid down.

Furthermore, an asiento's stipulations cannot be accepted literally. The asiento was considered a great commercial prize, but not for the sake of profits to be made on the slave trade. Quality standards and duty payments required by the Spanish government were too stiff to allow a high profit on slaves alone. The *asientista* counted far more on the opportunity for illicit sales of other goods to Spanish America in return for silver. . . . Few, if any, actually fulfilled the delivery stipulations of the contract. Their economic advantage was in pretending to carry more slaves than they actually did, leaving room to fill out the cargo with other goods. For this reason, delivery figures are likely to be inflated through the corruption of American customs-house officers, . . .

. . . Most asiento contracts gave the quantities to be delivered in *piezas de India,* not individual slaves. A pieza de India was a measure of potential labor, not of individuals. For a slave to qualify as a pieza, he had to be a young adult male meeting certain specifications as to size, physical conditon, and health. The very young, the old, and females were defined for commercial purposes as fractional parts of a pieza de India. This measure was convenient for Spanish imperial economic planning, where the need was a given amount of labor power, not a given number of individuals. For the historian, however, it means that the number of individuals delivered will always be greater than the number of piezas recorded. Market conditions in Africa made it impossible to buy only the prime slaves and leave all the rest, but the extent of the difference varied greatly with time and place. The definition of a pieza and its fractional values also changed. The asiento of the Portuguese Cacheu Company in 1693, for example, provided for an annual delivery in Spanish America of 4,000 slaves, so distributed in sex, age, and condition as to make up 2,500 piezas de India. This implied the expectation that the number of individuals was 60 per cent greater than the number of piezas. In this case, though, it made little difference: the company failed to meet either standard of delivery. At other times, the relationship between piezas and individuals was much closer. . . .

. . . While it was to the advantage of the official

asientista to deliver fewer slaves than required, the unfilled demand created a market for smuggled slaves that met no quality standards and paid no duties. This part of the slave trade to Spanish America was apparently very profitable in most periods, but extremely difficult to estimate. . . .

In spite of these uncertainties, the asiento figures have a considerable value, not as a record of the number of slaves delivered but as a rationally conceived estimate of manpower requirements. In this sense, they are not unlike the production targets in a modern planned economy. . . . The contracts from 1595 to 1773 therefore come to 648,688 slaves, or an annual average of 2,882 for 1595–1640 and 3,880 for 1641–1773. . . .

By now, the problem of estimating the slave imports into Spanish America should be clear. Was New Granada of the late eighteenth century like Jamaica, or like Argentina? The part of the viceroyalty that was to become Venezuela had a plantation component, . . . The rest of the viceroyalty (the present-day republics of Colombia, Panama, and Ecuador) presents another problem. Placer gold mining [panning and surface mining, as opposed to deep-pit mining] in Colombia depended on the slave trade much as a plantation sector would have done, but the mulatto population of Colombia was 40 to 50 per cent of the total by 1800. This suggests a growing African-derived population in one sector and a naturally decreasing slave population in another. . . .

The island colonies—Cuba, Puerto Rico, and the Spanish part of Hispaniola—were a backwater of the Spanish empire up to the middle of the eighteenth century. They had few settlers of any kind, and their slave populations were a small part of the total. Comparatively large numbers were free settlers of partial African descent. Given the fact that the slave trade to these islands had been gradual over several centuries, both the slave populations and the free black populations probably attained natural growth by the mid-eighteenth century. The mulatto population certainly did. Then, beginning in Cuba in the 1760's and in Puerto Rico somewhat later, these islands finally entered the South Atlantic System and developed a plantation sector worked largely by newly-imported slaves from Africa. As the plantation sector grew, it changed the demographic pattern of the islands. For this sector at least, a naturally declining slave population appeared, and the demographic pattern, like the economic pattern, came to resemble that of Jamaica or Saint Domingue a century earlier. Although Spanish Santo Domingo missed the new phase on account of the anarchy and warfare that spread from French Saint Domingue after the great slave revolt of 1791, Cuba and Puerto Rico began to import slaves in greatly increased numbers at the precise period when the slave trade to continental Spanish America showed signs of tapering off. . . .

. . . [T]he total slave imports into Spanish America were in the vicinity of 1,552,000 over the whole period of the slave trade. Some of the estimates on which this figure is based are geographical import estimates, while others are flow estimates for the whole trade to the Spanish empire over a period of time. One way of simultaneously checking the result and establishing the possible pattern of geographical distribution within Spanish America is to set these estimates against those that appear in the literature for particular countries. The calculations for Cuba and Puerto Rico have been given. Authorities on regional history have produced import estimates for Mexico at 200,000 during the whole of the slave trade, and for Venezuela at 121,000. For the Plata basin, we have the import estimates worked out by Elena de Studer, which are roughly equivalent to imports into the present Argentina, Uruguay, Paraguay, and Bolivia [about 100,000]. . . . For Chile, Rolando Mellafe estimated . . . about 6,000.

These partial estimates by geographical region . . . add

up to 1,301,000 slaves imported and cover all important regions—except Santo Domingo, Colombia, Panama, Ecuador, and Central America. If the balance of 251,000 that remains after this figure is subtracted from the over-all total estimate of 1,552,000 can fit comfortably into these countries, the broad accuracy of the estimates would be confirmed. Santo Domingo can be dealt with by an educated guess, based on the general level of economic development there in the sixteenth and seventeenth centuries. It was more important than either Cuba or Puerto Rico in those early centuries, but its slave imports were cut off sharply in the 1790's. It might therefore be allowed 30,000.

The northwest corner of South America is a more difficult region to deal with at the present state of knowledge. Cartagena was a very important entrepôt in the Spanish slave trade of the sixteenth and seventeenth centuries. Panama served as the trans-shipment point to the Pacific coast of South America, and the dominant racial strain all along that coast south to the Gulf of Guayaquil is African. Furthermore, the placer gold mines of western New Granada were worked mainly by African slaves, and the gold camps are known to have had an extremely high ratio of men to women. This implies a very high rate of net natural decrease and thus a high ratio of imports to surviving slave populations. The population of unmixed African descent in New Granada in 1810 is estimated at 72,270, but the proportion of mulattos to the total population was already 50 per cent by 1800. This suggests that the population of African descent contained a high proportion of creoles, which means that it may well have been growing by natural increase. This supposition is further supported by the fact that the Negro population of Colombia has remained at about the same percentage of the total since the latter part of the eighteenth century. Taking the combination of high wastage in the mining camps and comparatively early development of natural growth, and having the import estimates for Mexico and Venezuela for comparison, an overall figure of 200,000 for Colombia, Ecuador, and Panama might be a reasonable guess.

This leaves a balance of 21,000 for Central America. The number may be a little high, but it is not drastically out of line with the Mexican figure, with qualitative impressions, or with the later population of African descent.

. . . The slave trade to Brazil has received a great deal of attention from historians, but it continues to pose some difficult problems. The Portuguese imperial bureaucracy was not so tightly organized as that of Spain, and the slave trade was not so closely controlled. Archival data are therefore fewer to begin with, and in Brazil they are scattered among the half-dozen principal ports of entry. Since the trade was open to Brazilian as well as Portuguese shipping most of the time, metropolitan sources tend to be weak, though the Portuguese posts in Angola have produced longer time-series of slave exports than any other part of the African coast.

Like the historical work on the slave trade elsewhere, the range of estimates for total Brazilian slave imports is extremely wide, with some of the older and more offhand guesses running as high as 50 million slaves for the whole period of the trade. The passage of time, however, has tended to lower the estimates and finally to bring about substantial agreement. . . .

For present purposes, the figure of 3,646,800 is accepted as the total estimate for the slave trade to Brazil, mainly because it is the sum of the estimates by time period of Mauro and Goulart. It is not necessarily any more accurate than any other estimate in that vicinity, and it may well be higher than the actual figure; but the evidence now available tells little about the amount of downward revision that may be required. . . .

The most important West African source of slaves for Brazil was the Bight of Benin. When the Dutch captured Elmina castle in the 1630's, they first tried to cut the Por-

A Speculative Geographical Distribution of Slave Imports during the Whole Period of the Atlantic Slave Trade (000 Omitted)

Region and country		No.		%
Grand total		9,566		100.0*
Old World traffic		175		1.8
Europe		50		0.5
Madeira, Canaries, Cape Verde Is.		25		0.3
São Thomé		100		1.0
North America		651		6.8
Territory of the United States		427		4.5
British North America	399		4.2	
Louisiana	28		0.3	
Middle America		224		2.3
Mexico	200		2.1	
Central America and Belize	24		0.3	
Caribbean Islands		4,040		42.2
Greater Antilles		2,421		25.3
Haiti	864		9.0	
Dominican Republic	30		0.3	
Cuba	702		7.3	
Puerto Rico	77		0.8	
Jamaica	748		7.8	
Lesser Antilles		1,619		16.9
US Virgin Is.	28		0.3	
British Virgin Is.	7		0.1	
Leeward Is.	346		3.6	
Guadeloupe	291		3.0	
Martinique	366		3.8	
St. Vincent, St. Lucia, Tobago, & Dominica	70		0.7	
Grenada	67		0.7	
Trinidad	22		0.2	
Barbados	387		4.0	
Dutch Antilles	20		0.2	
Bahamas	10		0.1	
Bermuda	5		0.1	

South America		4,700	49.1
The Guianas		531	5.6
Surinam & Guyana	480	5.0	
French Guiana	51	0.5	
Brazil		3,647	38.1
Bahia	1,200	12.5	
Other	2,447	25.6	
Spanish South America		522	5.5
Argentina, Uruguay, Paraguay, & Bolivia	100	1.0	
Chile	6	0.1	
Peru	95	1.0	
Colombia, Panama, & Ecuador	200	2.1	
Venezuela	121	1.3	

*Percentages have been rounded off.

tuguese out of the Guinea slave trade altogether. This proved to be impossible in practice, and the Portuguese were allowed to return—but only on payment of a 10-percent duty on all trade goods brought to the coast, payable at Elmina. But payment did not open up the trade of the Gold Coast itself, it merely bought Dutch permission to trade at four ports on the Bight of Benin—Grand Popo, Ouidah, Jaquin, and Apa. As a result the Portuguese took to calling this area the Costa da Mina, and in time the term spread in Portuguese usage to include more loosely any part of the broad region from Cape Mount to Cape Lopez, as Portuguese trade spread somewhat as well. In 1721 the Portuguese built their own fort at Ouidah, and they less often paid blackmail to the Dutch; but their greatest trading interest remained in the Bight of Benin.

The best available data for measuring the level of Portuguese trade on the Costa da Mina are the recorded imports into Bahia. That province had a special interest in the Mina trade, with a marked market preference for "Minas" or West Africans over "Angolas" or Bantu-speaking peoples, and Bahia had the added advantage of producing a type of tobacco that was highly prized in West Africa—not merely in preference to other American tobacco, but also in preference to other Brazilian tobacco, even that from neighboring regions. . . .

. . . The real beginning of the downward spiral of African slave exports . . . came with the 1790's—not, as often pictured, after the passage of the British act abolishing the slave trade in 1808. . . .

It is clear from these data that no coastal region exported slaves at a consistently high rate. Nor is the export curve of any region closely tied to the export curve from Africa as a whole. The consolidated slave exports from West Africa . . . apparently responded to the demand of the European slave dealers and ultimately to the rhythm of war and peace between European powers on the Atlantic, but no coastal zone responded in quite that pattern. The high point for the Senegambia, for example, was in the 1710's, possibly even earlier. Sierra Leone reached one peak of export in the 1740's, followed by a second in the 1780's—a pattern in common with that of the Gold Coast. Exports from the Windward Coast also reached two decennial maxima, this time in the 1740's and 1760's. The Bight of Benin, on the other hand, shows a beginning pattern nearly reciprocal to that of the Gold Coast. While the Gold Coast exports were rising steadily from the 1710's to the 1740's, those from the Bight of Benin were falling, though they rose suddenly in the 1780's to more than twice the low point of the 1770's. . . . [T]he Bight of Biafra was a negligible supplier until the 1730's, but its export then grew very rapidly to levels that were more consistently maintained than those of any coastal zone other than Senegambia. . . .

In short, the exports of an individual region responded far more to local supply conditions than they did to the demand of European traders. . . .

The Bight of Biafra seems to be an exception to the prevailing West African pattern of slave supply dependent on political events. Here political change followed the appearance of European demand: Throughout the region, political reforms led to more efficient institutions for gathering slaves and transporting them to the coast, including devices like the manipulation of the Arochuku oracle among the Ibo to produce slaves for export without depending on large-scale warfare. The sustained high level of exports from the Bight of Biafra may possibly be explained by the success of these innovations.

A similar response may also explain the immense increase in slave exports from Central Africa in the 1780's. . . .

Mozambique also became a significant source of slaves for the Atlantic trade in the 1780's.

. . . [N]ew supplies from Mozambique . . . depended on an African response to demand. In this case, the innovators were not coastal traders but the Yao of the interior, who turned from their customary ivory trade to supply slaves as well, drawing on the area bordered by the Zambezi in the south, Lake Nyasa to the west, and the Rovuma River to the north. . . .

The dimensions of the nineteenth-century slave trade have always been a matter of controversy—political controversy at the time and historical controversy since. This outcome is hardly unexpected. . . .

The largest single importer was certainly Brazil. . . . [I]mports into Brazil were highly concentrated. The east-west coast took a bare 1 per cent of the identified imports. Southern Brazil took less than 1 per cent. But 80 per cent were drawn to the developing sugar and coffee estates of Rio de Janeiro and São Paulo, while Bahia and the northeast, the older home of the sugar industry, took only about 13 per cent.

The African origins of these slaves retained some aspects of the eighteenth-century pattern and lost others. Angola in the narrow sense now supplied a smaller proportion of Brazilian imports than the estimated 68 per cent that held for the period 1701–1810, but the shift was only a few miles up the coast to the region of Congo North. Since this region seems to have been the "Angola" of the French and English slavers in the eighteenth century, its export capacity was now available to serve Brazil. . . . Bahian captains bound for the Bight of Benin usually registered for a voyage to Malembo, Cabinda, or São Thomé, thus securing papers that would account for their legitimate presence near the Bight. Therefore, almost all the traffic shown in the table as originating in Congo North with destination Bahia came in reality from the Bight of Benin. Ships from Rio de Janeiro, on the other hand, lacked the old connection of the tobacco trade. Their trade with Congo North probably represents a genuine shift in source of supply.

Even with these biases taken into account, West Africa appears to have supplied a smaller proportion of Brazilian slave imports than it did in the eighteenth century. . . . Instead, Brazil began to draw more slaves than ever before from southeast Africa.[1]

The retention of old patterns is especially clear in comparing the origin of the imports into northern and northeastern Brazil. Pará and Maranhão had traditionally drawn their slaves from Guinea-Bissau, . . . Bahia, . . . had always shopped for slaves on the Costa da Mina, and it continued to do so as much as possible.

Still another curiosity of the Brazilian slave trade is the great variation in the size of the cargo. It was not only variable according to the African region of export, but increased in a regular manner from the north and west, where the mean number of slaves landed per vessel was smallest, to the south and east, where it was largest. The preference for larger ships in the long voyage to the Indian

[1] Curtin's data for Cuba (table 72 and pp. 243–249 *passim*) indicate similar provenience patterns: roughly one-third from the Bight of Benin, one-third from Mozambique, and one-fourth from Angola and Congo North.—Ed.

Ocean is clear, but the regular progression along the West African coast is not so obvious. . . .

The [nineteenth-century] West African slave trade now flourished in only two regions—the Bights taken together, and Sierra Leone . . . between Liberia and the Republic of Sierra Leone, or else from the river mouths to the north, in present-day Guinea-Conakry and Guinea-Bissau.

The Bights of Benin and Biafra, however, were more important than the conventional Sierra Leone, and this again is supported by . . . samples. They disagree only as to the detail, and especially as to which of the Bights held a larger share of the trade. . . .

It is now possible to look at the long-term movement of the Atlantic slave trade over a period of more than four centuries. The following table sums up the pattern of imports for each century. . . . Together, these data make it abundantly clear that the eighteenth century was a kind of plateau in the history of the trade . . . the period when the trade reached its height, but also a period of slackening growth and beginning decline. [The] trends are not surprising. They run parallel to the growth of the South Atlantic System traced in the literature on qualitative evidence.

ESTIMATED SLAVE IMPORTS INTO THE AMERICAS, BY IMPORTING REGION, 1451–1870 (000 OMITTED)

Region and country	1451–1600	1601–1700	1701–1810	1811–70	Total
British North America	—	—	348.0	51.0	399.0
Spanish America	75.0	292.5	578.6	606.0	1,552.1
British Caribbean	—	263.7	1,401.3	—	1,665.0
Jamaica	—	85.1	662.4	—	747.5
Barbados	—	134.5	252.5	—	387.0

Leeward Is.	—	44.1	301.9	—	346.0
St. Vincent, St. Lucia, Tobago, & Dominica	—	—	70.1	—	70.1
Trinidad	—	—	22.4	—	22.4
Grenada	—	—	67.0	—	67.0
Other BWI	—	—	25.0	—	25.0
French Caribbean	—	155.8	1,348.4	96.0	1,600.2
Saint Domingue	—	74.6	789.7	—	864.3
Martinique	—	66.5	258.3	41.0	365.8
Guadeloupe	—	12.7	237.1	41.0	290.8
Louisiana	—	—	28.3	—	28.3
French Guiana	—	2.0	35.0	14.0	51.0
Dutch Caribbean	—	40.0	460.0	—	500.0
Danish Caribbean	—	4.0	24.0	—	28.0
Brazil	50.0	560.0	1,891.4	1,145.4	3,646.8
Old World	149.9	25.1	—	—	175.0
Europe	48.8	1.2	—	—	50.0
São Thomé	76.1	23.9	—	—	100.0
Atlantic Is.	25.0	—	—	—	25.0
Total	274.9	1,341.1	6,051.7	1,898.4	9,566.1
Annual average	1.8	13.4	55.0	31.6	22.8
Mean annual rate of increase*	—	1.7%	1.8%	−0.1%	

* These figures represent the mean annual rates of increase from 1451–75 to 1601–25, from 1601–25 to 1701–20, and from 1701–20 to 1811–20.

4

THE MIDDLE PASSAGE

The "middle passage" was a euphemism for the horrors endured by the captured African before he ever set a chained foot on American soil. To transport slaves, small ships of 40 to 400 tons were often used. During the eighteenth century the most common slave ship in use was a square-sterned 140 tonner, 57 feet long, with 9-foot holds and only 5 feet of space between decks. The larger frigates (200 to 400 tons) were 77 feet long and 10 feet wide, with separate quarters for men, women, and children.[1]

From Bryan Edwards, *The History, Civil and Commercial, of the British Colonies in the West Indies*, vol. 2 (London: n.p., 1794), pp. 107, 127; James Barbot, "A Voyage to New Calabar," in *A Collection of Voyages and Travels*, eds. Awnsham Churchill and John Churchill (London: n.p., 1732), pp. 459–460; J. Smith, *Trade and Travel in the Gulph of Guinea* (London: Simpkin and Marshall, 1851), p. 186; Thomas Phillips, "A Journal of a Voyage Made—from England—to Barbadoes," in *A Collection of Voyages and Travels*, eds. Churchill and Churchill, p. 218; William Bosman, *A New and Accurate Description of the Coast of Guinea* (London: J. Knapton, D. Midwinter, 1705), pp. 363–364; Charles Boxer, *Salvador de Sá and the Struggle for Brazil and Angola, 1602–1686* (London: Athlone Press, 1952), pp. 230–231; Alexander Falconbridge, *An Account of the Slave Trade on the Coast of Africa* (London: n.p., 1788), pp. 23, 27–28; "Journal of a Cabin Boy," quoted in *Slave Ships and Slaving*, vol. 15, ed. George Francis Dow (Salem: The Marine Research Society, 1927), pp. xxxi–xxxii; James Barbot, "A Voyage to Congo," in *A Collection of Voyages and Travels*, eds. Churchill and Churchill, p. 513; Olaudah Equiano, *The Interesting Narrative of the Life of Olaudah Equiano, or Gustavus Vassa, the African*, vol. 1 (London: n.p., 1789), pp. 42–57 *passim*.

The narrative sequence followed below is from Robert I. Rotberg, *A Political History of Tropical Africa* (New York: Harcourt, Brace & World, 1965), pp. 143–153. Reproduced by permission of the author.

[1] Anonymous, *Liverpool and Slavery* (Liverpool: n.p., 1884), pp. 30–31.

*The hands and feet of male slaves were usually
shackled during their voyage. There was little fresh
air in the holds, which were often intolerably hot.
Sanitary conditions were primitive, water was a
scarce commodity, and the food was barely edible.
The passage from West Africa to America lasted
from six to ten weeks, while that from East Africa
often took up to four months. Under such conditions
disease was rampant and mortality rates were high,
even among the ships' crews. Ships' doctors on these
voyages often reported finding dead cargo chained
to the living!*

*Without qualifying the misery of the slaves in
transit, it should be noted that extreme hardships
were borne by almost all workers, slave or free, in
this capitalistic and exploitative enterprise. Such
miserable conditions could be expected to exist
given European attitudes, class relationships, and
travel facilities at the time. Philip Curtin demon-
strates that the death rate per voyage among ships'
crews was even higher than that among slaves.[2] The
reading of novels, memoirs, and other accounts of
sixteenth- to nineteenth-century naval life and ship
travel—for example,* Mutiny on the Bounty, Two
Years Before the Mast, *and* Damn the Defiant—*will
put the horrors of a transoceanic crossing into better
perspective.*

*The main narrative that follows is by an Ibo,
Olaudah Equiano, who was kidnapped as a boy from
his home in Benin, Nigeria. Olaudah worked first
as a slave for other Africans; eventually, he was
taken to America, where he was sold as a slave in
the United States and then in the West Indies. He
later served with Quakers, earned his freedom, and
became involved in the antislavery movement. His*

[2] Philip D. Curtin, "Postscript on Mortality," in *The Atlantic
Slave Trade,* pp. 275–286. See also, Philip D. Curtin, " 'The White
Man's Grave': Image and Reality, 1780–1850," *Journal of
British Studies,* 1 (November 1961), 94–110 and "Epidemiology and
the Slave Trade," *Political Science Quarterly,* 83 (June 1968),
190–216.

*memoirs, published in 1789, represent a unique ac-
count by an African of the process into and out of
enslavement.*

Adam (a Congo) . . . boy . . . came from a vast distance inland, was waylaid and stole . . . by one of his
countrymen. It was early in the morning, and the man hid
him all day in the woods, and marched him in the night.
He was conducted in this manner for a month, then sold
to another Black man for a gun, some powder, and shot,
and a quantity of salt. He was sold a second time for a
keg of brandy. His last mentioned purchaser bought several other boys in the same manner, and when he had
collected twenty, sent them down to the sea-coast, where
they were sold to a captain of a ship. . . .

[Through almost the entirety of western Africa, African
merchants maintained marshaling yards and *barracoons*
(warehouses) where slaves were stored, fattened, oiled,
and otherwise prepared for purchase. Traders displayed
their wares in age-old fashion.]

. . . [E]ach brought out his slaves according to his
degree and quality . . . and our surgeon examin'd them
well in all kinds . . . for the [overseers] . . . [H]aving
liquor'd them well and sleek with palm oil, 'tis no easy
matter to know an old one from a middle-age one. . . .

[But merchants desired to fill their ships with healthy
slaves.]

The Invalides and the Maimed being thrown out . . .
the Remainder are numbered, and it is entered who delivered them. . . . [A] burning Iron . . . lyes in the Fire;
with which ours are marked on the Breast. . . . [W]e yet
take all possible care that they are not burned too hard,
especially the Women, who are more tender than the
Men. . . .

[In Catholic Angola slaves were taken by the hundreds
to priests for baptism before the voyage to the New
World.]

"Look, you people are already children of God; you

are now going to the land . . . where you will learn things of the Faith. . . . [N]ow go with a good will." . . .

The place allotted for the sick negroes [on the ship] is under the half deck, where they lie on bare planks. . . . [T]hose who are emaciated frequently have their skin, and even their flesh, entirely rubbed off, by the motion of the ship. . . . And some of them, by constantly lying in the blood and mucus . . . have their flesh rubbed off much sooner. . . .

. . . Exercise being deemed necessary for the preservation of their health, they are sometimes obliged to dance. . . . If they go about it reluctantly, or do not move with agility, they are flogged. . . . The poor wretches are frequently compelled to sing also; but . . . their songs are generally . . . melancholy lamentations of their exile from their native country. . . .

. . . Upon the negroes refusing to take sustenance I have seen coals of fire, glowing hot, out on a shovel, and placed so close near their lips, as to scorch and burn them. . . . I have also been informed, that a certain captain in the slave trade, poured melted lead on such of the negroes as obstinately refused their food. . . .

. . . The negroes . . . were confined closely to the lower hold and this brought on a disease called opthalmia, which produced blindness. . . .

Equiano: A Slave Narrative

. . . When I was carried on board I was immediately handled, and tossed up, to see if I were sound, by some of the crew; and I was now persuaded that I had got into a world of bad spirits, and that they were going to kill me. . . . When I looked round the ship too, and saw a large furnace or copper boiling, and a multitude of black people of every description chained together, every one of their countenances expressing dejection and sorrow, I no longer doubted of my fate; and, quite overpowered with horror and anguish, I fell motionless on the deck and fainted. When I recovered a little, I found some black people about me, who I believed were some of those who brought me on board and had been receiving their pay; they talked to me in order to cheer me, but all in vain. I asked them if we were not to be eaten by those white men with horrible looks, red faces, and long hair. They told me I was not; and one of the crew brought me a small portion of spirituous liquor in a wine-glass; but, being afraid of him, I would not take it out of his hand. One of the blacks therefore took it from him, and gave it to me, and I took a little down my palate, which, instead of reviving me, as they thought it would, threw me into the greatest consternation at the strange feeling it produced having never tasted any such liquor before. Soon after this, the blacks who brought me on board went off, and left me abandoned to despair. I now saw myself deprived of all chance of returning to my native country, or even the least glimpse of hope of gaining the shore, which I now considered as friendly; and I even wished for my former slavery, in preference to my present situation, which was filled with horrors of every kind, still heightened by my ignorance of what I was to undergo. I was not long suffered to indulge my grief; I was soon put down under the decks, and there I received such a salutation in my nostrils as I had never experienced in my life; so that, with the loathsomeness of the stench, and crying together, I became so sick and low that I was not able to eat, nor had I the least desire to taste any thing. I now wished for the last friend, death, to relieve me; but soon, to my grief, two of the white men offered me eatables; and, on my refusing to eat, one of them held me fast by the hands, and laid me across, I think, the windlass, and tied my feet while the other flogged me severely. I had never experienced any thing of this kind before; and, although not being used to the water, I naturally feared that element the first time I saw it; yet, nevertheless, could

I have got over the nettings, I would have jumped over the side; but I could not; and, besides, the crew used to watch us very closely who were not chained down to the decks, lest we should leap into the water: and I have seen some of these poor African prisoners most severely cut for attempting to do so, and hourly whipped for not eating. This indeed was often the case with myself. In a little time after, amongst the poor chained men, I found some of my own nation, which in a small degree gave ease to my mind. I inquired of them what was to be done with us? They gave me to understand we were to be carried to these white people's country to work for them. I then was a little revived, and thought, if it were no worse than working, my situation was not so desperate: but still I feared I should be put to death, the white people looked and acted, as I thought, in so savage a manner; for I had never seen among any people such instances of brutal cruelty; and this not only shown towards us blacks, but also to some of the whites themselves. One white man in particular I saw, when we were permitted to be on deck, flogged so unmercifully with a large rope near the foremast, that he died in consequence of it; and they tossed him over the side as they would have done a brute. This made me fear these people the more. . . .

. . . The stench of the hold while we were on the coast was so intolerably loathsome, that it was dangerous to remain there for any time, and some of us had been permitted to stay on the deck for the fresh air; but now that the whole ship's cargo were confined together, it became absolutely pestilential. The closeness of the place, and the heat of the climate, added to the number in the ship, which was so crowded that each had scarcely room to turn himself, almost suffocated us. This produced copious perspirations, so that the air soon became unfit for respiration, from a variety of loathsome smells, and brought on a sickness amongst the slaves, of which many died, thus falling victims to the improvident avarice, as I may call it, of their purchasers. This wretched situation was again aggravated by the galling of the chains, now become insupportable; and the filth of the necessary tubs, into which the children often fell, and were almost suffocated. The shrieks of the women, and the groans of the dying, rendered the whole a scene of horror almost inconceivable. Happily perhaps for myself I was soon reduced so low here that it was thought necessary to keep me almost always on deck; and from my extreme youth I was not put in fetters. In this situation I expected every hour to share the fate of my companions, some of whom were almost daily brought upon deck at the point of death, which I began to hope would soon put an end to my miseries. Often did I think many of the inhabitants of the deep much more happy than myself; I envied them the freedom they enjoyed, and as often wished I could change my condition for theirs. Every circumstance I met with served only to render my state more painful, and heighten my apprehensions and my opinion of the cruelty of the whites. One day they had taken a number of fishes; and when they had killed and satisfied themselves with as many as they thought fit, to our astonishment who were on the deck, rather than give any of them to us to eat, as we expected, they tossed the remaining fish into the sea again, although we begged and prayed for some as well as we could, but in vain; and some of my countrymen, being pressed by hunger, took an opportunity, when they thought no one saw them, of trying to get a little privately; but they were discovered, and the attempt procured them some very severe floggings.

One day, when we had a smooth sea, and moderate wind, two of my wearied countrymen, who were chained together (I was near them at the time), preferring death to such a life of misery, somehow made through the nettings, and jumped into the sea; immediately another quite dejected fellow, who, on account of his illness, was

suffered to be out of irons, also followed their example;
and I believe many more would very soon have done the
same, if they had not been prevented by the ship's crew,
who were instantly alarmed. Those of us that were the
most active were in a moment put down under the deck;
and there was such a noise and confusion amongst the
people of the ship as I never heard before, to stop her,
and get the boat out to go after the slaves. However, two
of the wretches were drowned, but they got the other,
and afterwards flogged him unmercifully, for thus attempting to prefer death to slavery. In this manner we continued to undergo more hardships than I can now relate;
hardships which are inseparable from this accursed trade.
Many a time we were near suffocation, from the want of
fresh air, which we were often without for whole days
together. This, and the stench of the necessary tubs,
carried off many. . . .

[Insurrections were suppressed brutally.]

. . . About one in the afternoon . . . we according to
custom caused them, one by one, to go down . . . to have
each his pint of water. . . . [M]any of them . . . had
pieces of iron. . . . Thus armed, they fell in crowds and
parcels on our men . . . [W]e stood in arms, firing on
the revolted slaves . . . [T]hey gave way . . . and many
of the most mutinous leapt overboard, and drown'd
themselves. . . .

[Once in the Americas they were again oiled and
shaved and displayed for sale.]

It was the practice . . . to open the sale on shipboard,
the males being arranged in one part of the ship, and the
females in another. . . . [C]rowds of people went on
board, and began so disgraceful a scramble . . .

[In other parts of the New World slaves were sold on
shore.]

. . . [O]n a given signal . . . the buyers rush at once
into the yard where the slaves are confined, and make
choice of that parcel they like best. . . . In this manner,

without scruple, are relations and friends separated, most of them never to see each other again. . . . O, ye nominal Christians! Might not an African ask you, learned you this from your God? . . . Surely this is a new refinement in cruelty, which, . . . adds fresh horrors to the wretchedness of slavery.

I I I

Life and Labor of Blacks and Mulattoes in Spanish America

We purchase slaves to cultivate our plains
We don't want saints or scholars to cut canes;
We buy a negro for his flesh and bone,
He must have muscle, brains, he need have none.
But where, you ask me, are the poor old slaves?
Where should they be, of course, but in their graves!
                                    —*Juan Francisco Manzano**

If scholars have learned anything about slavery in the last few decades, it is that the institution was neither static nor monolithic and that from region to region massive discrepancies existed between laws regulating slavery and the system in practice. Constant factors such as climate and topography; more variable factors such as ecology and demography; social, political, and economic conditions—all affected the evolution of slavery throughout

---

* Translated by R. R. Madden from Canto II, "The Sugar Estate," in *Poems by a Slave in the Island of Cuba* (London: Thomas Ward and Co., 1840), p. 44.

America. Furthermore, the system functioned differently in a slave society (e.g., nineteenth-century Cuba), whose economic system depended entirely on slavery and where slavery was the dominant capital-labor relationship, than it did in a nonslave society (e.g., sixteenth-century Mexico), where slavery was simply one of several possible capital-labor relationships.

We are also just beginning to get a fuller picture of the types and degrees of slavery that existed in Spanish America. For example, not all slaves in the New World were field hands. Some of the more favored blacks and mulattoes were kept as domestics; the most classic account of this privileged position is Gilberto Freyre's study.[1] Next in favor were urban slaves. Our evidence indicates that they were generally better off than their counterparts in the mines or plantation fields. Slaves in urban areas were often skilled laborers and artisans who had almost total freedom of movement and could hire themselves out or be hired out, paying their owner a fixed rent and keeping the remainder. (Slaves who were hired out were designated negros de aluguel; those who hired themselves out were called negros de ganho.) Thus these slaves possessed both time and money to become involved in community affairs, to form brotherhoods and cabildos, and to purchase their own freedom. Such blacks eventually acculturated and assimilated, becoming Latin Americans rather than Afro-Americans. Of course, conditions for gaining freedom were something less than ideal. Many urban slaves were exploited by poor owners, and in areas where jobs were lacking, males turned to thievery and vagabondage, and females to prostitution.[2]

[1] See Gilberto Freyre, The Masters and the Slaves (New York: Knopf, 1963) for the study of domestic slavery that influenced Tannenbaum.

[2] See Analola Borges, Alvarez Abreu y Su Extraordinaria Misión en Indias (Tenerife: n.p., 1963), pp. 138–139; and Jaramillo Uribe, "Esclavos y Señores en la Sociedad Colombiana del Siglo XVIII," Annuario Colombiano de Historia Social y de la Cultura, 1, (1963).

Placer and pit-mining, truck farming, and cattle ranching, all made use of slave labor. Yet, the greatest number of slaves, at least in Brazil, the Spanish Caribbean, and coastal northern Spanish America (that is, present-day Venezuela, Colombia, Ecuador, and Peru) were utilized in plantation agriculture. While we might expect this form of slavery to breed some of the worst conditions, once again circumstances varied: types of crops, levels of technology, degrees of exploitation, and varying market conditions serve to complicate efforts to generalize. For example, in Venezuela cacao slaves had spare time to earn money for manumission. However, increasing capitalization (and other factors) in the Cuban sugar-growing industry caused a depressed manpower situation that made for particularly brutal conditions of slavery.

Treatment of slaves seems to have coincided with patterns of labor. The most repressive conditions seem to have occurred where there was maximum utilization of manpower and money. In some cases, slaves represented more than 50 percent of the plantation's total investment, and since that investment was inelastic the slaves had to be kept working. Often slaves on such plantations worked from early dawn until midnight; this was true especially at harvesting time. Such excessive labor left little time for family or personal life. Moreover, any kind of resistance was often met with severe punishment or even death.[3] However, under other forms of servitude, slaves might enjoy numerous privileges, and many seem to have maintained as free a family structure as their masters.

In Mexico (New Spain) cacao, cotton, wheat, indigo, and, especially, sugar were of prime importance to the economy. The most important sugar plantations "consti-

[3] See Stanley J. Stein (Selection 15); Gilberto Freyre, *O Escravo nos Anúncios de Jornais Brasileiros de Século XIX. Tentativa de Interpretação Antropológica, Através de Anúncios de Jornais, de Características de Personalidade e de Deformação de Corpo de Negros* (Recife: n.p., 1963); and A. Ramos, "Castigos de Escravos," *Revista do Arquivo Municipal de São Paulo,* IV, 42 (1938), 79–104.

tuted the first great feudal estates and, as early as the sixteenth century, anticipated the classical Mexican hacienda."[4] Black slaves worked on all the plantations of Mexico, but they proved particularly capable in the sugar-refining processes. By the seventeenth century most sugar refineries utilized 20 to 40 black workers, and some had as many as 200.[5] A declining labor force brought racially mixed groups to work together—village Indians as well as black and mulatto slaves. By 1800 many mill areas had sizable settlements of slaves and free mestizos.

Until James Lockhart published *Spanish Peru*, very little was known of the society that developed during the conquest of Peru.[6] Lockhart described an urban-centered, young, multiracial society. Among the various groups in Spanish Peru were the Africans who had come as servants and auxiliaries during the earliest explorations and military expeditions. Many of these hispanicized *ladinos* earned their freedom participating in the first conquests in the New World. African slaves in early Peruvian societies also functioned as foremen in the Indian villages, as artisans, as soldiers, and as urban workers.

In northern Spanish America, Africans and their descendants formed an important labor force. In three provinces of the western Andes, they were the chief source of manpower in the gold mines.[7] As elsewhere, conditions among mining slaves also varied. Those who

[4] See François Chevalier, *Land and Society in Colonial Mexico* (Berkeley and Los Angeles: University of California Press, 1963), pp. 74–83.

[5] *Ibid.*, p. 80.

[6] A new and important study, Frederick P. Bowser's *The African Slave in Colonial Peru, 1525–1650* (Stanford, Calif.: Stanford University Press, 1973) appeared while this volume was undergoing editorial routine. It discusses the use of African slaves for silver mining, their role in Peru's economy, their daily life, and devices for assimilation.

[7] The two largest mining areas in Spanish America, Mexico and Peru-Chile, employed relatively few Africans in the mines. Indian labor was utilized instead.

worked in the placer mines toiled under relatively mild conditions, and received Sundays and religious holidays off. Many used their free days for extra work at the mines, thereby accumulating money to purchase their freedom. Deep-pit mining, on the other hand, was much more costly of human lives, and, in Spanish America, somewhat more deleterious to Indians than Africans.[8]

The African provided much of the agricultural labor in Venezuela and in sections of Colombia and Ecuador. Blacks on Venezuela's cacao plantations, like those in the placer mines, were permitted spare time to cultivate plots of trees and earn money for manumission. Thereafter, they could retain the plot they had worked.[9]

By the late eighteenth century Africans were arriving in the Platine provinces (Argentina, Uruguay, and Paraguay) at a rate of 2,500 a year. Thousands were transported from Buenos Aires and Montevideo across the Andes to Chile, or from Panamá down to Guayaquil and the Peruvian coast. The great river valleys of New Granada were settled with and worked by black slaves, and Cartagena became a great slave-trading market supplying the interior with black and mulatto labor for mines, mills, farms, and cattle haciendas. Slaves in this last group— the cowboys—had a certain amount of freedom and responsibility, and they were apt to be treated well. Moreover, it was easy for such slaves to escape from the ranches—and many did.[10]

While the Platine became an important transshipment point, it was permanent host to relatively few Africans.

[8] See Charles R. Boxer (Selection 13); and Robert C. West (Selection 7).

[9] See Federico Brito Figueroa, "La Investigación Sobre Historia de la Formación de la Propiedad Territorial Agraria en Venezuela," in *La Obra Pia de Chuao, 1568–1825*, eds. Eduardo Arcila Farias, et al. (Caracas: Ediciones de la Biblioteca Ciudad Universitaria), pp. 124–161.

[10] See Fernando H. Cardoso, *Capitalismo e Escravidão no Brasil Meridional* (São Paulo: Corpo e Alma do Brasil, 1962), pp. 136–139; and David M. Davidson (Selection 18).

At the end of the nineteenth century Argentina counted among her people fewer than 5,000 of African ancestry, Uruguay about 6,000, and Paraguay practically none.[11]

The most important area of African influence in Spanish America was Cuba. Between 1763 and 1838 Cuba changed from an underpopulated and underdeveloped backwater of towns, cattle ranches, and tobacco farms to an island dominated by sugar and coffee plantations. Sugar had been produced in Cuba since the late sixteenth century, but for 200 years it was overshadowed by tobacco and cattle. After 1763, however, several interrelated circumstances changed the mixed economy of Cuba to one dominated by sugar plantation agriculture. Shifts in international market demands, English occupation of Havana (1763–1764), the economic and administrative reforms of Charles III, liberalization of trade and the related increases in importation of African slaves—all were enormous stimuli to an agricultural transformation in Cuba. The Cuban economy was also affected by conditions in Spain during the late eighteenth and early nineteenth centuries. As the Spanish crown grew gradually poorer, lands that had previously been held in usufruct were offered for sale and purchased by Creoles, who subsequently developed plantations.

Cuba had one of the longest traditions of slavery in the Americas. Before the sugar revolution, however, slaves lived with relatively few restrictions. Many were in domestic service, some worked together with their masters on *vegas* or haciendas, and relations between masters and slaves were relatively amiable. Scholars before Knight tended to use this preplantation model for purposes of comparison with slavery in the United States. The result,

---

[11] See Elena F. S. Studer , *La Trata de Negros en el Rio de la Plata Durante el Siglo XVIII* (Buenos Aires: Universidad de Buenos Aires, Departamento Editorial, 1958) ; and Irene Diggs, "The Negro in the Viceroyalty of the Rio de la Plata," *Journal of Negro History,* 36 (July 1951), 281–301.

of course, was a confirmation of the Tannenbaum thesis that Ibero-American slavery was more lenient than the United States variety. Yet, as Knight suggests and Manzano confirms, life for the Afro-Hispano was less than idyllic.

The following selections demonstrate the variations in labor patterns that existed among blacks and mulattoes in Spanish America. They also provide examples for contrast with slavery in Brazil, as well as in the English, Dutch, and French colonies of the New World.

5

WARD BARRETT

SLAVERY AND THE MEXICAN SUGAR HACIENDA

In his study of African slave labor on the plantation, geographer Ward Barrett selected several mills in different areas of Mexico for comparison. He found that, in general, these plantations were burdened with mortgages and other financial obligations, and that they changed ownership frequently. An exception, however, was the mill established by Hernán Cortés in 1535, which remained in the Cortés family until the twentieth century.

Ward Barrett is Chairman of the Department of Geography at the University of Minnesota.

Spaniards were fond of remarking that Negro slaves formed the core of the labor force, and it is true that they dominated in mill and boiling-house, in accordance with law; contrasted with the total inputs of Indian labor, however, the importance of Negro slaves at the Cortés plantation occupied second place.

The first large importation of Negro slaves by Cortés

Barrett, Ward. *The Sugar Hacienda of the Marqueses del Valle.* University of Minnesota Press, Minneapolis. Copyright 1970 University of Minnesota, pp. 78–86, 97–99.

for use on his plantations occurred in 1544, when a shipment arrived for the Tuxtla mill. Cortés had contracted . . . for the shipment of 500 Negroes . . . two-thirds to be male and the rest female, between the ages of 15 and 26. A receipt for one shipment of 100 in fulfillment of the contract shows that Cortés' agent refused 2, and described most of the 98 acceptable Negroes as thin and tired. Delivery of the next large shipment . . . occurred in January 1579, when 40 were sent via Spain—only 5 were females —to the mill at Tuxtla. In later years the lots were much smaller; one major lot in 1598 contained only 19 individuals (3 females), and the major feature of later purchases of imported slaves remained their small size. Many were bought in Mexico City and had spent time there before being sent to the plantation. Information . . . demonstrates the decrease in reliance on imported slaves between 1579 and 1623.

After 1623, purchases of small groups or of individuals were common: in 1655 and 1656, 21 slaves were bought from as many different persons in Mexico; 19 were mulattoes born in Mexico, and only 2 were identified as African. Subsequent purchases in the 1670's and 1680's were of small groups containing hardly any persons born in Africa, and many were mulattoes. Whether this changing pattern of purchase at Atlacomulco duplicates a more general pattern for Mexico I do not know; . . .

The Atlacomulco data are nevertheless adequate to discuss the long-term relative importance of purchase of slaves and their acquisition by birth on the plantation. About half (445) of all the slaves concerning whom I have information were born on the plantation, and their numbers were approximately equally male (218) and female (227). Over the long run of the slaveholding history, therefore, it might be useful to state as an approximation that for every slave bought, one was born at the plantation. Since many of the latter died before reaching maturity, however, it is obvious that purchase of slaves was more important than local reproduction in maintaining the work force.

. . . It was customary to include in inventories information concerning whether the slave had been born in Africa or was a creole (criollo): thus it is possible . . . to classify [slaves] by place of birth. . . .

Of . . . 889 individuals [one particular inventory], approximately one-third were Negroes born in Africa, and it appears likely as well that more than half of all 889 were full-blooded Negroes, the difference representing creole Negroes. [In New Spain during the sixteenth and seventeenth centuries], half came from the Senegambian coast and interior, . . . Approximately half as important numerically were slaves brought at a later date from the Congo basin and coast and from Angola. . . .

. . . More difficult than identifying place of birth is the identification of an individual's racial heritage. This is largely due to the fact that the sixteenth-century inventories describe the offspring of African-born slaves as criollo, perhaps because most of the first and second generations of slaves born on the plantation were in fact full-blooded Negroes. Not until the inventory of 1585 were mulatto children identified, but this cannot be taken as proof that none existed before the 1580's.

. . . [P]ersons who were identified as mulattoes or who had at least one mulatto parent numbered only half the total number of Negroes, yet there remains the large group of 229 criollos that may have contained sufficient mulattoes to raise their numbers to one-third of the entire slave population.

The proportion of Indian-Negro crosses within the mulatto group, in contrast to Negro-Spanish or Spanish-Indian, is difficult to fix because of the wide range of meaning of the word "mulato." According to Aguirre Beltrán . . . the Indian-Negro mixture predominated over the others, and although the word "zambaigo" designated this type it was little used, being rapidly replaced by "mulato," which was also applied to persons of Indian and Spanish blood mixed with Negro. . . .

Since the purchase of mulattoes was uncommon, the members of this group were almost entirely native to the plantation. . . . [O]nly 9 mulatto women and 24 men were purchased, most of them bought in the mid-seventeenth century by Governor Valles (2 women and 17 males) and in 1721 from the small hacienda Atotonilco (6 females and 4 males). The "mulato" group inevitably became dominant as time passed, since the word was applied to so wide a range of racial mixture, and slaves were no longer purchased on the scale that they had been in the sixteenth and very early seventeenth century.

. . . An overview of the slaveholding history of the plantation . . . shows that Negro slave labor was important numerically only in the second half of the sixteenth century and the first two decades of the seventeenth. Peak numbers were held in 1566, when there were 155 slaves described in the inventory, two-thirds of them male. An effort was made to obtain slaves to comply with the late sixteenth century edict prohibiting the use of Indians in millwork, allowing their use only in the fields, but important purchases had already been made by 1596 before the edict, probably as a result of decrease in the Indian labor supply. After 1607 the slave population declined, reaching a low in 1655, but a few purchasers and reproduction kept the population between 50 and 60 until about 1700. A major purchase was made in 1721, with the acquisition of all the slaves of Atotonilco. No attempt was made after this to acquire many other slaves nor even to recapture the many who fled, an important source of loss in the middle eighteenth century, with the result that finally the small slave population consisted primarily of the very old, the young, and the sick and disabled, and probably made little contribution to the work of the plantation. Nevertheless, because many of the few slaves in the late seventeenth and eighteenth centuries were specialists in various branches of plantation work, including such key posts as sugarmaster, and could do the work of salaried Spaniards, their contribution to the labor force was important.

. . . [B]irths and deaths as well as purchases and sales of individuals were itemized in numerous annual accounts. This information, combined with the few remaining examples of lists accounting for the distribution of weekly rations and the more numerous lists accounting for distribution of the annual clothing allowance in some accounts, enables fixing with varying degrees of precision the birth and death dates of 740 (slightly more than 80 per cent) of the total of 916 slaves. The latter figure is a minimum but nearly complete figure of the total number of slaves held between 1549, the year of the first inventory, and about 1800. The information also permits estimation of the years of work contributed by 833 slaves (nearly 90 per cent of the total), . . .

[T]he distribution at Tlaltenango of age groups of Negro slaves in 1549 [is shown in the accompanying table].

Age	Male	Female
0-6	7	11
7-15	0	0
16-25	3	2
26-35	9	8
46-55	9	0
56-65	0	1
66-105	0	0
106-110	1	0

. . . Without additions by purchase, however, the rate of decline of the slave population might have been greater than that of the regional population, but interpretation is complicated by the imbalance in numbers between males and females that persisted from the mid-sixteenth century.
. . . [T]he average value of all slaves fell after 1607 to

remain at a plateau between 1613 and 1693, after which began a persistent decline in value that characterized the eighteenth century until at least 1764. It appears, rather, that the price of slaves followed the price of sugar, with the rate of decline in the values of both being especially noticeable between 1746 and 1764.

. . . Calculation of the average number of years at work at the plantation was based on the assumption that most persons were counted in the work force between the ages of 10 and 60 years. There are numerous items in the inventories that show 10-year-old boys, for example, to have been carreteros or irrigation assistants; in addition, the 1575 rental contract states that all adult slaves were valued at $400, and all under 12 were valued at $300, suggesting that a more or less important contribution to work was made at the age of 12. At the other extreme, it seems a reasonable assumption that some work was performed until the age of 60, [but] values began to decline at approximately 50 years of age. In all cases where data concerning the working ability of an individual were available, the figures for the individual years were adjusted in the light of such information. Although, as with the figures showing average age at death and the length of association with the plantation, it is not possible to state precisely the lengths of time involved . . . I have not indicated the ranges . . . for length of association, since it is nearly identical with the range of average age at death. In nearly all cases, the average number of years at work has been estimated within a much smaller range, . . .

For persons born in the first four decades of the sixteenth century, the average years at work were about 20. The average working life then declined, finally stabilizing between about 10 and 15 years for persons born between 1550 and 1620. Over the long period from about 1620 to 1710, average working life increased, reaching a peak of slightly over 20 years for those born near 1710. Following this peak, average working life declined again.

[There are] data concerning average length of association with the plantation . . . bearing on questions concerning the profitability of slavery. . . . [T]he length of time that the average individual was supported by the plantation but not working . . . was rather small until, beginning with individuals born about 1670, it became almost half as great as the length of the working life. The resultant increase in the costs of support at both ends of the working life thus worked against the gains of a longer working life that characterized the late seventeenth century.

. . . [I]t appears that all employees, slave and free, Negro, Indian, and mulatto, were subjected to the same rigorous discipline; even Independence did not bring release from this rule. However, the plantation records themselves do not speak concerning this point, and in fact I find it very difficult to place discipline on a scale ranging between extreme permissiveness and extreme harshness.

All the colonial inventories list items used to discipline slaves: stocks, collars, chains, leg-irons. Many inventories contain descriptions of slaves who were difficult or chronic runaways. The data give the impression of a somewhat turbulent group of workers in frequent conflict with the mayordomo, but both sides had the opportunity to appeal to the Governor of the Estate to uphold their cause. Although to the slaves the Governor must have been rather a remote figure known only through occasional visits to the plantation that were accompanied by a certain amount of ceremony, they could and did appeal to him when they felt they were mistreated; the mayordomo, on the other hand, could invoke the distant Governor as arbiter in cases that he felt required severe discipline without himself appearing to have full responsibility for the final decision.

Some show of discipline was intended to forestall poor behavior: de Ribaguda Montoya wrote to the Governor in 1952 when the milling was about to begin that he intended to gather the Negroes together the day before milling began to speak to them about proper behavior and performance. His talk would contain the information that they were to obey the Governor, that they would be treated well if they obeyed, but punished "con rigor" if they did not. To dramatize his intentions, he would select a Negro with whom he was extremely annoyed and give him four lashes: . . . Complaints about the difficulty of controlling the slaves are so numerous in the few surviving letters of the mayordomos that one can only conclude that their relations were one of the most unpleasant features of the work as far as the mayordomos were concerned.

On the other hand, the Negroes complained to the Governors about the mayordomos, and could take legal action against them. . . .

Flight offered an apparently easy solution [to rigorous discipline]. In this case, however, the slave's side was not likely to be heard by the Governor; in fact, I have seen no explanation apart from comments by the mayordomos intended to minimize their own responsibility for events. . . . The mayordomo Urtado wrote pointedly to the Governor on 27 November 1702 that two slaves had fled . . . In other cases . . . the motive of flight was said to be robbery. There were numerous bands of highwaymen consisting of escaped slaves, mulattoes, and Indians, particularly on the road to the capital, attracted by shipments of money used for weekly salary payments at the haciendas.

The data on frequency of flight from the plantation are inadequate, since most are found in inventories and data from annual accounts suggest that reliance on the inventories results in a marked underestimate of the real frequency. Slaves described as runaways in the inventories were in general never found, but many of the annual accounts describe the costs of recapturing slaves who managed to escape for only a short time. Thus, while the inventories describe only 7 slaves as runaways in the two decades 1580–99, in 1581 alone, according to the annual account, at least 20 slaves fled but were recaptured. In part of 1584 and 1585, 13 fled, and in 1594 it cost $191 to bring 3 runaways back from the Mixteca. According to the inventories, at least 67 persons escaped permanently or for periods longer than a year between 1544 and 1799, a figure that must be much lower than the number of slaves whose flights were of short duration.

The distribution in time of the 67 more successful flights is significant. Before 1699, 27 persons were described in inventories as runaways, but 35 were so described in the much shorter period 1740–99, 19 of them in the two decades 1740–59. These data substantiate the impression, readily gained from scanning the records, that not only were there more runaways in the mid-eighteenth century than at any other time, but less trouble was taken to capture them than formerly. Thus, of the 7 males described in inventories as captured after having fled, all are mentioned in inventories belonging to the decades 1580–1679, and I have found no reference to recaptured slaves after the latter date. Part of the explanation of the increase in successful flight may be that it was easier for the predominantly mulatto slaves to disappear into a larger free mulatto population. The decrease in the numbers of males who fled after 1759 is due to the simple fact that there were very few males left on the plantation. Many who did not flee were physically handicapped in some way, but on the other hand some handicapped males did take flight.

Mention in inventories of slaves in irons or with scars from irons also changed. In the years from 1580 to 1659, seven males and one female had such marks, but none are so described after the latter date, and eighteenth-century inventories show a decrease in prison equipment.

. . . The rental contracts generally contained a clause stating that slaves should be treated well and fairly, punished neither excessively nor harshly. Although the owner was expected to bear the risk of death by natural causes, the renter was held responsible for the value of slaves who died as a result of harsh punishment or excessively hard work. The governors instructed the administrators to take good care of the slaves, and in numerous instances the administrators found themselves obliged to write to the governors for supplies—particularly clothing—for the slaves.

In their letters to the governors, the mayordomos never praised any of the workers, Negro, Indian, mulatto, or Spanish, for the quality or amount of work done. Instead, they complained frequently about the difficulty of managing the entire labor force. In their view, the slaves' attitude toward work was a racial trait, . . .

The comments of the mayordomos and the directives of the Estate officials suggest that, to them, society consisted of a set of fixed and hierarchical types, and that members of the upper social levels who had to supervise or control workers should assume, ideally, a tutelary and responsible relationship with them. [Praise was accorded] persons who displayed more or less ideal behavior toward their "gente" or local populace generally by providing some schooling for children or by avoiding the common practice of charging high prices at the plantation stores: celebrating these instances implies that many poor persons did not receive such treatment.

Religious teachings were a major source of the paternalistic attitude toward labor. All of at least the major plantations had a chapel, and at Atlacomulco all the resident personnel attended services together. For slaves, as for freedmen and Spaniards, all of the events of the life cycle important in Catholic practice received due attention: baptism, last rites, and Christian burial were routine, marriage within the Church was the ideal, and all the costs were borne by the plantation owners. The patron saint of the plantation was recognized by an annual fiesta, and . . . many other similar religious ceremonies were held . . .

. . . [C]osts fell into two classes, the costs of purchasing slaves and their maintenance. The purchase prices of nearly all the slaves bought for the plantation are available, but the costs of their maintenance are somewhat more difficult to establish.

. . . [I]nventory evaluations [show] for various dates the complicated dependence of value on age, skill, sex, health, and racial composition. I have selected these dates as adequately representing other years when inventory values were stated.

Age emerges as the most obvious factor in determining value, with the data showing that from 1596 to 1754 the value of a slave increased from birth until about the age of 25, after which it leveled off; aging did not operate so consistently to depress value as did maturation to increase it, but the data—particularly of the 1740's—suggest that after about the age of 45 or 50 value began to decrease. Thus the 20 years from age 25 to 45 were regarded as the most productive in the life of a slave. Skills of males were also important, and in cases where these were described, the sugarmaster was usually the most valuable slave, as might be expected: no other skill possessed by a worker so greatly or directly affected the profitability of a plantation. In general, males were more valuable than females, but in the years near 1600, when it seems to have been hoped that natural increase would supply at least part of the slave labor demanded by the viceregal edicts and therefore the value of females were enhanced, the most valuable slaves were two females valued at $500 each. Chronic or permanent physical disability operated to depress the value of a slave, and the variations in disabilities were so great as to provide the major source of scatter on the diagram. It seems likely that at a given age mulattoes had less value than at least Negroes born in Africa, but since the Atlacomulco data deal with two so markedly different populations—an early one dominated by African-born and later ones dominated by mulattoes—no certainty attached to this conclusion.

. . . The value of mature Atlacomulco slaves peaked in the late sixteenth and early seventeenth centuries, but by 1655 had reached a level it maintained with little variation for more than a century; purchase of the Atotonilco slaves in 1721, some of whom had children, probably helped to maintain the average value for a while. The effect did not persist, however; within a decade the value of a mature slave had sunk by $100 to a low level that reflected a growing indifference to the maintenance of this class of labor. The decline in value between the decades about 1600 to the year 1655 indicates not only the effect of the many factors discussed above, but probably also the partial return of Indian labor to the service of the plantation and possibly a change in the value of the peso. The slaves present in 1754 were nearly all mulattoes, mostly immature or disabled, and few gave long service to Atlacomulco.

. . . [T]he total costs of maintaining and buying Negroes, heavy in the 1580's and 1590's, owing to numerous purchases, were greater from 1583 to 1600 than the costs of all Indian labor but . . . from 1621 to 1624 the costs of both kinds were more nearly equal.

. . . Whether or not imported Negro slaves and their descendents worked harder and more efficiently than did Indians is a question with a long history and some relevance to this discussion. If these differences were real and large, they may mean that Negro labor was in fact cheaper than Indian when the daily cost of Negro labor was about the same as that of Indian, as in the 1620's.

The only extensive comparison that I have found describes conditions in the 1650's. It consists of sworn testimony submitted by witnesses supporting the Governor Diego Valles in a suit he brought against the Estate for the labor of 53 Negro slaves missing at the time he assumed responsibility for the plantation. Since Valles was then forced to rely heavily on Indian labor and demanded compensation for his expenses, the testimony centered on the wages that might be earned by Negroes in order to fix

the amount owed Valles by the Estate. Not surprisingly,
Valles' witnesses agreed that the Negroes deserved a
higher wage than did Indians, but since many of the witnesses were owners or managers of haciendas their testimony deserves consideration. The lawyers of the Marqués
did not contest their testimony, and it seems reasonable to
assume from their statements that a difference in productivity did exist.

The arguments of the witnesses may be reduced to a
number of points on which there was general agreement.
Negroes were claimed to work longer hours than did
Indians, from 3 or 4 A.M. to 10 or 11 P.M., whereas Indians worked from 8 or 10 A.M. until 4 or 5 P.M. Indians
would not work at night, but Negroes would; since night
work was done only in the mill where Indians were not
allowed to work at all, there can be no disagreement concerning at least this point. Indians required more supervision than did Negroes: when they finished an assignment,
they did nothing else if not directed, whereas Negro slaves
worked continuously. Someone had even to bring the
Indians to work. The quality of Indian work was poor:
. . . but we have seen that the Cortés mill could not have
continued without it at any time before the nineteenth
century. Negro slaves were capable of becoming skilled
workers—smiths, cartwrights, and sugarmasters—and
many did so at Atlacomulco. It is true that fewer Indians
assumed these positions of responsibility.

The ratio of value of Negro labor to that of Indians
was stated as 2:1, 3:1, and 4:1, with even higher relative
value placed on the work of skilled Negro workers. However, the difference in wages actually received, or that
should have been received, at the time was stated merely
to be at least 4:3 or 5:3, much lower than the difference
in actual wages had been a century before, when Negro
slaves used at Axomulco were paid for at the rate of $3
monthly, and Indians doing the same work received only
$1. If we accept these statements and ratios as expressive

of actual differences, the small difference between the costs of Negro and Indian labor in the period 1581–1624 means that the former was indeed more profitable. The comments that I have summarized from the mid-1650's show that this advantage persisted until at least that date. Perhaps the apparent difference did not persist into the eighteenth century, because Estate officials did not make strong efforts to maintain Negroes as even the skilled core of the labor force then.

6

JAMES LOCKHART

AFRICANS IN SIXTEENTH-CENTURY PERU

Until the mid-1550s Spanish blacks were the only significant group of non-African blacks in Peru, a factor of considerable importance in the development of Peru. In the following selection, James Lockhart discusses the Africans and the Afro-Peruvians, their roles in a Spanish colonial society, and their influence on Peruvian culture.

James Lockhart, Professor of History at the University of California, Los Angeles, is the author of several articles and two books on colonial Latin American social history.

Planned or accidental, ethnic diversity was an element of prime importance in determining the Africans' role in Peru. It meant that Africans lived and acted almost entirely within the Spanish context. Most Africans must have had to speak Spanish to each other. Separated from the Indians by race, culture, and mutual hostility, cut off from one another by their diversity, Africans counted in

From James Lockhart, *Spanish Peru, 1532–1560: A Colonial Society* (Madison: University of Wisconsin Press; © 1968 by the Regents of the University of Wisconsin), pp. 174–198 *passim.*

the conquest and occupation of Peru mainly as so many more Spaniards, so many more spreaders of Spanish language and European ways.

The only African traits that could at all assert themselves were the very general patterns that were more universal than language. African-type dancing was one of these, and appeared wherever Africans could congregate. Kingship was another. The few independent communities of renegade Negroes which managed to exist in certain parts of Peru for a few years operated under that African political institution. It would be of great interest to know what language the renegades spoke. Probably it was Spanish. Or possibly these communities enjoyed some degree of success because they had been able to concentrate enough people from one or another of the ethnic groups to form a strong nucleus. In any case, ethnic diversity was one effective deterrent to slave rebellions. . . .

For years the Spanish Negroes were the only significant group of non-African Negroes in Peru. Though much is hidden behind the all-inclusive term "creole," it appears that very few Negroes born in other parts of the Indies ever reached Peru. Only isolated examples occur, mainly from the Isthmus and the Antilles. The first major addition to the Negroes born outside Africa came in the mid-1550's, when a generation of Peruvian-born Negroes reached saleable age, according to the criterion of the time. . . .

"Ladino" and "bozal" were two words that did heavy duty in the description of slaves. Buyers wanted to know two things, whether or not a slave was experienced, used to life outside Africa and among Europeans, and whether or not he spoke Spanish. Two sets of terms were really needed to express all this, but, in the peculiar conditions of slavery in the Indies at the time, experience and Spanish speaking so nearly coincided that one set of terms sufficed. "Bozal" basically meant just an inexperienced new arrival from Africa, and "ladino" merely meant

Spanish-speaking, but they were used as opposite poles, "bozal" to mean a new slave who therefore knew no Spanish, and "ladino" to mean a Spanish-speaking slave who was therefore experienced. . . .

To express all kinds and degrees of mixtures of Negroes with other races, only one word, "mulatto," was in common use. Mulattoes were not generally thought of as a group distinct from Negroes; a mulatto was a type of a Negro. . . .

Most Negro slaves went through life with no more than a simple Christian name like Pedro, Antón, or Catalina, often qualified by the word Negro. Generally Negroes assumed surnames only when they were freed, . . .

. . . [I]n the period of 1530–60 Negro slaves did not yet ordinarily arrive in Peru by whole boatloads, as they did in the Caribbean. Negroes got to Peru by miscellaneous and various means, as the Spaniards themselves did. Many Negroes came with their permanent owners, or with Spaniards who, as a sideline, were speculating on the sale of two or three slaves. Small private activity may have accounted for as many Negroes as the more or less official trade carried on by large merchants. . . .

The vast majority of Negro slaves changed hands in small transactions, mostly sales of one slave, less often of two or three. Many of these sales can be called primary; that is, they represented the sale of a newly arrived Negro, by the merchant or speculator who imported him, to the person who was going to own him permanently. But many other transactions were part of a constant, disturbingly prevalent process of resale. Among various reasons for the frequency of resale, the most basic was the peculiarly insistent demand for Negro slaves. In a general market situation where most prices, despite violent short-term fluctuations, were remarkably stable over the years, and prices of livestock and food staples actually fell, the price of Negro slaves rose steadily, giving owners a constant opportunity to make a profit by reselling. It was very common for a slave to have had two or three previous owners at time of sale . . .

. . . When, as often happened, Negro slaves were sold along with the land they cultivated, the livestock they cared for, or the tools they worked with, the slave was an element of continuity while the masters changed. At times this became a conscious process of capital formation. A Spanish artisan could acquire untrained Negroes, equip and train them, and sell them as a highly valuable independent unit. Some of the largest sales recorded were of gradually accumulated, trained teams of Negro slaves sold together with the other assets of the company that owned them. In these cases the lives of the Negroes and the operations of the companies remained largely unaffected by a changeover at the top.

After an initial period of instability, the price of Negro slaves was constantly on the rise during the period from 1530 to 1560. . . .

Negro slave owning was very widespread in Peru; not every Spaniard owned Negro slaves, but it can be said that there was no stratum of Spanish Peruvian society which did not include owners of slaves. A complete list of slave owners would include artisans of many kinds, priests, lawyers, notaries, merchants, sailors, and free Negroes, as well as captains and encomenderos. Negro slaves were never the monopoly of the great captains. . . .

. . . With practically all encomenderos and artisans owning several slaves, and many other Spaniards, from rich to poor, at least owning personal servants, or slaves to care for land and stock, it is apparent that Negroes were present in very substantial numbers. All in all, it seems probable that on the coast at least, there were as many Negroes as Spaniards. In the first coastal censuses, around 1570, Negroes had overtaken Spaniards, and may have already done so by 1560. . . . Negroes were present in the highlands in substantial numbers, but less numerous than on the coast.

While there is no sure way of knowing who owned the most Negroes, something can be said about the type of ownership represented by the two most prominent groups of owners, encomenderos and artisans. The encomenderos were purely consumers. The artisans were partly consumers, and partly trainers of slaves, and therefore speculators and sellers. When, in 1560, officials attempted to fix the prices of Negro slaves, forty residents of Lima protested. Of the forty, twenty-one are identifiable as artisans, while not a single encomendero joined the protest.

Whatever else they may have been, most Negro slaves in Peru were personal servants. Though the proportion of full-time personal servants to agricultural workers and artisan slaves is not known, slaves in the latter two categories also performed as servants, and certainly were thought of as such. Personal service was the role most closely associated with Negroes in the minds of the Spaniards. Only those slaves who spent or lost their lives in the migrant gangs organized for gold mining completely escaped the category, and such slaves do not seem to have been really numerous except during the Carabaya gold rush in the Cuzco area in 1542 and 1543. Large encomenderos might own a whole houseful of Negro servants. A notary, priest, or merchant would often have only one, preferably female, as general housekeeper.

Negro slaves were in great demand as servants for two main reasons. The first had to do with their utter foreignness. [It was felt that] foreign slaves who are isolated from the populace at large . . . cannot melt into it. . . .

The second reason why Negroes were desired as servants was that they were one essential part of the general pattern of Spanish ambitions. No encomendero felt happy until he owned a large house, land, livestock and . . . Negro servants. Most Spaniards could not hope to achieve this goal in its entirety, but they aimed at least for two essentials, a house (which could be rented) and Negroes.

One of the most important yardsticks for a Spaniard's contribution to any of the various war efforts was the number of Negro servants he brought to the battle with him. . . .

Negro artisan slaves were at the top of the ladder in the slave world, the most highly skilled and the highest priced, with a certain measure of intrinsic freedom. Doubtless they were less numerous than ordinary personal servants and field workers, but there were enough to form the backbone of the skilled labor force working in the shops of Peruvian Spanish artisans.

There were Negro slaves working in all the trades then common in Peru, but their distribution did not necessarily follow the relative numbers of Spanish artisans. Negroes were especially well represented in basic trades like carpentry and tailoring. A disproportionate number of Negro artisans were blacksmiths and swordsmiths, practitioners of those most basic trades of all, which made the whole Spanish conquest and occupation possible. All the trades involving mass production, like tanning or confectionery, needed and employed Negroes. But though there were many Spanish silversmiths, few Negroes were trained to the trade. Silversmiths were more assayers and general experts on metals and mining than producers, and what productive work they did was often of high technical difficulty. Further, silversmiths, like stonemasons, enjoyed a certain social prestige, and the Spaniards wanted to preserve such roles for themselves.

Negroes from the Iberian peninsula contributed more than their share to the class of Negro artisans. . . . The Spanish Negroes were relatively predominant because they arrived in the Indies already trained. An even spread among the African ethnic groups shows that no one group proved to be more adept or inept at Spanish artisanry than the others.

Every Spanish artisan who had enough capital bought one or more Negro artisan slaves, or, if these were not available, bought ordinary slaves and trained them in the trade. This led to the development of complete shop units which consisted of a Spanish artisan manager and several Negro artisans, with the addition, in some trades, of some less skilled Negroes. A tailor shop in Lima in 1550 consisted of a Spanish hosier and four slave tailors, three Negroes and an Indian. A confectionery in 1552 had a Spanish confectioner, a Negro slave confectioner, and three untrained Negro slaves.

The next step was the development of independent units of slave artisans which could function without the direction of an expert Spaniard. Spanish artisans sold these units, equipped with tools, for a small fortune to wealthy people who lived in remote areas like Upper Peru or Chile, or were undertaking expeditions. Forges were the most common such units. In 1554 a Spanish smith sold a forge, two Spanish Negro smiths, and two African Negro helpers, to a lawyer going to Chile, for 2,000 pesos, enough to buy a mansion or a ship. The Spanish smith continued his operations in Lima. He must have accumulated the forge unit specifically for resale. Other Spanish slave owners participated in this process of training slaves to increase their value, by putting their slave boys into apprenticeship with Spanish artisans, on the same basis as any other apprentice, except that the slaves returned to their owners at the end of the term.

Some very highly skilled Negro artisans carried the tendency toward independence even farther, achieving much of the substance of freedom without its forms. The price of a Negro master artisan . . . alone entitled him to careful treatment. Men of this type sometimes reduced their slavery to the level of an obligation to share their profits. In Arequipa in 1550, two Negro slave artisans were running a shop together and remitting the profits to their respective owners. One Negro carpenter, . . . the slave of an encomendero, actually entered into a company with a Spanish carpenter on equal terms, or indeed as the senior partner.

The category of artisan slaves merged imperceptibly into the category of slaves with less valuable skills who were employed in large teams or gangs. On the borderline between these two types were the Negro muleteers. Of the three main carriers of goods in the highlands—Indian porters, llamas, and mules—trains of mules were the fastest and most reliable, and the most valuable goods were generally entrusted to them. A pack train consisted of a Spanish muleteer, several mules, and some Negroes who cared for and loaded the mules; Negro slaves had a practical monopoly of the function of accompanying pack trains. Most trains were of moderate size, with ten to twenty mules and, ideally, one Negro for every three mules. The merchants who were the chief owners of pack trains often sold them as a unit, mules, tackle, Negroes, and all.

Certain types of Spanish enterprises employed semi-skilled Negroes in relatively large teams of ten to twenty. These were, principally, the carting companies of Lima, the coastal fisheries, and some incipient large cattle owners. The teams were overwhelmingly male, with only one or two Negro women cooks. . . .

Large-scale use of unskilled Negro slaves on plantations was not yet a factor of importance in Peru by 1560. Only one such operation is known to have existed, in Nazca, on the southern coast, where a royal official and encomendero ran a sugar plantation and also carried on stock-raising and general agriculture, with the labor of Negro slaves. . . .

The most frequent use of groups of unskilled Negroes was in mining, particularly gold mining. Even this was not of really basic importance; the great silver mines of highland Peru were always worked by Indians, with an exception or two. Gold mining was thought to be appropriate for Negroes because gold mines were mainly in hot, low-lying river areas. Even so, gold mining was far from a Negro monopoly. There were two major gold rushes in Peru within our period, one in Carabaya, a low-altitude area in the jurisdiction of Cuzco, in 1542 and 1543, and the other in the Quito area in 1545 and 1546. . . . In Carabaya, . . . Spaniards brought in numbers of Negro slave gangs. Less intensive gold mining with Negroes took place intermittently in various parts of Peru.

Mining gangs usually consisted of ten or fifteen raw African Negro slaves and a slave woman, Negro or Indian, to cook for them, directed by a Spaniard who might be their owner or part-owner, or just a miner-foreman. Occasionally gangs were larger. In the 1540's Francisco de Barrionuevo, a former governor of Panama, extracted gold in south and central Peru with a large force of forty-five Negroes. Though he at that time had no encomienda, the possession of so much economic power put him fully on the level of an encomendero. . . . That in time Barrionuevo gave up his mining ventures and accepted a relatively small encomienda in La Paz is representative of a general trend, the gradual fading out of Negro mining, after initial high hopes. Negro gold miners had the worst lot of all Negro slaves, tramping in gangs from one steaming river site to the next, out of contact with either the Indian or the Hispanic world, except for their Spanish overseer.

Whenever mining gangs or other kinds of work teams were made up of encomienda Indians, Negroes assumed a different role. In these situations a few Negro slaves became a permanent cadre, aiding the skilled Spaniard who directed the work, guarding the plant or equipment when the seasonal Indians were gone, and probably serving as overseers. . . .

Small-scale agriculture was one of the main areas of endeavor of Negro slaves, comparable in importance to personal service and artisanry. In Lima as in other towns, the surrounding agricultural land was divided out to encomenderos and others, in quite small parcels, at the city's founding, in this case in 1535. By the early 1540's at latest, the environs of Lima had become an impressive garden spot, full of closely spaced small holdings where Spanish agriculture was practiced, with irrigation, to supply Lima's markets. Almost every one of these holdings, called chácaras or estancias indiscriminately, had one or more Negroes working on it. In Arequipa the situation was much the same, and apparently in Trujillo as well. It is doubtful that nearly as many Negroes did agricultural work in Cuzco and Upper Peru, but the pattern did extend that far, . . .

In Lima, some Negro field workers lived in the city and went out daily to work, while others lived fulltime on the chácaras, to the distress of law-enforcement officers. Many or most of these Negroes were without any direct Spanish supervision. The agriculture they carried on was totally unspecialized. In accordance with their masters' wishes, they attempted to raise all kinds of grains, vegetables, and fruits on each plot, and if possible, a few animals as well. A fair amount of speculation in land did not affect the field workers greatly, because they were sold with the land they worked on.

The picture of life on the chácaras remains hazy, but it is clear that the Negroes did the daily work required throughout the year, and counted on seasonal help by Indians for harvesting. By the 1550's, some of the holdings were imposingly complete units, like a chácara for wheat and maize in the valley of Surco, maintained by a Negro slave farmer and carpenter, which had a house, garden, dovecot, plows, and two oxen. There were yet more ambitious chácaras where it was apparently intended that Negroes would do the bulk of the work even at harvest time. . . .

Outside the immediate environs of the cities, small landholdings devoted mainly to intensive agriculture gave way to larger, more loosely defined properties where stock raising took precedence over agriculture, and, in distant plains, superseded it entirely. . . . Whatever they were called, they had Negro slaves working on them.

As large-scale ranching began to develop in the 1550's, whole teams of Negroes worked at cattle herding. Even in the 1540's, there were some good-sized establishments, like the six Negro slave men and women who cared for a herd of cattle and goats in the Lima area in 1547. But most characteristic were the lone Negroes living deep in the country, far from the Spaniards, in charge of several cows, goats, or pigs. Herdsmen were more closely attached to the stock than to the land; whereas field Negroes were sold along with the land they worked, herdsmen were sold together with the herds.

The list of country Negroes is completed by the *tamberos* and the woodcutters. Tamberos were in charge of tambos, the roadside inns of the Incas; in the name of their encomendero masters, they sold provisions to the travelers and provided them with free wood and fodder. (There were Spanish tamberos, too, particularly on well-traveled routes where business was good.) Negroes had the reputation of being particularly hard on the Indians who supplied the provisions. The Negro woodcutters lived in the cities, but went out periodically with a mule or a lame horse to the nearest wooded area to fetch firewood to sell in the city markets.

While the great majority of Negro slaves worked directly for their owners, the practice of hiring out slaves did exist. When a special project demanded temporary extra labor, slaves would be rented from any owners who could spare them. At least one owner in Lima kept slaves specifically to be hired out for general labor, such as rowing boats, acting as servants, guarding cattle, or, in one case, digging in Francisco Pizarro's garden for gold presumed to be buried there. The price for hiring unskilled slave labor was exorbitant, . . . A special practice was the hiring out of valuable artisan slaves to Spanish artisans for a year at a time for . . . enough [money] to buy an ordinary slave permanently.

Despite occasional disappointments, Spaniards placed

extraordinary trust in their Negro slaves. Agricultural slaves had infinite opportunities to run away. Negro herdsmen not only could run away, but were in complete charge of easily movable property that had an especially high value in a country only in the process of being stocked with European varieties. The degree of independence of Negro master artisan slaves has also already been seen.

Some slaves were allowed to lend and borrow money, and it was common for Negro slaves to be entrusted with merchandise to sell. . . .

When Spaniards knew individual slaves really well, they gave them the kind of absolute confidence they otherwise extended only to close blood relatives. In 1553 a Spanish muleteer fell ill while taking his pack train, loaded with merchandise, from Arequipa to Potosí. He returned to Arequipa for treatment, leaving the senior Negro slave muleteer in charge of the merchandise, the mules, and the other Negroes, with 30 pesos in silver to spend on food and maintenance. The pack train and the merchandise, worth several thousand pesos, represented the Spanish muleteer's life savings and more.

Why Negro slaves in Peru, presented with such multiple opportunity, did not all run away, may seem a mystery. Part of the explanation is the lack of a place of refuge. Most Spanish settlements were far away from such dense tropical forests as protected runaway slaves in Panama and the Antilles. Runaway Negroes could not hope to be received among the Indians, to whom Negroes were merely another type of intruder. In any case, hiding among the Indians was impossible for Negroes because their distinctive physical appearance made them readily identifiable. In effect, runaways had only one place to go, some other Spanish settlement than the one they were in. Slaves who had a specific fear or grievance could at times find temporary refuge in the Spanish monasteries, but this was hardly running away.

In conditions like these, the recovery of runaway Negro

slaves was a relatively easy, even a predictable process. The Spaniards were so confident of recovering runaways that it was not at all uncommon for a runaway slave, while still absent, to be sold without conditions, at a good price, to a new owner. . . .

Since runaway Negroes could not live among the Indians and were quickly detected in the cities, the only way they could hope to maintain themselves was by organizing bands of cimarrons or renegades in the countryside. Geography kept Peru from becoming a land of cimarrons like Panama, but there were usually a few small bands in operation in some part of the country. . . .

The Spaniards felt little or no reluctance to liberate individual Negro slaves. Negroes in Peru started obtaining their freedom very early, by 1536 at the latest, and the movement continued with increasing momentum right through 1560. Most of the Negroes freed had to buy their liberty in one way or another. Charity played an important role, even when freedom was bought, but it came into full operation only when the owner no longer needed the slave, or the slave was not in the prime of life. Spaniards made true grants of freedom in their testaments, or when they left for Spain; also to aged slaves and to infant children of slaves. Such grants were in their sum effect a significant factor, but they cannot be said to represent the ordinary avenue to freedom.

Slaves somehow managed to accumulate the money to free themselves. If there was any legal obligation on the part of masters to liberate slaves for their just price, the masters did not recognize it. Some owners let their slaves go cheaply as an act of charity, others for a good price. Others held out for exorbitant amounts; . . . Either slaves were allowed to earn money on the side, or they received some sort of pay or allowance from their masters. However they did it, it was a difficult process. . . . Many slaves could not get the money together, and relied on loans, or worked out the equivalent of the price. The loans came from various sources, often from other Negroes who were already free and solvent. Loans might take the form of an advance in pay from the new freedman's employer.

Along with the flood of the newly freed was a trickle of Negroes who arrived in Peru already free.

Free Negroes were an important class of people. Though it is impossible to estimate their absolute numbers, . . . they were numerous indeed. In Lima they were already considered a problem as early as 1538. As was true of Negro slaves, more free Negroes lived on the coast than in the highlands, but they were to be found in the highlands too.

The freedom that Negroes bought was far from absolute. In all kinds of legal records, Spaniards were careful to see that freedmen were specifically called free Negroes, the only ordinary exceptions being some light mulattoes. Spanish legal authorities, often calling free Negroes simply slaves, continued to claim farreaching jurisdiction over them. Freedmen were periodically ordered to register and to take positions with Spanish masters. Once authorities issued a peremptory order for all free Negroes to leave the country; another time all freedmen were to join an unpaid, involuntary street-cleaning force. All such orders and schemes failed, partially or completely, because of the social reality. Though Spaniards as a group were disturbed to see the rise of a class of independent Negroes (whose contribution to slave delinquency is undeniable), Spaniards as individuals tolerated them and found them useful. Not a single free Negro left Peru; . . .

Legislation requiring former slaves to take Spanish masters was more serious. First, it had a strong nuisance value, forcing the freedmen into at least ostensible and sporadic compliance. More basically, such ordinances had a certain shaping effect on the lives of free Negroes; they were the legal precipitation of the Spaniards' determination not to let Negroes take over positions and functions that they desired for themselves. Artisans' shops run inde-

pendently by free Negroes, for example, were in constant
jeopardy. With this upper limit, freedmen enjoyed the
legal privileges of Spaniards (and it should be remembered that even Spaniards were subject to orders to find
a job or leave town). A freedman could own and bequeath any kind of property, marry, and carry on
litigation.

The standard Spanish ambitions of acquiring a house,
a wife, land, fine clothes, and Negro slaves were also the
ambitions of free Negroes. Successful free Negroes were
particularly anxious to enjoy the respectability conferred
by marriage; most prominent free Negroes were married,
usually to free Negro women, or less often, to Negro slave
women or Indian women. The status of free Negroes was
judged by the same set of criteria as that of Spaniards.
Francisco Hernández, the recognized leader of Lima's
free Negro community, was married, propertied, and had
been in Peru from the early days of the conquest.

Free Negroes formed a coherent group or community,
much like the Basques or foreigners, but even more tightly
knit. Negroes married within the community, had their
closest friends and worst enemies within it, loaned each
other money, and preferred to do all kinds of business
with each other. In the late 1540's the free Negroes organized a cofradía or religious brotherhood, over Spanish
opposition.

Since practically all free Negroes had been slaves, there
was a close relationship between the occupations of the
two groups. The activities of freedmen can be described
summarily by saying that they merely did all the same
things slaves did, except that they did them as independent
operators or as wage earners. Personal service, agriculture,
and artisanry were the primary occupations for Negroes,
whether free or slave. As in other ages and countries,
many freedmen maintained a close relationship with their
former masters. Slaves ordinarily took their master's surname at the time of freedom; many either continued to
work for their masters, or stayed dependent on them in-

directly, living on or near the master's properties. The very word "freedman" (*horro*) could be synonymous with servant. Free Negro servants got a yearly wage . . . which was not much less than the wage of an unskilled Spaniard.

Naturally there were some opportunities denied to slaves but open to freedmen—particularly activities having to do with owning property. Agricultural workers were anxious to have their own fields or cháracas, and often succeeded in getting them, buying land sometimes from Spaniards, sometimes from Indian caciques. The free Negroes sent to Carabaya did not become mere mining employees as planned; soon they were the owners of agricultural land cultivated by Indian labor. Many free Negroes bought houses in the cities to live in, and some owned property which they rented out as a source of income. Freedmen also owned their own Negro slaves; a prominent Negro . . . might own several. Negroes loaned money, primarily to other Negroes but also to Spaniards, . . . Few if any succeeded in becoming long-distance whole-sale merchants, but they did speculate on merchandise by having merchants invest money for them.

As independent operators, freedmen might do miscel-laneous things, from selling llamas to running a tavern, but tended to concentrate on certain types of enterprises, by operation of the process that has always led to the economic specialization of foreign minorities. Negro women were associated with, though they did not monop-olize, the business of baking bread and biscuit to sell in city markets. Since independent Negro artisanry encoun-tered resistance, much Negro effort was channeled into the construction of adobe walls and fences, an activity Spaniards did not resent. (In the highlands, where Span-ish artisans were not so overwhelmingly numerous, inde-pendent Negro artisans seem to have had an easier time of it.) Many of the town criers and executioners in Peruvian cities were free Negroes, because few Spaniards would consent to hold the post.

In Chile a free Negro became an encomendero; in

Puertoviejo a member of the city council and royal official was said to be a Negro and former slave. But these were fringe areas; in central Peru, the kind of complete success and social acceptance represented by encomendero status and high office was far out of the reach of free Negroes, though some did achieve wealth and started to improve their social status outside the Negro community. . . .

The fate of the children of free Negroes is little more than a subject for speculation. The records for the period up to 1560 contain remarkably little about them, beyond the facts that their parents could bequeath them property, and that some of them were put into apprenticeship with Spanish artisans. There is little reason to doubt that the second generation was headed into the path marked by the first; but whether free Negroes were a truly self-perpetuating class, or sustained themselves by each generation's contribution of new freedmen, is a question to be answered by research in documents of a later period.

Free Negroes present a double image. In the official municipal records they appear as a band of troublemakers, abetting runaway slaves, covering up thefts, fomenting unrest. In the notarial records they appear an industrious and useful class of people who seized every opportunity given them, and did much to build up the country for themselves and the Spaniards. . . .

Africans, or Negroes as we must call them, since some of them were born in Spain or the Indies, were a factor of absolutely first importance in Peru in the conquest period. They were an organic part of the enterprise of occupying Peru from its inception. The dominance of Spanish language and culture was never threatened, but in terms of ethnic or racial groups, the conquest of Peru was carried out by an equal partnership. Negroes were in a hundred ways the agents and auxiliaries of the Spaniards, in effect doubling their numbers, making the Spanish occupation a much more thorough affair than it could have been without them. Far from their own roots, apart from the Indians, the Negroes assimilated Spanish culture with amazing speed, and were for the main part the Spaniards' willing allies, in spite of the cimarrons. And this willingness is understandable. Though Negroes were subordinated to Spaniards, they were not exploited in the plantation manner; except for mining gangs, Negroes in Peru counted as individuals.

7

ROBERT C. WEST

PLACER MINING
AND AFRICAN LABOR

*The economy of New Granada (Ecuador, Venezuela,
Colombia, and Panama) was based primarily on
mining throughout much of the colonial period.
African slaves were imported by the Spanish crown
to replace Indian labor in the mines because the
government wished to protect these natives of
Spanish America from extinction. In the following
selection, geographer Robert West, of the Louisiana
State University, describes the utilization of African
slaves and free labor in the gold placer mines of
western Colombia.*

Western Colombia was the largest mining area in the
Spanish colonies in which Negro slaves eventually replaced Indian labor. . . . [A]fter 1510, subsequent to the
decimation of the native population, some blacks were
brought into gold fields of Hispaniola and Cuba; also,
Negroes mined most of the gold in Veragua (northern

From Robert C. West, *Colonial Placer Mining in Colombia,* Louisiana State University Studies, Social Science Series, no. 2 (Baton
Rouge: Louisiana State University Press, 1952), pp. 83–90. Reprinted
by permission of the Louisiana State University Press.

coast of Panama) and in Venezuela. But in terms of numbers of slaves engaged in mining, these areas were sec-
ondary to New Granada. . . .

Small numbers of Negro slaves were brought into New
Granada with the first Spanish settlers. On most of their
entradas, Spaniards took along Negroes as personal or
household servants, for such servitude had long been
established in the Peninsula. . . . [I]n the 1530's slaves
were brought into the Sinú area from Cartagena to dig
gold from Indian graves. Later, in 1549, a royal order
specified that only Negroes were to be employed in grave
robbing; Indians were to be exempt from such work. By
1544, and probably earlier, blacks were working in the
mines around Popayán, and by 1550 Spaniards had introduced gangs of Negro slaves into the mines of Buriticá.
The influx of Negroes into mining areas, however, did
not become noticeable until the end of the sixteenth century, when it was apparent that the Indian population had
collapsed. Since reliable data are incomplete and scattered, estimates of the number of Negroes brought into
New Granada during the colonial period are extremely
hazardous. By 1590 at least a thousand slaves were imported annually through Cartagena, and most of these
were sold eventually to miners. During the sixteenth century most of the slaves destined for the mining industry
were shipped into lowland Antioquia and the Cauca and
Magdalena valleys, where the Indian element had been
severely reduced.

. . . Throughout the remainder of the colonial period
the importation of Negroes into western Colombia was
sporadic. Although the supply of slaves from Africa to
Cartagena was under government regulation, arrival of
slave ships was uncertain. Moreover, the high cost of
transport into the interior often made the price of slaves
prohibitive to many miners. At the close of the seventeenth century and during the first quarter of the eighteenth, many blacks were taken into the Chocó and other

Pacific coastal areas. By 1787, however, the provinces of Antioquia, Chocó, and Popayán, which included the principal placer mines of New Granada, contained only seventeen thousand Negro slaves.

Most of the slaves that entered the mines of New Granada were imported directly from Africa—mainly from the Guinea coast, the Congo, and Angola. Customarily, a Negro slave was given the surname corresponding to the name of his tribal language, or sometimes from the name of the slaving station from which he was obtained, . . . Negroes born in the New World usually took the surname "Criollo." . . . Thus from the name lists in account books of the mines, a rough, though sometimes erroneous, idea can be obtained of the provenience of the blacks of any one camp. The language and most of the native culture of a given slave were quickly lost when he was forced to work with Negroes of diverse tribes and to learn Spanish, the lingua franca of the land. Blacks from the Guinea coast were preferred by most miners, while those of the Congo and the Carabali Negroes were considered rebellious.

Slaves destined for the mines of western Colombia entered through the port of Cartagena, one of the largest colonial slave marts of the Spanish mainland. Mineowners obtained slaves chiefly through itinerant merchants, who purchased Negroes in Cartagena and, together with other types of merchandise, shipped them up the Magdalena and Cauca rivers in canoes. Rarely did a merchant carry more than 25 to 30 slaves at one time. During the eighteenth century *bozales* . . . were valued at 300 pesos, whereas *criollos* brought from 400 to 500 pesos. Young females were often valued as highly as males, for women were used not only for breeding and as household servants but also as agricultural workers and mine laborers, particularly in the placers.

Miners were often sorely pressed to raise sufficient funds to pay for slaves brought in by merchants. As early as

1595 many established miners of Zaragoza were forced to borrow money or purchase on credit in order to obtain an adequate number of Negroes to form a labor gang, or *cuadrilla*. Throughout the colonial period the loudest complaint of the miner concerned the high prices and the irregular supply of Negro slaves.

. . . The colonial mineowner of western Colombia was usually known as a *señor de cuadrilla*—an indication of the importance attached to slave gangs in the mines. The size of the *cuadrilla* ranged from five or six to more than one hundred blacks, depending upon the extent of the workings and the capital of the *señor*. Often only half of the slave gang was employed in mining; the others, called *piezas de roza*, were required to grow food for the camp in fields nearby. Both the mining and farming *cuadrillas* were composed of men and women. Negresses, like Indian women, proved to be excellent divers and panners in the placer mines. In sluicing operations it was usually the task of the women to scrape the sluice with the *almocafre* and to pan with the batea, while the heavy work with the iron bar was assigned to the men. Still today the tradition of female labor is common in small placer workings in the Chocó and Antioquia, where much of the gold and platinum is panned by women and girls.

The slaves of a *señor* were managed by a white or mulatto overseer (*administrador de minas*), who was well versed in mining techniques. A rich *señor* with many mines and *cuadrillas* usually resided in one of the large towns, such as Zaragoza or Popayán, and only occasionally visited his workings; poor mineowners were often the administrators as well, living in the camp with their small *cuadrillas*. At the head of each labor gang was a Negro slave captain (*capitán de cuadrilla*), a trusty whose duties included the disciplining of his gang, the distribution of food, and the collection of the weekly take of gold for his administrator. The Negro *capitán* was an important person; he was something of a chief, and held the respect of his gang. He was likewise respected by his master, who often gave him special rations to induce him to keep his people . . . working. Occasionally a female *capitana* had charge of the women of the gang. Today within the Chocó, Negro mining gangs, which now work on a share basis, are still led by a person called the *capitán* or *cabo de cuadrilla*.

. . . Examination of account books of the mines and documents pertaining to official inspections reveals that in general slaves in the mining camps of New Granada received humane treatment. As the blacks were valuable chattels, it behooved the *señor de cuadrilla* to feed his slaves adequately and to administer medicine to the sick.

The slave food ration varied from region to region, but generally it consisted of plantains, maize, salt, and fresh or salted meat. The ration of plantains was especially common in the west-coast lowlands. There, each Negro received six plantains a day, a small weekly portion of maize and salt, and, in some camps, two pounds of salt pork or beef per week. In other areas, such as Popayán and Antioquia, each slave recived a weekly ration of twenty-five pounds (one almud) of shelled maize, which with salt and an occasional quantity of meat represented a substantial diet. Sometimes local crop failure resulted in famine and actual starvation in some mining districts.

Although in the hot lowlands clothing was not essential, most mineowners supplied their blacks with pieces of woolen and cotton cloth for shirts and breechclouts at least once a year. In high, cooler areas such as Remedios a piece of cotton cloth sufficiently large to cover the body was given to each slave every six months. At the present time most Negro-male miners in the Chocó work only in breechclout, while the women wear ragged cotton dresses. Until a few years ago it was quite proper for any Negro male to enter a Chocoan town dressed only in breechclout. Today he is liable to arrest by village authorities if so attired.

Disease seems to have been rampant among the Negroes in the mining areas. While partially immune to malaria, the blacks were often ravaged by measles and smallpox, but yaws . . . various intestinal diseases, syphilis . . . leprosy, and tuberculosis . . . appear to have been the principal maladies. To combat illness among their slaves, the *señores* went to some expense to keep special foods and medicines in the mining camp. Chickens were imported into Zaragoza and Remedios from the Valley of Aburrá (Medellín) mainly for broth and eggs to feed ailing Negroes; hams and fresh and salt pork were usually on hand for convalescents and for women bedridden after childbirth. Various medieval remedies, . . . purges, salves and oils of many sorts, herbs, verdigris, honey and refined sugar, and wine, filled the medicine chest. Some miners even hired itinerant "barbers and surgeons"—the doctors of the day—to let blood from sick slaves and to pull ailing teeth. According to one *señor de cuadrilla* of Zaragoza, writing in 1632: ". . . the expense incurred for medicines is necessary in this land, for without medicinal care it would be impossible to keep a slave gang, because of the continual sickness of the Negroes. . . ."

The high incidence of disease among the Negroes in the mines was reflected in a high mortality rate. A continual influx of new slaves was necessary to replace the dead, and when such were not available, gold production decreased sharply. Moreover, infant mortality must have been high; for instance, in Remedios (1632) a *cuadrilla* of ninety-four slaves, thirty-eight of whom were women of childbearing age, contained only eleven children under ten years.

Since the sixteenth century it was customary for mine-owners of New Granada to give Negro slaves rest on Sundays and other religious holidays. On such days, partly to keep them out of mischief, Negroes were permitted to work the mines on their own account; all gold obtained thus belonged to them to spend as they saw fit—for food (usually meat and delicacies), tobacco, and cloth. The mining camps consequently became attractive markets for itinerant merchants from Cartagena, Bogotá, and Quito.

Through the system of free-labor days any slave could theoretically accumulate sufficient gold to buy his freedom. That privilege, however, was enjoyed chiefly by the captain of the *cuadrilla*; for, receiving the greatest portion of the take, he was the better able to save the necessary amount demanded for liberty (300 to 400 pesos).

Despite such limited privileges, the slaves occasionally rebelled and fled into the wilderness to escape servitude and hard labor in the mines. By 1576 a large number of blacks from Buriticá and other mining areas of Antioquia had fled into the Chocó. For many years during the last quarter of the sixteenth century small groups of slaves had been slipping away from the mines of lowland Antioquia and had established themselves in fortified settlements (*palenques*) in swampy jungles between the Cauca and Nechí rivers. Some of these settlements contained more than a hundred Negro men and women. From their *palenques* the runaway Negroes (*cimarrones*) raided outlying mining camps and preyed on shipping along the Cauca and Nechí. A particularly bad rebellion which occurred in Zaragoza in 1598 forced the Spaniards to organize a military campaign to rout the Negroes from their fortified villages. Throughout the remainder of the colonial period the Spanish miners of Antioquia and the Chocó were pestered by periodic outbreaks of Negroes in the mines and raids by *cimarrones*.

. . . By the end of the colonial period a sizable group of free Negroes (*libres*) had evolved in the mining areas of New Granada. The free element was composed mainly of Negroes who had been able to buy freedom, the runaways, the mulattoes (offspring of white and Negro unions), and the few individuals who had been emancipated by compassionate masters. Almost invariably the *libres* continued in the mining profession, usually working either as independent gold washers or as free laborers in

Spanish mines; some even acquired ownership of small placers and one or two slaves. In 1809 it was estimated that more than 80 per cent of the gold produced in Antioquia was mined by free labor, the rest by slaves. Moreover, by the end of the eighteenth century a large part of the Negroes of the Chocó had acquired free status. Thus when general emancipation of the New Granadan slaves took place in 1851, an occupational precedent had been long established, and most of the freed blacks continued as miners, forming the labor base of the present industry in the lowlands of western Colombia.

Chiefly from the free-Negro and mulatto miners developed the renowned *mazamorrero* of Colombia—the itinerant gold panner, who with his family wanders up and down streams working small bar or terrace deposits. Many follow dredges or work on the margins of large hydraulicking operations, panning tailings for gold. Today the *mazamorrero* is by law permitted to operate within two hundred meters of any dredge, and he may pan in all streams without filing claim, regardless of legal ownership of the land. Although the term *mazamorrero* was applied to Indian panners at the beginning of the seventeenth century, the profession became well established only by the end of the colonial period. The term itself derives from the word *mazamorra*, the name given to sand and gravel sluice tailings, which were often reworked by free Negroes and Indians.

The old colonial mining areas where Negro labor predominated are today among the major regions of black or mulatto population of Colombia. The inhabitants of the entire Pacific coast, including the Chocó, are chiefly Negro; and the rural lowlands of Antioquia, those of the Cauca and the lower Magdalena, and the Patía Basin are populated mainly by Negroes, mulattoes, and sambos (mixed Indian-Negro). Even on the high, cold Antioquian Batholith there exist small communities of Negroes, descendants of the slave population that once worked the placers of the Río Chico and Río Grande near Santa Rosa.

8

JUAN AND ULLOA

EIGHTEENTH-CENTURY SPANISH AMERICAN TOWNS: AFRICAN AND AFRO-HISPANIC LIFE AND LABOR IN CITIES AND SUBURBS

In the spring of 1735 two young Spanish naval lieutenants joined an expedition of French scientists on a journey through northern Spanish America and the Caribbean. Among the cities they visited were Cartagena, a major port for Spanish America's slave commerce; Porto Bello, on the Isthmus of Panama, during the galleon season the greatest fairground in the Americas; Panama City, "about 30 minutes west of Porto Bello"; Quito, captial of present-day Ecuador; and Lima, the capital of Peru. The narrative left us by these two Spaniards, Juan and Ulloa,

From Don Jorge Juan and Don Antonio de Ulloa, *A Voyage to South America: Describing at Large the Spanish Cities, Towns and Provinces, etc. on that Extensive Continent; Undertaken by Command of the King of Spain by Don George Juan, and Don Antonio de Ulloa.* Translated by John Adams, 2 vols. (London: n.p. 1806), bk. 1, chaps. 2, 4; bk. 2, chaps. 2, 5, 6; bk. 3, chap. 5; bk. 5, chap. 5; bk. 7, chap. 5.

provides an excellent picture of eighteenth-century South American society.

Cartagena

The inhabitants may be divided into different castes or tribes . . . Whites, Negroes, and Indians. . . .

The class of Negroes is not the least numerous, and is divided into two parts; the free and the slaves. These are again subdivided into Creoles and Bozares, part of which are employed in the cultivation of the haziendas, or estancias. Those in the city are obliged to perform the most laborious services, and pay out of their wages a certain quota to their masters, subsisting themselves on the small remainder. The violence of the heat not permitting them to wear any clothes, their only covering is a small piece of cotton stuff about their waist; the female slaves go in the same manner. Some of these live at the estancias, being married to the slaves who work there; while those in the city sell in the markets all kinds of eatables, and dry fruits, sweetmeats, cakes made of the maize, and cassava, and several other things about the streets. Those who have children sucking at their breast, which is the case of the generality, carry them on their shoulders, in order to have their arms at liberty; and when the infants are hungry they give them the breast either under the arm or over the shoulder, without taking them from their backs. This will perhaps appear incredible; but their breasts, being left to grow without any pressure on them, often hang down to their very waist, and are not therefore difficult to turn over their shoulders for the convenience of the infant. . . .

. . . [M]en without employment, stocks, or recommendation; who, leaving their country as fugitives, and, without license from the officers, come to seek their fortune in a country where they are utterly unknown; after traversing the streets till they have nothing left to procure them lodging or food, . . . are reduced to have recourse to the last extremity, the Franciscan hospital. . . . The Negro and Mulatto free women, moved at their deplorable condition, carry them to their houses, and nurse them with the greatest care and affection. If any one die, they bury him by the charity they procure, and even cause masses to be said for him. The general issue of this endearing benevolence is, that the Chapetone, on his recovery, during the fervour of his gratitude, marries either his Negro or Mulatto benefactress, or one of her daughters. . . .

Chocolate, here known only by the name of cacao, is so common, that there is not a Negro slave but constantly allows himself a regale of it after breakfast; and the Negro women sell it ready made about the streets, at the rate of a quarter of a real (about five farthings sterling) for a dish. . . .

The passion for smoking is no less universal, prevailing among persons of all ranks in both sexes. . . . This custom the ladies learn in their childhood from their nurses, who are Negro slaves. . . .

. . . [H]ere is an office for the assiento of Negroes, whither they are brought, and, as it were, kept as pledges, till such persons as want them on their estates come to purchase them; Negroes being generally employed in husbandry and other laborious country works.

Porto Bello

At the east end of the town, which is the road to Panama, is a quarter called Guiney, being the place where all the Negroes of both sexes, whether slaves or free, have their habitations. This quarter is very much crowded when the galleons are here, most of the inhabitants of the town entirely quitting their houses for the advantage of letting them, while others content themselves with a small part in order to make money of the rest. The Mulattoes and other poor families also remove, either to Guiney, or to cottages already erected near it, or built on this occasion. Great numbers of artificers from Panama likewise, who flock to Porto Bello to work at their respective callings, lodge in this quarter for cheapness. . . .

Whilst the assiento of Negroes subsisted either with the French or English, one of their principal factories was settled here; and was of considerable advantage to its commerce, as being the channel by which not only Panama was supplied with Negroes, but from whence they were sent all over the kingdom of Peru: on which account the agents of the assiento were allowed to bring with them such a quantity of provisions as was thought necessary, both for their own use, and their slaves of both sexes.

Panama

The Peru and Guayaquil vessels, unless at the time when the armada is here, return empty, except when they have an opportunity of taking Negroes on board; as, while the assiento subsists, there is at Panama a factory, or office, which corresponds with that at Porto Bello; and hither the Negroes are brought. . . .

The owners of the Negroes employ the most proper persons for this fishery; which being performed at the bottom of the sea, they must be expert swimmers, and capable of holding their breath a long time. These they send to the islands, where they have huts built for their lodgings and boats which hold eight, ten, or twenty Negroes, under the command of an officer. In these boats they go to such parts as are known to produce pearls, and where the depth of water is not above ten, twelve, or fifteen fathoms. Here they anchor; and the Negroes having a rope fastened around their bodies, and the other end to the side of the boat, they take with them a small weight, to accelerate their sinking, and plunge into the water. On reaching the bottom, they take up an oyster, which they put under the left arm; the second they hold in their left hand, and the third in their right; with these three oysters, and something another in their mouth, they rise to breathe, and put them in a bag. When they have rested themselves awhile, and recovered their breath, they dive a second time; and thus continue, till they have either completed their task, or their strength fails them. Every one of these Negro divers is obliged daily to deliver to his master a fixed number of pearls; so that when they have got the requisite number of oysters in their bag, they begin to open them, and deliver the pearls to the officer, till they have made up the number due to their master; and if the pearl be not formed, it is sufficient, without any regard to its being small or faulty. The remainder, however large or beautiful, are the Negro's own property, nor has the master the least claim to them; the slaves being allowed to sell them to whom they please, though the master generally purchases them at a very small price.

These Negroes cannot every day make up their number, as in many of the oysters the pearl is not at all, or but imperfectly formed; or the oyster is dead, whereby the pearl is so damaged, as to be of no value; and as no allowance is made for such pearls, they must make up their numbers with others.

Besides the toil of this fishery, from the oysters strongly adhering to the rocks, they are also in no small danger from some kinds of fish, which either seize the Negroes, or, by striking on them, crush them by their weight against the bottom.

Every Negro, to defend himself against these animals, carries with [him] a sharp knife, with which, if the fish offers to assault him, he endeavors to strike it in a part where it has no power to hurt him; on which the fish immediately flies. The officers keep a watchful eye on these voracious creatures, and, on discovering them, shake the ropes fastened to the Negroes' bodies, that they may be upon their guard; . . .

Quito

The commonalty may be divided into four classes; Spaniards or Whites, Mestizos, Indians or Natives, and Negroes, with their progeny. These last are not proportionally so numerous as in the other parts of the Indies; occasioned by it being something inconvenient to bring Negroes to Quito, and the different kinds of agriculture being generally performed by Indians.

Lima

The inhabitants of Lima are composed of whites, or Spaniards, Negroes, Indians, Mestizos, and other casts, proceeding from the mixture of all three. . . .

The Negroes, Mulattoes, and their descendants, form the greater number of the inhabitants; and of these are the greatest part of the mechanics; though here the Europeans also follow the same occupations, which are not at Lima reckoned disgraceful to them, as they are at Quito; for gain being here the universal passion, the inhabitants pursue it by means of any trade, without regard to its being followed by Mulattoes, interest here preponderating against any other consideration. . . .

. . . [D]omestick services [are] performed by Negroes and Mulattoes, either slaves or free, though generally by the former.

9

FRANKLIN KNIGHT

SLAVE SOCIETY IN CUBA

In Slave Society in Cuba *Franklin Knight examines
the stresses put on traditional institutions by economic changes, in particular, the effect, of such
changes on race relations. His is a detailed picture
of an oppressive society and how the black man
fought it. To conclude his analysis, he also offers a
comparison of the situation in Cuba with that in
Puerto Rico.*

*Knight is Associate Professor of History at the
Johns Hopkins University. He has written exten-
sively on slavery in Cuba.*

Cuban slave society, like any other slave society, was subdivided into castes and classes. The castes corresponded
very roughly to the racial divisions in which membership
was hereditary and defined by laws: the white population
first, and then, in descending order of social rank, the free
persons of color and the slaves. A class stratification
characterized each caste. The term class is appropriate
in this context, referring as it does to those who had a
certain degree of social mobility, and whose status and

From Franklin W. Knight, *Slave Society in Cuba During the Nineteenth Century* (Madison: University of Wisconsin Press; © 1970
by the Regents of the University of Wisconsin), pp. 59–61, 63–65,
72–82, 133–134, 190–191.

position were not necessarily either heritable or legally prescribed. This combination of caste and class provided a certain stability to the society by allowing a dynamism within the separate classes of each racial group, while retaining and constraining the various elements within the castes.

The two classes within the slave caste were the urban and domestic, and the field slaves. Arriving Africans joined either of these two classes. But the number of domestic and urban slaves in the nineteenth century was relatively small, and the chance of a recent arrival finding his way into this group was extremely slim. A small minority of the slaves lived in the towns, where they were employed mainly as domestic servants, or in minor skills and simple professions (though these services formed an important economic function in the society as a whole). The vast majority of the Africans imported during the nineteenth century—more than 80 per cent of those brought in between 1840 and 1860—ended up working on the plantations of the interior. It was precisely this preponderance of rural slaves which made Cuban slave society in the nineteenth century a plantation society, and hence distinct from Cuban slavery in the earlier period. . . .

. . . [U]rban slavery could not be considered the norm for the society. . . . Any attempt to generalize about Cuban slavery must bear in mind some important distinctions, and not the least of these is the separate environment of the two slave groups. The two classes were a world apart. Urban slaves had some unique opportunities and resources which their rural counterparts lacked or were denied. Moreover, the entire organization of urban and domestic slavery in Cuba, as in other parts of the world, lent itself to moderation and liberality. . . . [C]onditions surrounding urban slaves were more closely comparable to the conditions of the master group than to the conditions of rural slaves.

The urban slave enjoyed advantages denied his rural

counterpart in three crucial areas: in the method of labor and participation in the cash economy; in social and sexual conduct; and in the available legal resources.

Urban slaves fell into three large groups. Many were domestic helpers, with some women being wet nurses for the infants of the white people, and females in general dominating the domestic occupations. Many others conducted some specific occupation—coachmen, carpenters, dressmakers, gardeners, musicians—or small trade. A third group hired out their labor either for their own gain, or for their master's. No group, however, was entirely exclusive, and sometimes circumstances superseded preferences. . . . [W]ithin the urban slave community during a certain period in the nineteenth century it was considered somewhat ignominious to be rented, as such a gesture indicated the poverty and low social position of the owners.

Writers on slavery generally conceded that the urban slaves, regardless of their occupations, established an understanding and a relationship with their masters which was completely absent elsewhere. Not only was the life of slaves in the towns far less regimented, but also the opportunities to get cash enabled them to buy their freedom with relatively greater facility than rural slaves. Urban slaves also mixed with the free colored people, and escaped from their masters with greater ease.

With far more cash and far more freedom, the urban slave both fed and dressed himself better, and enjoyed himself more. Instead of the striped, coarse clothes and simple dress of the plantation slave, the urban slave was sometimes smartly—if uncomfortably—uniformed if he were a coachman or she a preferred domestic helper. Otherwise, the slaves in the city generally dressed in the style of the whites. In the towns, too, the slaves participated in a wide variety of common attractions, ranging from membership in an Afro-Cuban *cabildo*, or lodge, to dances and drinking in their *bodegas*, or taverns. Such forms of entertainment took place with their friends of the same accepted "tribe," or the *carabelas*—their shipmates from Africa. Sexual union was facilitated by the consistently larger proportion of black women in the towns. Apart from this, sexual relations with the whites were common, and often rewarding for the black parties involved. For not only did the whites offer handsome material rewards in cash or other valuables which assisted in *coartación*, the method by which the slave gained his freedom, but also, albeit quite rarely, they gave their slaves freedom in their wills. . . .

CUBAN SLAVE POPULATION

Year*	Urban	% of all slaves	Rural	% of all slaves	Total slaves
1855	70,691	19.0	304,115	81.0	374,806
1856	66,132	17.8	305,243	82.2	371,375
1857	65,610	17.5	307,375	82.5	376,899
1871	55,830	20.9	231,790	79.1	287,620

* All figures are for January.

Most rural slaves found themselves working on tobacco farms, coffee plantations, or sugar plantations. Rural life and conditions for the slaves were so far removed from city or great house conditions that banishment to the plantation was a frequent threat against recalcitrant slaves. . . .

There was a general consensus that conditions of labor varied according to the nature of the agricultural enterprise. The tobacco farms were thought to offer the easiest life, followed by the coffee plantations, where the work was not very arduous. Life on the sugar plantations, however, was seen in Hobbesian terms as "nasty, brutish, and short." The life and conditions of any particular group of slaves depended, of course, on the personality of the master. Notwithstanding, two factors corresponded to make the labor and living conditions on the coffee and tobacco farms more favorable than on the sugar plantations. In the first place, the nature of the tasks differed and the need for regimentation was less: only sugar demanded a great number of workers who had to accomplish their tasks in a very important and specific period of time. In the second place, many white planters lived on their farms, and often worked with their slaves in tending and reaping the harvests of tobacco or coffee. . . .

By the middle of the nineteenth century, tobacco-farming was an activity of free white and free colored people, with very little use of slave labor. . . .

For the Cuban [sugar] slave the year had two significant divisions: *zafra*, or crop-time; and *tiempo muerto*, or dead season. These two divisions not only composed his yearly cycle but also decided his daily activities.

The beginning of the calendar year often coincided with the beginning of the harvest. All the slaves were given the first of two changes of clothes (the other being given at the end of the harvest). Each man received one loosely-fitting cotton shirt, and one pair of pants, which reached just below the knees, a woolen cap, a short, thick flannel jacket, and a blanket. Each woman received one striped cotton dress and a cotton scarf. . . . At the end of the harvest, the rations were almost identical, except that the men were given straw hats instead of woolen caps. A holiday usually followed this first distribution of clothing, the signal that the harvest was about to begin.

Before the actual work began, however, it was important that all the slaves knew precisely where they worked, and the order of their rotation. At the first session on a new estate, this was done by an assembly of the entire working force, and their division. First the men for the boiler house were called forward. They were the strongest men in the force, and were handed over to the maestro de azúcar. The number of boilers determined the number of men. Each boiler needed about 7 attendants, with an additional 4 or 5 for odd jobs. A factory of 5 boilers had about 39 men.

The cartmen who hauled the canes were next selected. If the estate lacked its own domestic railroad, the number of cartmen was equal to the number of men in the boiling house, since they took over the first night shift from these men, after their own day's work in the fields. For that reason they had to be the second strongest team of men.

Following in descending order of strength came the cutters. Numbering about fifty for a medium-sized estate, they had to be taught the way of cutting in order to achieve maximum safety and maximum output. The cutter held the cane in his left hand, then first cut off the leaves with one swift stroke of his machete. He then cut the cane as near as possible to the ground with a second stroke of the machete, and threw the stalk behind him. At nights the canecutters relieved the men in the purging house, and those carrying the bagasse on the compound.

Lesser duties followed in this order of selection: 25 men for the purging house; 50 women and boys to collect the cane, stack it, and help to load the carts; 4 boys to change the teams of oxen; 2 older men and women to collect the cane which fell from the carts or railway wagons along the way; 8 men to take away the green bagasse (crushed canes) from the mills; 10 men to carry the dry bagasse and tend to the fires; and 60 additional women and a few boys to attend to the cooking, and to serve water to the men in the fields.

Harvest was the time of work for everyone on an estate. It presented a scene of concentrated and determined labor. During these months, the slaves averaged a workday of nearly twenty hours, even on the best-run estates. The slaves worked almost to the maximum of their physical ability. . . .

In order to keep the slaves awake, and as a stimulus to work, the whip became the chief instrument of the mayorales and contramayorales. . . .

Indeed, the need for continuous labor was so great at this time that the handbook recommended that the men in the boiler house be given their night meals on the job. Nevertheless, despite the rigorous regime of crop-time, many reporters remarked that the slaves not only survived, but even displayed a robust physical appearance.

The second distribution of clothing signalled the end of harvest. The slaves cleared the land and planted new fields of sugar cane, weeded the old fields of "ratoon" cane, and cut wood to prepare for the next harvest. These occupations were time-consuming and made reasonably heavy demands on the labor force.

. . .The planting season usually lasted from September to December. More often, however, the scarcity of labor forced the planters to continue the operation long after the close of the conventional season. At such times the planters might be forced to hire additional slaves to cut wood or tend the cattle. . . .

Many attempts were made to use steam-driven plows to replace the hand plows used by the slaves. But although the machines were far more efficient, their high cost, coupled with the fact that they could not be easily operated by slaves, tended to make them prohibitive for all but the richest planters. . . . Following the path of least resistance, many planters preferred to take fullest advantage of the wretched system of slavery while it still existed, or sought simply to replace their slave labor by equally wretched indentured Asians.

One of the innovations of plantation agriculture in Cuba, at least in the history of slavery there, was the provision of facilities for medical care for the sick, and a nursery for the small children. The sick room, or miniature hospital, catered to the small eventualities of the estate. It possessed all the medicine required for the frequent injuries, small infections, or the colds and influenza epidemics which accompanied the rainy summer months.

Many slaves used the facilities of the infirmary as an excuse for procrastination. The result of this was that some planters were particularly skeptical about admitting the illnesses of their slaves. In the earlier days of slavery, some plantation owners had held the assumption that it was more economical to work a slave to death as quickly as possible and then replace him with a new purchase than to care for the slave properly and encourage reproduction. . . .

According to the handbook for slave-run sugar estates, pregnancy and birth were not classified as illnesses. Forty-five days after giving birth, a mother went back to work, often in the fields, while the offspring was given to the *criollera*, an old slave woman who supervised the nursery.

Under the arduous conditions of labor, the rural slave population found it impossible to maintain its own equilibrium of births and deaths. One important factor, of course, was the tremendous imbalance of the sexes on the plantations, where productive males outnumbered productive females by over 2:1, as very few planters made any attempt to supply an adequate number of females to satisfy the males on their estates. Women were considered to be less productive than men. Apart from the sexual imbalance, women could not produce healthy babies under conditions of labor entirely devoid of hygiene, and where they often had to do field work for the entire time of their pregnancy. The practice of having women in their ninth month of pregnancy working alongside men and cutting canes in the field perhaps contributed to a number of deformed or stillborn babies. Many women lost their babies during the terrible punishments they underwent for individual misdemeanors.

Corporal punishment was at once a measure of discipline and of intimidation for the slaves. The slave code of 1842 sanctioned the more popular forms—flogging, stocks, shackles, chains, and imprisonment—which were administered on the estates.

Flogging was the most common and the most convenient form of punishment. It was legally limited to twenty-five lashes, but was often given on a brutal installment plan called the *novenario* which consisted of nine strokes daily over a period of nine days. . . .

Next in popular use on the plantations came the stocks and shackles. . . . Both forms had many styles. The most common form of stocks consisted of an enormous, fixed board with holes through which fitted the head, hands, and feet of the delinquent slaves, either separately, or in any combination. . . .

Shackles varied from simple chains and padlocks attached to the ankles or wrists and fastened around the neck to the types that were attached to a large log, which the slave had to lift whenever he desired to move from one place to another. . . .

The degree to which these measures operated depended on the individual slave master and the supervisory personnel on the estate, who had the authority to inflict punishment in the absence of the proprietors. All the above forms of physical abuse remained on the law books until 1882.

The slaves never remained indifferent or acquiescent to their conditions. Not many were literate and therefore able to leave a written account of their impressions and experiences, although at least one probably did. Instead, the reactions of the slaves must be deduced from their actions.

As long as the Cuban economy had remained relatively underdeveloped, and the increase of Africans small, the social problems of a multiracial society were neither obvious nor frightening. Both elite and subordinate groups had the kind of close, personal relationship characteristic of patriarchal societies. On the one hand, the number of slaves held by any one master was unlikely to be very

large. On the other hand, the absence of any great economic incentive on the part of the master permitted him
to be fairly liberal in his regimentation of the lives of the
slaves. . . . [W]ith the harsher conditions of a plantation
type of slavery, . . . resistance became more widespread.
The slaves resisted slavery in many ways. Some simply
poisoned their masters, destroyed machines, or set cane-
fields on fire. Such manifestations of resistance, however,
neither alleviated their suffering nor affected their status,
and represented individual responses of anger, jealousy,
or revenge in particular situations.

Far more serious reflections on the general state of
slavery came from the evidence of voluntary abortions,
suicides, and runaways. . . .

Wherever the plantation society existed—as indeed,
wherever slavery existed—slaveowners faced the recur-
rent problem of escapees. . . . But it was not merely that
the masters feared losing forever the slave who might
have intended to desert only temporarily in the initial
stages. Rather it was more significant that the master
could not afford to lose a slave who might be required
for the harvest time. Part of the idea of leniency, therefore, stemmed from the acute shortage of laborers on the
island. Masters could have been motivated by kindness
and economic considerations with equal validity. But
lenience did not seem to reduce the desire for freedom.
This desire could be frustrated; it could never be extin-
guished.

Desertion, temporary or permanent, was as common
among urban slaves as it was among plantation slaves.
Slaves with ideas of permanent escape created their
abodes in the most inaccessible parts of the mountains.
Called *cimarrones*, or maroons, these runaways in their
villages or *palenques* often defied the concerted attacks of
the whites for extremely long periods. Not only did they
carry on their own regular social and political organiza-

tion independent of the white society, but they practiced cultivation to supplement foraging and stealing from the plantations. Their weapons for defense included machetes stolen from the plantations—still one of the most useful devices in Latin America and the Caribbean—poisoned arrows and wooden spears with improvised iron heads. In addition, the maroons also defended their villages with sharpened bamboo poles, fixed firmly in the ground, and covered with dried leaves.

The main Negro palenques were in the mountains of the east, . . . Some runaways, however, did not live in the palenques, but rather led a wandering life in the country, or drifted to the larger towns where they tried to blend in with the free colored population. White response to the *apalencado,* or Negro slave living in the palenque, was considerably less lenient than to the temporary absconder, who, by the intervention of a third party, called a *padriño,* could be pardoned and restored to the farm. Many whites were semiprofessional slavehunters. These *ranchadores,* accompanied by bloodhounds, led expeditions into the mountains, often to eliminate a troublesome palenque, or its diminutive, the ranchería, but more often to get the four dollars per head reward each captive brought from the *capitanes de partido* (the district military or judicial commanders). Sometimes large military expeditions went out to destroy the more formidable maroon villages in the mountains.

The most emphatic form of resistance of slavery consisted of open rebellion. In a number of cases, most notably in 1825 and 1843 in Matanzas, the slave revolts revealed widespread planning, and even included whites and free persons of color. Far more frequently, however, all the slaves on a single estate would erupt in violence, destroying property and killing those whites they could get their hands on. Spontaneous uprisings, confined to the slaves of the same owner, were very common throughout the Caribbean region. . . .

The opinions expressed about slave mortality as about everything else in the island differed considerably. The only general consensus seemed to be that mortality rates were higher in the rural areas than in the towns, and highest of all on the sugar plantations. Both in town and country, infant mortality was extremely high. One infant sickness alone, . . . called *espasmo*, . . . was purported to have been responsible for over 50 per cent of infant slave deaths. Adult mortality, however, was far less uniformly presented. . . .

. . . The most reasonable figure seems to be about 4 per cent—a mortality rate comparable with that of other West Indian islands during their plantation era.

The prevalence of diseases certainly played a part in the high mortality figures. Nevertheless, conditions of labor for the Cuban slaves in the nineteenth century were also responsible. . . . [B]etween the last years of the eighteenth century and the decade beginning in 1840, the slave numbers on the sugar estates were maintained exclusively by new purchases. Nor could the slaves be expected to reproduce or resist diseases when they suffered from sexual imbalance, dietary deficiencies, and consistent overwork. . . .

. . . [S]lavery was slowly changing the traditional pattern of [Cuban] society. The sugar revolution and slavery had brought to the fore of the society a new landowning and slaveholding oligarchy who were keenly interested in making money and running profitable plantations. . . . [T]he new system changed the ratio of the races on the estates, and demanded a more regimented organization of the labor force than the previous systems. . . . [T]he new plantation owners, particularly in the sugar areas, lived in the towns, and used intermediaries recruited from among the lower levels of the white element to assume most of the onhand, upper managerial tasks of the estates. And as the number of slaves increased, the white supervisors in particular and the white caste in general feared violent, physical retaliation by their slaves, as well as the loss of their "property" and, of course, their laborers. This increasing fear of a body of oppressed men did not permit a more lenient attitude toward the slaves, and the slave laws of 1842 reflected this change.

Slavery was an institution which affected the entire Cuban society. While the majority of white persons were by no means large landholders requiring a great number of African workers, almost every family desired or possessed slaves of some sort. Owning a slave was a significant social index: the more slaves any person had, the more social prestige accrued to him. . . . [E]ven the poor whites . . . who worked in the fields along with the slaves strongly aspired to be slaveowners themselves some day. They were the most overtly racist group in the island and in the minor positions of responsibility which they attained they often sharpened racial tensions by their attitudes.

A very wide difference existed between the numbers of slaves owned by urban white people, under better conditions, and those held by rural planters. According to the census data, the slaves of the towns were either domestics or hired hands. But more important than occupation was the pattern of slaveholding: in the towns, the individual master held far fewer slaves than in the plantation areas.

. . . The census of 1857 gave 22,753 persons owning 65,568 urban slaves, a mean holding of nearly 3 slaves per owner. Havana, the capital city, had 29,420 slaves, owned by 9,421 persons—a mean holding of 3.1, not significantly different from the urban pattern throughout the island. . . .

The total of 307,375 registered slaves in the rural areas had 26,358 owners, an island-wide average holding of 11.6 slaves per owner. But the picture was very different in the plantation areas: 483 rural owners had more than 80 slaves each, yielding a total of 95,523 slaves for a mean holding of 197 slaves each. In other words, less than 1 per cent of the slaveowners of Cuba held more than 25 per cent of all the slaves in the island. . . . These slaveowners . . . were very influential men in political affairs, and owned the largest sugar estates. . . .

The difference that the rise of the slave plantations made to the sharpening of racial attitudes may be seen by comparing the development of slavery and society in both Cuba and Puerto Rico at the time. Until the later eighteenth century, both islands had a mixed economy, with relatively amicable relations between the races, and no sharper economic, social, and political deprivation of the nonwhites above and beyond the built-in inequality of Spanish colonial society, based on the purity of blood. But with the rise of sugar cultivation during the nineteenth century, Cuba became a slave plantation society, and Puerto Rico did not.

During the nineteenth century, Puerto Rico intensified and extended its sugar industry, but managed to continue the mixed economy. Even though the landless were regimented, the previous uncomplicated relations between the races were not disrupted—only a massive importation of slaves could have ended the interdependence of the various groups. The island built up its own large intermediate group of free colored persons, akin in culture and language to the elite, which supplied the labor for which African slaves were required in Cuba. But the predominance of mulattoes—as opposed to freed blacks—in the free colored segment meant that "passing as white" was much easier, and the society could level itself upwards. Social mobility in Puerto Rico was possible for most people, who suffered from no practical inequalities and were not visually and culturally distinct from the elite.

The Cuban trend reversed itself once the sugar revolution had brought the flood of Africans to the plantations. The intermediate free colored population not only was swamped by the immigrants, but was restricted to the towns and the eastern part of the island where the opportunities were more abundant. Two consequences of the influx militated against the development of a situation similar to that in Puerto Rico. In the first place, the greater majority of the immigrants, owing to their cultural and linguistic deficiency, were suitable only for the regimented routine of the plantations. It took two generations, generally, for the slave to acquire the language and skills which equipped him for urban life. And while the urban setting afforded more avenues of mobility, the prevalence of the "plantation values" meant that only in the case of the fortunate few with mixed blood was the passage relatively easy. In the second place, the free colored population was predominantly black. Thus the physical characteristics of the majority of this intermediate group distinguished them from the elite and facilitated separatist tendencies.

This later phase of Cuban slavery closely resembled the other West Indian islands while the plantation was the dominant form of economic enterprise. The economic basis of Negro slavery greatly modified the inheritance of culture or the intervention of any religious denomination. Roman Catholicism and the Iberian heritage played no significant role in the variations which developed in the institutions of slavery and race relations in Cuba and Puerto Rico during the nineteenth century.

10

JUAN FRANCISCO MANZANO

AUTOBIOGRAPHY OF
A TEEN-AGE SLAVE

Information on the treatment of children under slavery is rather sparse; however, the following account by an ex-slave gives us some picture of what it was like. Juan grew up in Cuba during the early decades of the nineteenth century, when that island still lacked adequate labor to meet the increasing demand for sugar cultivation.† The selection here touches on several as yet unexamined aspects of slave life: the position of the favored slave, the workings of coartación *(manumission through self-purchase), and religious instruction of slaves.*

My master took a fancy to me, and it is said I was more in his arms than in those of my mother. She had all the privileges of a slave who had acted as a dry-nurse, and also partly as a wet-nurse, *media criandera;*[1] and having married one of the head slaves of the house, and given a little Creole to her mistress, I was called by this lady, "the

---

From *Poems by a Slave in the Island of Cuba, Recently Liberated.* Translated by R. R. Madden (London: Thomas Ward & Co., 1840), pp. 56–71.

† In *Slave Society in Cuba*, Knight points out (p. 29) that as late as 1827 Cuba only had 286,942 slaves in a total population of 704,487.

[1] This term is applied to a negress who at the same time suckles her own infant and that of her mistress.

child of her old age." I was brought up by the side of my mistress without separating from her, except at bed-time, and she never went out without taking me in her volante. . . .

It would be tedious to detail the particulars of my childhood, treated by my mistress with greater kindness than I deserved, and whom I was accustomed to call "my mother." At six years of age, on account, perhaps, of too much vivacity, more than anything else, I was sent to school to my godmother every day at noon; and every evening I was brought to the house, that my mistress might see me, who seldom went out without seeing me, for if she did, I roared and cried, and so disturbed the house, that sometimes it was necessary to send for the whip, which nobody dared to lay on me, for not even my parents were authorised to flog me, and I knowing this, often took advantage of it. . . .

I also knew my catechism well, and as much of religion as a woman could teach me. I knew how to sew tolerably, and to place the furniture in order. On one occasion, I was taken to the Opera, and received some presents for reciting what I heard, but many more for the sermons, and my parents got what I received in the drawing-room.

But passing over much of my early history, in which there was nothing but happiness, I must not omit the circumstances which happened at my baptism; on that occasion, I was dressed in the same robe in which the Senora Donna Beatrice was baptized, which was celebrated with great rejoicings, my father being skilled in music, and playing on the flute and clarionet; and my mistress desiring to solemnize that day with one of her noble traits of generosity, in part liberated my parents by "coartacion," giving them the power at any time of purchasing their liberty at the sum of three hundred dollars each; what greater happiness could be looked for at her hands.

At the age of ten, I was placed under the care of my godfather; having learned something of my father's trade, which was that of tailor, previously, to being sent to the estate. My mother gave birth to two other children. One of them, for what reason I know not, was made free—and this one died. My father lamenting his death, saying, "if things had been otherwise, I might have been content, my two living children are slaves, and the one that was free is dead;" whereupon my generous mistress had a document prepared, in which it was declared that the next child they should have should be free; and it happened that twins were subsequently born, who are still living, and both were freed. My parents now were removed to the estate of the Molino, where they were placed in charge of the house, and about this period the Marquesa died there. I was sent for in her last illness. . . . [A]ll night long all the negroes of the estate made great lamentation, repeated the rosary, and I wept with them.

I was taken to the Havana, to my godfather, with whom I soon learned my mistress had left me; for some years I saw nothing of my father. . . .

After some time I was taken to the house of Donna Joaquina, who treated me like a white child, saw that I was properly clothed, and even combed my hair herself; and as in the time of the Marquesa de J., she allowed me not to pray with the other negro children at church—and at mealtime my plate was given to me to eat at the feet of the Senora Marquesa de P., and all this time I was far away from my father and mother. . . .

I had already at the age of twelve years composed some verses in memory, because my godfather did not wish me to learn to write, but I dictated my verses by stealth to a young mulatto girl, of the name of Serafina, which verses were of an amatory character. From this age, I passed on without many changes in my lot to my fourteenth year; but the important part of my history began when I was about eighteen, when fortune's bitterest enmity was turned on me, as we shall see hereafter.

For the slightest crime of boyhood, it was the custom to shut me up in a place for charcoal, for four-and-twenty hours at a time. I was timid in the extreme, and my prison, which still may be seen, was so obscure, that at mid-day no object could be distinguished in it without a candle. Here after being flogged I was placed, with orders to the slaves, under threats of the greatest punishment, to abstain from giving me a drop of water. What I suffered from hunger and thirst, tormented with fear, in a place so dismal and distant from the house, and almost suffocated with the vapours arising from the common sink, that was close to my dungeon, and constantly terrified by the rats that passed over me and about me, may be easily imagined. . . .

I would roar aloud and pray for mercy; and then I would be taken out and almost flayed alive, again shut up, and the key taken away, and kept in the room of my mistress, the Senora herself. On two occasions, the Senor Don Nicholas and his brother showed me compassion, introducing through an aperture in the door, a morsel of bread and some water, with the aid of a coffee-pot with a long spout. This kind of punishment was so frequent that there was not a week that I did not suffer it twice or thrice, and in the country on the estate I suffered a like martyrdom. I attribute the smallness of my stature and the debility of my constitution to the life of suffering I led, from my thirteenth or fourteenth year.

My ordinary crimes were—not to hear the first time I was called; or if at the time of getting a buffet, I uttered a word of complaint; and I led a life of so much misery, daily receiving blows on the face, that often made the blood spout from both my nostrils; no sooner would I hear myself called than I would begin to shiver, so that I could hardly keep on my legs, but supposing this to be only shamming on my part, frequently would I receive from a stout negro lashes in abundance.

About the age of fifteen or sixteen, I was taken to

Matanzas once more, and embraced my parents and brothers. . . .

We passed five years in Matanzas, where my employment was to sweep and clean the house as well as I could at sunrise, before any one in the house was up; this done I had to eat myself at the door of my mistress, that she might find me there when she awoke, then I had to follow her about wherever she went, like an automaton with my arms crossed. When breakfast, or the other meals were over, I had to gather up what was left, and having to put my hand to clear away the dishes, and when they rose from table I had to walk behind them. Then came the hour of sewing, I had to seat myself in sight of my mistress to sew women's dresses, to make gowns, shifts, robes, pillow-cases, to mark and to hem fine things in cambric, and mend all kinds of clothing.

At the hour of drawing, which a master taught, I was also present, stationed behind a chair, and what I saw done and heard, corrected and explained, put me in the condition of counting myself as one of the pupils of the drawing-class. One of the children, I forget which, gave me an old tablet, and a crayon; and with my face turned to the wall, the next day I sat down in a corner, and began making mouths, eyes, ears, and going on in this way, I came to perfect myself, so that I was able to copy a head so faithfully, that having finished one, my mistress observing me, showed it to the master, who said that I would turn out a great artist, and that it would be for her one day a great satisfaction that I should take the portraits of all my masters.

At night I had to go to sleep at twelve or one o'clock, some ten or twelve squares of buildings distant, where my mother lived (in the negro barracones). . . .

Some attacks of ague, which nearly ended my days, prevented me from accompanying my mistress to Havana. When I recovered, no one could enjoy himself in two years as I did in four months; I bathed four times a-day, and even in the night, I fished, rode on horseback, made excursions into the mountains, ascended the highest hills, [ate] all kinds of fruits; in short, I enjoyed all the innocent pleasures of youth. In this little epoch I grew stout and lively, but when I returned to my old mode of life, my health broke down again, and I became as I was before.

When I recovered sufficiently, my first destiny was to be a page, as well in Havana as in Matanzes; already I was used to sit up from my earliest years the greatest part of the night, in the city, either at the theatre, or at parties, or in the house of the Marquis M——— II——— and the Senoras C., from which we went out at ten o'clock, and after supper play began, and continued till eleven or twelve; . . .

We were returning from the town late one night, when the volante was going very fast, and I was seated as usual, with one hand holding the bar, and having the lanthorn in the other, I fell asleep, and it fell out of my hand; on awaking, I missed the lanthorn, and jumped down to get it, but such was my terror, I was unable to come up with the volante. I followed, well knowing what was to come, but when I came close to the house, I was seized by Don Sylvester, the young mayoral. Leading me to the stocks, we met my mother, who giving way to the impulses of her heart, came up to complete my misfortunes. On seeing me, she attempted to inquire what I had done, but the mayoral ordered her to be silent, and treated her as one raising a disturbance. Without regard to her entreaties, and being irritated at being called up at that hour, he raised his hand, and struck my mother with the whip. I felt the blow in my own heart! To utter a loud cry, and from a downcast boy, with the timidity of one as meek as a lamb, to become all at once like a raging lion, was a thing of a moment—with all my strength I fell on him with teeth and hands, and it may be imagined how many cuffs, kicks, and blows were given in the struggle that ensued.

My mother and myself were carried off and shut up in the same place; the two twin children were brought to her, while Florence and Fernando were left weeping alone in the hut. Scarcely it dawned, when the mayoral, with two negroes acting under him, took hold of me and my mother, and led us as victims to the place of sacrifice. I suffered more punishment than was ordered, in consequence of my attack on the mayoral. But who can describe the powers of the laws of nature on mothers? [T]he fault of my mother was, that seeing they were going to kill me, as she thought, she inquired what I had done, and this was sufficient to receive a blow and to be further chastised. At beholding my mother in this situation, for the first time in her life, (she being exempted from work) stripped by the negroes and thrown down to be scourged, overwhelmed with grief and trembling, I asked them to have pity on her for God's sake; but at the sound of the first lash, infuriated like a tiger, I flew at the mayoral, and was near losing my life in his hands; but let us throw a veil over the rest of this doleful scene. . . .

. . . The volante was ready to go to town, and I was to ride behind; but alas! I was little aware what was to come in the next hour! Instead of riding in the volante, I was taken to the stocks, which were in a building, formerly an infirmary, and now used for a prison, and for depositing the bodies of the dead till the hour of interment. My feet were put in the stocks, where shivering with cold, without any covering, they shut me in. What a frightful night I passed there! My fancy saw the dead rising and walking about the room, and scrambling up to a window above the river and near a cataract, I listened to its roar, which seemed to me like the howling of a legion of ghosts. Scarcely day-light appeared, when I heard the unbolting of the door; a negro came in followed by the overseer wrapt in his cloak; they took me out and put me on a board fixed on a kind of fork, where I saw a bundle of rods. The overseer, from under a handkerchief over his mouth, roared out, "tie him fast;" when my hands were tied behind like a criminal, and my feet secured in an aperture of the board. Oh, my God! Let me not speak of this frightful scene! . . .

Some time after, it happened that a carrier brought to the house some chickens, some capons, and a letter, and as I was always on guard like a sentinel, it was my misfortune to receive them; leaving the fowls outside, I took in the letter. . . . Two weeks after this, I was called to an account for one capon missing, I said without hesitating, that I received three capons, and two chickens, which I delivered. Nothing more was said of the matter, but the following day . . . my mistress ordered me to go to the mayoral's house, and tell him—I do not remember what. With sad forebodings, and an oppressed heart, being accustomed to deliver myself up on such occasions, away I went trembling. When I arrived at the door, I saw the mayoral of the Molino, and the mayoral of the Ingenio, together. I delivered my message to the first, who said, "Come in man," I obeyed, and was going to repeat it again, when Señor Dominguez, the mayoral of the Ingenio, took hold of my arm, saying, "it is to me, to whom you are sent;" took out of his pocket a thin rope, tied my hands behind me as a criminal, mounted his horse, and commanded me to run quick before him, to avoid either my mother or my brothers seeing me. Scarcely had I run a mile before the horse, stumbling at every step, when two dogs that were following us, fell upon me; one taking hold of the left side of my face pierced it through, and the other lacerated my left thigh and leg in a shocking manner, which wounds are open yet, notwithstanding it happened twenty-four years ago. The mayoral alighted on the moment, and separated me from their grasp, but my blood flowed profusely, particularly from my leg—he then pulled me by the rope, making use at the same time, of the most disgusting language; this pull partly dislocated my right arm, which at times pains me yet. Getting up, I walked as well as I could, till we arrived at the Ingenio. They put a rope round my neck, bound up my wounds, and put me in the stocks. At night, all the people of the estate were assembled together and arranged in a line, I was put in the middle of them, the mayoral and six negroes surrounded me, and at the word "upon him," they threw me down; two of them held my hands, two my legs, and the other sat upon my back. They then asked me about the missing capon, and I did not know what to say. Twenty-five lashes were laid on me, they then asked me again to tell the truth. I was perplexed; at last, thinking to escape further punishment, I said, "I stole it." "What have you done with the money?" was the next question, and this was another trying point. "I bought a hat." "Where is it?" "I bought a pair of shoes." "No such thing," and I said so many things to escape punishment, but all to no purpose. Nine successive nights the same scene was repeated, and every night I told a thousand lies. After the whipping, I was sent to look after the cattle and work in the fields. Every morning my mistress was informed of what I said the previous night.

At the end of ten days, the cause of my punishment being known, Dionisio Copandonga, who was the carrier who brought the fowls, went to the mayoral, and said that the missed capon was eaten by the steward Don Manuel Pipa, and which capon was left behind in a mistake; the cook Simona was examined and confirmed the account. I do not know whether my mistress was made acquainted with this transaction; but certain it is, that since that moment, my punishment ceased, my fetters were taken off, and my work eased, and a coarse linen dress was put on me. But the same day an accident happened, which contributed much towards my mistress forgiving me.

After helping to load sugar, I was sent to pile blocks of wood in one of the buildings, while so employed, all of a sudden the roof with a loud crash gave way, burying under its ruins the negro Andres Criollo; I escaped unhurt through a back door. The alarm given, all the people came to the rescue of poor Andres, who with great difficulty and labour was taken from under the ruins, with his skull broken, and he died in the Molino a few hours after. Early next morning, as I was piling the refuse of sugar canes, there arrived the then Master Pancho, and now Don F., followed by my second brother, who was in his service, and who intimated to me that his master was coming to take me back to the house. This was owing to my brother, who hearing of the accident and my narrow escape, begged earnestly of his young master to intercede with his mother on my behalf, which he easily obtained. I was presented to my mistress, who for the first time received me with kindness. But my heart was so oppressed, that neither her kindness nor eating, nor drinking could comfort me; I had no comfort except in weeping; my mistress observing it, and to prevent my crying so much, and the same time being so very drowsy, ordered me to move about, and clean all the furniture, tables, chairs, drawers, &c. All my liveliness disappeared.

I V

Life and Labor of Blacks and Mulattoes in Portuguese America

LAMENT OF A LATIN AMERICAN SLAVE

"The life of a black slave
Is a burden of pain;
Working all day:
Without the night to rest."
　　　　　　　—Morales de los Rios Filho*

From the late sixteenth to the early eighteenth centuries, Brazil's economy was based on sugar, and even after the decline in its total production, this commodity continued to influence developments in the Northeast. Northeastern plantation life has formed the largest chapter in the written histories of Brazil, but it is usually presented from the vantage point of the elites, for there is available little concrete information about the bulk of the population.

---

* Translated by Richard Mazzara from *O Rio de Janeiro Imperial,* p. 62.

In the early decades of Portuguese colonial rule in America, black slaves were utilized on the growing number of sugar farms in rural areas, where they toiled at planting, weeding, felling trees, and cutting cane. It has been estimated that "the sugar growing parishes of the Recôncavo often had a two to one ratio of slave to free inhabitants [and] slaves constituted the largest portion of the cane grower's original investment."[1]

The major urban area in Brazil, at that time, was Bahia (Salvador), a center of social, economic, political, and religious interaction, a place quite different from the relatively parochial master-slave world of the hinterlands. Bahian society was a mix of Portuguese, Indian, African, and New Christian (converted Jews). Early in the sixteenth century Sudanese blacks from the Guinea coast comprised most of the African population in Brazil, but by the end of the sixteenth century most blacks were from Angola (the Bantu). A dispute raged over the relative merits of each: the seemingly stronger, more hard-working, and more rebellious Sudanese were relegated to the plantations, while the Bantu, more susceptible to disease and apparently more suited to domestic labor, were kept in the cities. As a result, Bantu were predominant in Bahia during the seventeenth century.

The 1680s marked a crisis in Brazil; external pressures, such as foreign competition and a decline in sugar prices, combined with numerous bad harvests and sociopolitical changes within the country to shake the economy. Merchants moved to assume political power, as the planters retreated from urban life and began to develop a more isolated, self-contained life style. This also meant a contraction in labor and, consequently, a reduction in social mobility for free laborers. Deprived of their potential

[1] Stuart Schwartz, "Free Farmers in a Slave Economy: The *Lavradores de Cana* of Bahia, 1550–1750," paper delivered at the Newberry Library Conference on colonial Brazil, November 1969.

power, this group no longer needed to support traditional sociopolitical patterns.[2]

At precisely this time gold strikes occurred in the neighboring area of Minas Gerais (between 1693 and 1695). Discontented free-white citizens and freed blacks migrated toward these mining areas, while the owners of some declining plantations sold their slaves to mining groups. Some Africans accompanied their masters to the mines, thereby contributing much to the dredging of wealth for European empires.

By the end of the 1750s the gold and diamond mines had been exhausted, and the remainder of the eighteenth century signaled for blacks and mulattoes a return to labor on plantations and in the cities. But a new crop was rapidly acquiring favor with planters: coffee had begun to vie with sugar.

From 1822 to 1889 coffee continued to gain predominance in Brazil, creating several changes in the national power structure.[3] Coffee created a demand for a new kind of plantation in Brazil, and its products were subject to the vicissitudes of a new world market structure. The expansion of plantations also brought a tremendous influx of Africans to Brazil, creating new ethnic patterns and social stratification in central and southern central Brazil. In addition, the economic and political center of Brazil shifted from Bahia and Pernambuco to Rio de Janeiro and later São Paulo, where a new entrepreneurial class of coffee barons arose.

[2] *Ibid.*, pp. 44–48.

[3] For those students unfamiliar with Brazilian history, Brazil was "discovered" in 1500 by Pedro Cabral and colonized shortly thereafter by the Portuguese. It remained within Portugal's imperial orbit until 1822, when the son of Portugal's reigning house—which had fled to Brazil during the Napoleonic Wars—declared himself and Brazil independent of Portugal. After 1822 Brazil endured first the rule of her own emperor, Pedro I, then from 1831 to 1840 a regency, and finally a long rule under Pedro II from 1840 to 1889. In 1889 the empire was overthrown and a republic established.

It was in the context of these varied political and economic developments that Brazil's black and mulatto communities functioned. The following selections describe the varieties of life that existed for Afro-Brazilians.

11

WHO SHALL BE A SLAVE, AND WHY?

The commentary reproduced here is one of the few eighteenth-century printed works that criticize the status and treatment of Brazilian slaves. The only known copy of this pamphlet is in the library of Professor Charles Boxer. The dialogue accurately reflects a climate of opinion prevalent in the mid-eighteenth-century, Portuguese-speaking world. The lawyer represents numerous people who were aware of the evils of slavery, while the miner speaks for the great majority who believed blacks were born to serve whites.

MINER. Learned Sir, I have come here to sit at your feet and seek your advice concerning a most important matter.

LAWYER. Sit down, dear Sir. The problem is whether my few qualifications will be sufficient to advise you as wisely as I hope to do.

MINER. The fact is that I have a Negro whom I suppose must have been sent into this world for my Purgatory.

LAWYER. Well, let us continue; for it is always true

From *Nova e Curiosa Relação* (Lisbon, 1764). Translated by Ann M. Pescatello. The first translation of this pamphlet was made by Professor Charles Boxer and appeared as "Negro Slavery in Brazil" in *Race*, 5, no. 3 (January 1964), 38–47. This translation by permission of Charles Boxer.

that whoever deals with youths and with slaves needs patience.

MINER. Slowly, learned Sir. That patience is necessary in dealing with youths, I agree; for after all they are somebody's children, and they are white like ourselves. But I cannot stand to hear it said that patience is necessary in dealing with slaves; for after all they are Negroes, and as their owner has bought them for money he can do whatever he likes with them.

LAWYER. You seem to be very offended with the Negroes; all not withstanding however, one cannot deny the truth.

MINER. I am going to deny everything.

LAWYER. Whew, Sir! That's insane! How can you deny that which is right?

MINER. Yes, Sir. If it is anything in favor of Negroes or of slaves, I deny it absolutely.

LAWYER. You really do seem to be of a terrible disposition. But I presume that the misbehavior of one of your slaves has annoyed you so much that you feel compelled to give vent to your anger. However, I hope that, when you've calmed down, you will be prepared to agree with me, if by chance you understand and realize that what I am going to say is the truth.

MINER. Agreed. You have your say, and we will see if I can agree with it.

LAWYER. Now, Sir. One of the reasons which you give me for being patient with youths is that they are somebody's children?

MINER. Yes, Sir.

LAWYER. Well, then. This reason is equally applicable to our being patient with slaves, as they are also somebody's children.

MINER. But with a difference. For we whites are descended from Adam, and the Negroes are descended from Cain, who was black, and who died cursed by God himself, as the Scripture relates.

LAWYER. . . . Now, that Cain was accursed is a scriptural truth, but that he was a Negro, and the Negroes are his descendants—where did you find this information?

MINER. It is something which I have always heard ever since I was a boy.

LAWYER. Ah, well, in that case you are bound to believe in a lot of foolish things! . . .

MINER. But this is something which stares one in the face.

LAWYER. What, Sir! Since you quoted the Bible at me, hear me. It is certain, and a scriptural truth, that all men, women and children were drowned in the universal flood, with the exception of only eight persons who survived: Noah, his wife, their three sons, and three women who were wives of the said sons. It is also certain that the Bible does not state that any of them were black. Therefore, the blacks are not black because they are descendants of Cain.

MINER. Well then; why have they got that color, and we don't?

LAWYER. That problem, my good Sir, is a very intricate one and hard to resolve. . . .

MINER. I have heard it said that the blackness of the blacks is due to their being born in a very hot climate, and much nearer the sun.

LAWYER. That is a boy's tale. If that were really so, then anybody who was born in the country of the blacks would be black, while on the other hand everybody born in the country of the whites would be white . . . [W]e have not yet been able to ascertain the reason for the blackness of the black people.

MINER. Whatever the reason may be, the fact remains that they are black.

LAWYER. And what do you deduce from that?

MINER. I deduce that the Negroes are not people like ourselves.

LAWYER. Sir, the blackest man in all Africa, because he is a man, is just as much a man as is the whitest German in all Germany. There have been very famous black men and women, of whom we read in

History. . . . What doesn't Portugal owe to the blacks in its conquests in Brazil! They were the ones who threw the Dutch out of Pernambuco and Rio de Janeiro; and our Lord the King Dom Pedro II granted a habit of the Order of Christ to a black, who on that occasion successfully led the others; for that great king did not wish that the accident of color should deprive him of the honor to which his merits entitled him. And what have you got to say in view of these facts?

MINER. Then you are arguing that a black is just as good as a white.

LAWYER. Undoubtedly he is, in the sense in which I am speaking.

MINER. Well, if the blacks are just as good as we are, what is the reason that they are our slaves, and we whites are not their slaves?

LAWYER. I now see that you are very far from perceiving the truth. Sir, the blacks are not our slaves just because they are black. The Moors can also be enslaved, and what is more they are not black. Mulattoes, Kanarese, Chinese, and others can be enslaved, and they are not black. At one time the Tapuyás of Pará were reputed as slaves, certainly they are not black. I have seen in this city a boy who was about ten years old, with all the features of his face and the shape of his hair just as if he was a black, but his hair was very blond and his body exceedingly white, yet this boy was a slave. So that it is not owing to their color that the blacks are enslaved. There are other lawful and politic reasons why they can be enslaved. . . .

MINER. I am amazed at what you have told me about this matter; but I have always observed that in Brazil the Negroes are treated worse than animals, being punished very severely, and called by very insulting names, yet despite it all the blacks endure this.

LAWYER. From what I can see, you must be a miner, and have lived in Brazil. However, you must now have the patience to listen to me. All those punishments and insulting, or rather, scandalous names, if they exceed the limits of propriety, are all sinful, criminal and unjust.

MINER. Oh now, you must be joking! On a certain plantation in Bahia, I saw two Negroes killed in one day, their master standing by and ordering them to be flogged to death by other slaves. And on a farm in Rio de Janeiro, I saw a master kill a Negro with his own hands. Moreover, none of these men were punished for killing their slaves, nor did anybody take the slightest notice of it. For after all, if they killed Negroes, they were the ones who lost their money, and a man can do what he likes with his own.

LAWYER. Excuse me, Sir, because I simply must tell you that I cannot believe everything you say. I do not doubt but that those sugar-planters killed their slaves, in fact I can very readily believe it. But what I cannot believe is that they went unpunished for those crimes, unless the crime was unknown; and in that case, what you have told me proves nothing. It is also quite true, as you say, that these men lost their money when they killed their slaves. But what do you mean by this? Do you mean to imply that they did not commit murder? That they should not be severely punished? That they were not cruel? That they did not commit mortal sin? Ah, sir! how badly do they treat the wretched slaves in Brazil! But who treats them thus? Avaricious people! Godless people! People with the hearts of wild beasts!

MINER. How I would like, learned Sir, to see *you* trying to cope with 100 or 200 disobedient, treacherous, lazy and thieving slaves, and to see how you would treat them then.

LAWYER. I would probably treat them worse than does anybody else there. But what each one of us ought to do, is to treat his servants with charity, with zeal and for the love of God. Whoever does not have the patience to take trouble with slaves should

seek some other way of life. For it is more important
not to offend God than to gain profit from any
wordly concern whatsoever.

MINER. I see that you have become a missionary in
favor of the Negroes; but this is because you have
no experience of what they are really like. In short,
Sir, let us drop this futile argument and come to the
point of the purpose for which I came; although I
can see from our preliminary discussion that you
will decide against me.

LAWYER. I can assure you, and if necessary on oath,
that I will never advise you to do anything that will
go against my conscience, nor have I done so in anything that I have told you thus far.

MINER. Learned Sir, the fact is that I have a Negro
whom I bought about ten or eleven years ago. At
first he served me as he ought, and in view of this I
promised him that if he would continue to serve me
well, I would give him his freedom at the end of
ten years.

LAWYER. So far you did, if not what you were obliged
to do, at any rate something just and praiseworthy.
For I assure you that I cannot help feeling sorry for
the wretched slaves who have to toil all their life in
perpetual bondage.

MINER. What would you do, Sir, if you saw the
Negroes in Brazil working almost continually day
and night, and this while going naked? As a rule,
they are only given a little bit of manioc flour to eat;
and they have Sundays and some Saints' Days off,
so that they can earn something to keep themselves
from starving.

LAWYER. Although I have never actually witnessed it,
I am reasonably well informed about the hardships
that those wretches endure. But let us come to the
main point.

MINER. As I was saying, seeing that the Negro served
me loyally and readily in everything, and that even
after my promise his zeal was still greater, I secretly
resolved never to give him his certificate of manumission.

LAWYER. This was quite contrary to all justice. The very reason that you were the more obliged to keep your word to free him, you used as an excuse to go back on your word.

MINER. Even so, am I obliged to keep a promise which I made to my own Negro?

LAWYER. If your promise, or your word, was given for a just cause, who can doubt it?

MINER. But surely there is no reason why I should not deceive my own black?

LAWYER. On the contrary, Sir! We are always obliged to keep faith with everyone without exception.

MINER. Oh, nobody can tell me that! If I did that, I would be placed on a level with a Negro.

LAWYER. Then do you think that the privilege of being white gives you the right to lie as much as you like? But let us come to the point.

MINER. The Negro, seeing that I was not giving what I had promised, began to cool off in his zeal to serve me; and he displeased me so much that I resolved to sell him as a slave in Brazil, with the sole object of getting him killed by the harsh punishments in vogue there. The Negro, perceiving this, and having been so advised by others, went and enrolled as a Brother in one of their Brotherhoods, which they say has the privilege that the blacks belonging to this brotherhood cannot be sold as slaves for overseas. However, as soon as I heard about this, I gave him a severe beating; and . . . I resolved to sell him secretly and send him to Minas Gerais. However, last Sunday I went to confession and telling this to the confessor, he raised objections to it, telling me that I could not in conscience do such a thing. I now come to sit at your feet, so that you may reassure me on this point.

LAWYER. Sir, your confessor, like a wise and prudent man, has already told you what you ought to do. I can only add two words in confirmation. . . . Certainly anyone who disobeys the laws which the sovereigns lay on their vassals, commits a mortal sin. The privilege, which our kings granted to the blacks of that Brotherhood, is a law by which our monarchs order that such Brothers cannot be sold as slaves for overseas. It follows then that whoever violates this privilege commits a mortal sin . . . and thus it seems to me that this is a case of restitution, both to the said Brotherhood, in so far as it is concerned with that Brother, as with the said Brother, in so far as he is concerned as a member of the said Brotherhood.

MINER. Well, learned Sir, does this mean that I am not master of what is mine?

LAWYER. You can be, yes Sir, and you are; but with those restrictions and conditions stipulated by just laws.

MINER. I have a friend, who has done the same thing, and nothing of all this happened to him. . . .

LAWYER. . . . I will say what I believe: what you ought to do, is to fulfill your promise; or, at the very least, inflict no further affliction on your slave, who is sufficiently unfortunate in being one. It is a very common error to believe that the blacks were born solely in order to serve as slaves, but Nature itself loves men of all races without distinction. The way in which many masters treat their slaves is unjust. The latter ought to be punished when they do wrong, but the punishment should be in proportion to the fault. . . . I do not argue from this that slaves who disobey their masters should not be punished at all, but I stress that the punishment should not degenerate into cruelty. A conditional promise has the force of law. You promised to free your slave if he continued to serve you well; he not only continued to serve you well, but better still. You are, therefore, obviously bound to free him. You are also bound to respect the privilege which he enjoys as a member of his Brotherhood. Hence, if you take my advice, you should either give your slave a certificate of manumission, or else you should treat him kindly. . . .

MINER. Tell me, learned Sir, won't it be enough if I give this Negro his freedom in fifteen or twenty years time?

LAWYER.   Better late than never. But tell me, how old is this Negro?

MINER.   When I bought him he would have been about twenty-eight years old. I have had him about fourteen or fifteen years, so he must be over forty years old now.

LAWYER.   And you want to give him his certificate of manumission fifteen or twenty years hence? In other words, when he will no longer be able to work at all! In this way you are not doing a favor to your black, but merely trying to escape the responsibility of feeding him when he can no longer work. And in that case you are not only very far from keeping your promise but you are behaving tyrannically. Now tell me, what can be more contrary to reason, than to make use of a man as a slave for so long as he can work, and then when he no longer can, dismiss him and let him die of hunger! Look, I have told you what I think, and now you can go and do what you like. . . .

12

A. J. R. RUSSELL-WOOD

FEMALES, FAMILIES, PHILANTHROPY, AND FUNERALS—BLACKS IN BAHIA, 1550-1755

When Portugal established an overseas empire, she transferred to the New World many of her own political and social institutions. Among these were the lay brotherhoods that had arisen in Portugal to serve the needs of the urban poor. The brotherhoods initially drew their members from professional groups, but later both aristocratic and plebian elements were included. Ultimately, however, membership in such organizations became a matter of race and social class.

In his examination of the Misericórdia, A. J. R. Russell-Wood informs us not only of Brazilian atti-

From A. J. R. Russell-Wood, *Fidalgos and Philanthropists: The Santa Casa da Misericórdia of Bahia, 1550–1775* (Berkeley and Los Angeles, 1968), pp. 59, 61, 78, 134, 138–143, 182–183, 216–218, 222, 226–227, 255–257, 314. Originally published by the University of California Press; reprinted by permission of The Regents of the University of California. (Santa Casa of the Misericórdia was one of the innumerable brotherhoods in colonial Bahia; it exerted much control over other brotherhoods.)

tudes toward the welfare of blacks but also of some of the functions of the Afro-Baians within the community.

Russell-Wood is Associate Professor of History at the Johns Hopkins University and author of several articles on colonial Brazil.

There was a flourishing triangular trade of inter-complementary wares between Portugal, the west coast of Africa and Brazil. This was a trade of supply and demand. Portugal relied for its economic survival on the agricultural products of Brazil and the gold and ivory of Africa. Luanda and Bahia needed manufactured goods . . . foodstuffs . . . and certain luxury items. The sugar mills and plantations of Bahia depended on African slaves from Guinea and Angola for their manpower.[1] . . .

. . . A sugar plantation . . . was a community with its own chapel, resident chaplain and a social hierarchy at once staunchly rigid yet curiously flexible. Slave labour was the basis of this community, be it outdoors as culti-vators of the cane, herdsmen, shepherds, fishermen and boatmen, or in the domestic duties of the house. . . .

. . . Bahia was the leading city in Portuguese America during the sixteenth and seventeenth centuries. . . .

[The] outline of Bahian society . . . reveals two dis-tinct modes of life. On the one hand was the aristocracy who owned vast tracts of land . . . and whose children married within this society. On the other hand was a class of men who had advanced by personal effort to achieve financial and social position. The one was rural, the other urban. It was only among the bourgeoisie that there existed a class struggle. . . .

. . . [T]he native, be he Indian or Negro, was regarded

---

[1] Brazilwood had been Brazil's first major product. Within a few decades, however, sugar replaced Brazilwood in prominence and remained the largest export throughout the sixteenth and seven-teenth centuries.—Ed.

as inferior, but the extent of miscegenation compelled the authorities to adopt some policy. . . . In general, . . . offspring of white-Amerindian parentage, came off better . . . than . . . products of black and white sexual unions. [But the] Indian remained in the interior of the Captaincy of Bahia and consequently played no part in the urban life of the capital. The same cannot be said of Negroes and mulattoes who achieved a sufficiently high degree of social consolidation to found brotherhoods and provide a disrupting element in urban life by their aspirations.

In theory a Negro was either a freed man or a slave but in practice such a distinction was often forgotten and a Negro was simply a chattel at the disposal of a white person. . . . The accessibility of the monarch to . . . coloured subjects was . . . shown by the appeal of the Negro slave, António Fernandes, to Dom João V, alleging that he had been unjustly tortured.[2]

. . . The Crown was not deaf to . . . appeals and fully realised the appalling conditions in which the slaves were brought from Africa and then employed on the sugar plantations. Numerous decrees were issued to protect the Negro, such as those aimed at reducing the mortality in the slaving ships . . . by lessening the numbers of slaves crowded below decks, punishment for slave owners found guilty of cruelty, as well as measures to ensure that every slave received a decent burial. Although such decrees bore witness to the good intentions of the Crown, they were largely ineffective in reality, . . .

No order from a monarch some three thousand miles away could remove the ingrained prejudice of the white Bahians. . . . The scorn felt by white Bahians towards the coloured peoples . . . led the coloured population either to direct revolt or to establishing representative bodies to plead their case. . . . Flight offered a degree of

---

[2] Fernandes was the slave of the former Provincial of Bahia's Carmelites. His case will be discussed below.—Ed.

freedom. . . . Groups of slaves . . . fromed *quilombos* [runaway communities] in the interior and were often joined by freed slaves. . . .

The urban counterpart of the *quilombo* was the brotherhood. Many coloured brotherhoods were established in Bahia in the seventeenth and eighteenth centuries—there were some five for mulattoes and six for Negroes dedicated to the Virgin Mary alone—and testified to the social consolidation achieved by the coloured populace. In some cases the brotherhood was founded with the object of freeing its members from bondage: once free, a member contributed to the liberation of his brothers. The majority had wider terms of reference to project the interests of their members during life and to give them a decent burial at death. The most powerful coloured brotherhood of Bahia was that of Our Lady of the Rosary, the only brotherhood to hold annual elections of a king and queen. . . . In its early years membership was limited to Angolan Negroes but later it admitted Brazilian Negroes, mulattoes and even white people. It was the initially exclusive nature of the Rosary which resulted in the foundation of brotherhoods with more flexible terms of entry. One of these was the Brotherhood of St Anthony of Catagerona, founded in 1699 by a group of creole Negroes and Angolan Negroes. This brotherhood admitted anybody, irrespective of state or sex, but maintained the equal representation of Angolans and creoles on its board of guardians. Such was the profusion of these coloured brotherhoods that any person of colour, a slave or a freed man, African or Brazilian, could find a brotherhood to suit his condition.

The ethnic groups of white, Negro and mulatto founded brotherhoods in this chronological order. Once social consolidation had been achieved the conditions of entry to the respective brotherhoods were gradually relaxed. This is well exemplified in the attitudes of the black and white brotherhoods to Jews and those of other ethnic groups. The Rosary, initially exclusive, became more tolerant to the extent of admitting white people. Never did its statutes, or those of any other coloured brotherhood, discriminate against New Christians. There was a similar move towards greater tolerance among several of the white brotherhoods. As mulattoes achieved social standing and even administrative positions if they were not of too dusky a hue, and the Negroes gained their independence in increasing numbers, the white brotherhoods relaxed their conditions of entry. In fact, the Negro was well enough provided for by his own brotherhoods and did not need to apply to a white brotherhood for membership: but this tolerance enabled the light-skinned mulatto, the *branco da Bahia*, to gain entry to a society previously closed to him. . . .

. . . It is undeniable that the girls of the *senzalas*, or slave quarters, were often the concubines of the masters, the butts for the anger of jealous wives, and the playthings of adolescent sons. But there was another side to the picture of inter-racial contact which is usually forgotten. Many slave owners appear to have taken a genuine interest in the welfare of their slaves. The receipt ledgers of the Misericórdia frequently recorded payments . . . made by a plantation owner for the cure of a slave in the hospital of the brotherhood. João de Mattos referred in his will, with evident pride, to how he had arranged the marriage of one of his slave girls and had given her a dowry and some household possessions. Many slaves were granted their freedom as a reward for years of faithful service. A wealthy widow, Theodora de Góis, who died in 1693, granted her slave Luiza her freedom and ordered that a dowry of 100$000, clothing and gold trinkets be given her on marriage. This paternal attitude on the part of the white ruling classes towards the coloured population was not limited to slaves. Many families adopted coloured children. Pedro Viegas Giraldes and Felippe Correia, both benefactors of the Misericórdia in the seventeenth century, brought up mulatto children in their homes. The history of the relationships between masters and slaves white and black, was not always a chronicle of cruelty and exploitation. There was often an undercurrent of Christian idealism among the authoritarian and domineering plantation owners of colonial Bahia. . . .

. . . The first coloured brotherhood to enjoy the privilege of using a bier had been the Brotherhood of Our Lady of Succour (*Irmandade de Nossa Senhora do Amparo*) of free and captive mulattoes. In 1649 the Misericórdia had granted them this privilege on two conditions. The first had been that only slaves should be carried on this bier: all freed members of the brotherhood should be buried by the Misericórdia. The second condition had been that permission to use the bier did not imply possession, and the Misericórdia maintained the right to withdraw this privilege at any time. In 1656 the privilege of the Brotherhood of Our Lady of Succour had been challenged by the Brotherhood of Our Lady of Guadalupe of mulatto slaves. They had claimed that there were no longer any slaves belonging to the Brotherhood of Our Lady of Succour, and that the privilege of using a bier should be transferred to their brotherhood. The board of guardians of the Brotherhood of Our Lady of Succour had vigorously denied this and produced lists of slave members. Indeed, with the exception of the three officers (Judge, scribe and treasurer), the remaining eight members of the board of guardians were all slaves. The Misericórdia had confirmed the privilege of the Brotherhood of Our Lady of Succour to use the bier, and reached a compromise with the Brotherhood of Our Lady of Guadalupe. The former was to permit the brothers of the latter to use the bier, which would be carried by two members of each brotherhood. Should the Brotherhood of Our Lady of Succour fail to comply with the conditions laid down by the Misericórdia and bury freed members, the bier would pass to their rivals. These two brotherhoods were both small and exerted little influence in the city. The most powerful

coloured brotherhood of Bahia was the Brotherhood of
Our Lady of the Rosary. This brotherhood had branches
in most of the parishes but its most vocal group was in
the Pelourinho.

The Brotherhood of Our Lady of the Rosary also enjoyed the privilege granted by the Misericórdia of using
a bier for the funerals of its brothers. Although the majority of its members were slaves, it was also allowed to bury
its freed brothers. The only restriction imposed by the
Misericórdia was that only brothers should be carried on
its bier. . . .

In the eighteenth century an increasing number of
slaves gained their freedom. The Negro became a more
vocal element in urban society, although the majority of
administrative positions were still barred to all except
those of light hue. The Brotherhood of the Rosary was
the mouthpiece for Negro rights. In 1720 the Rosary
addressed a petition to Dom João V for the privilege to
possess a *tumba de arco*: this was a covered bier and
represented an advance on the mere litter, or *esquife,* they
had been permitted to use. The challenge to the Misericórdia was two-fold: first, for possession of a bier, a
privilege of the Misericórdia; secondly, for a covered bier,
whose use had previously been regarded as the exclusive
prerogative of the white population. This petition represented a demand by the leading coloured brotherhood to
the leading white brotherhood for equal privileges. The
Misericórdia, to whom the petition was referred by the
king, rejected it outright. The attitude adopted by the
Misericórdia and the wording of its rejection reveal the
socio-racial prejudice felt by white Bahians towards the
coloured population. . . .

Dom Pedro II had been much concerned about the
conditions of the Negro in Brazil. In 1684 he had introduced a law to reduce the mortality of slaves on the
crossing from West Africa to Brazil in the slave ships.
In 1688 he had ordered the Governor of Rio de Janeiro

to investigate all allegations of cruelty by the masters against their slaves, and to take legal action against the masters if these allegations were shown to be true. In 1693 he had written to the Chapter of the cathedral of Rio that measures should be enforced to ensure that the last sacraments were administered to all slaves on the point of death. It had been brought to the royal attention that this was not the case, partly because the priests demanded exorbitant fees, partly because the masters of the slaves refused to call a priest to a dying slave. Letters from the king to his governors and archbishops rarely produced practical results. Nevertheless, they were evidence of strong royal concern for the living conditions of slaves in Brazil. On 4 October 1693, the Mesa of the Misericórdia of Bahia had established the *banguê* [litter for the conveyance of dead slaves] for the burial of slaves. . . .

The Misericórdia records for the burial of slaves do not permit even approximate calculations for slave mortality. This was notoriously high, and the average working life of a slave on a plantation did not exceed ten years. Slaves in domestic service in the city could probably have expected a longer life span. Many achieved a degree of liberty. The women sold sweetmeats on the streets or acted as washerwomen or cooks. Some male slaves were qualified as masons, carpenters or painters and were themselves employers of slaves. The average number of slaves buried each year by the Misericórdia in the eighteenth century was in the region of 600. This represented only a small proportion of the number of slaves who died annually, but it must be remembered that the Negro brotherhoods had assumed responsibility for the burial of their own members, many of whom were slaves. . . .

The slave was a criminal scapegoat. He was frequently the instrument for the crimes of his master. When captured he received no defence and was unable to present his case. The master disowned him and the law condemned him. . . .

In Bahia the only case on which there is adequate information concerned the defence of a slave by the Misericórdia. . . .

. . . António Fernandes faced a charge of murder. Only two facts were certain: first, that one António Guedes and his slave disappeared in Bahia in 1718; secondly, that shortly afterwards António Fernandes was sent to Rio by friar Manuel to be sold. While in Rio it was alleged that António Fernandes had confessed to the double murder, saying he had acted on his master's orders. The Crown judge in Rio sent him back to Bahia to stand trial on the charge of murder. The charge was unsubstantiated. There was no evidence of the crime and the bodies of the murdered men were not discovered. The witnesses, who claimed to have heard António Fernandes confess to the crime, failed to recognise him in an identity parade. The accused pleaded innocence and the Misericórdia took up his defence. Despite the lack of evidence he was sentenced to be tortured. This sentence was justified by the legal authorities on two dubious grounds. First, that the accused was a 'base person and a slave'. Secondly, that in such a serious case mere hearsay was enough evidence to proceed to torture. One of the judges noted that, in any case, the severity of the punishment received at the hands of the law would have been no greater than the beatings António Fernandes suffered from his master. The lawyer of the Misericórdia appealed to the High Court but the appeal was rejected. A second appeal was also rejected and the lawyer was fined 20$000 for his temerity, whereupon he refused to continue the defence and resigned from his post as lawyer to the Misericórdia. The sentence was carried out and António Fernandes was tortured with brutal severity. The torture lasted four hours and the victim became unconscious twice. On each occasion the doctor and surgeon of the High Court were called to examine the accused to see if the torture could be continued. Only after he had fainted for the second time did the doctor and surgeon forbid further punishment on medical grounds, although the doctor affirmed that there had been no danger of death and the surgeon said that he had treated worse cases who had been sent to the Misericórdia hospital after torture. The stewards of the prisoners of the Misericórdia, who had also been called to assist the accused after each fainting, testified ambiguously that 'although he (António Fernandes) was mad with the pain of the torture, nevertheless we cannot be certain if his condition resulted from the torture alone or was simulated'. António Fernandes appealed to Dom João V, complaining of the 'inhuman tribulations and injustices' he had suffered. The king ordered a full enquiry in 1722. The Count of Sabugosa replied that the enquiry had shown that the torture had been justified and that there was no reasonable doubt as to the guilt of the accused. Nevertheless Dom João V, possibly aware that Sabugosa himself had been named unfavourably in the appeal of Fernandes, ordered a second enquiry to be made in 1723. This was to be conducted by the new Crown judge being sent to Bahia, Dr. Bernardo de Sousa Estrella. The king ordered that friar Manuel da Madre de Deus be expelled from the captaincy for the duration of the enquiry because his powerful influence might obstruct the course of justice. . . .

Purchase of a female slave gave the master the ownership not only of her body but of any children she might produce. . . . Although the capture of slaves in Africa had resulted in the atomisation of families, once these had settled in Brazil there was a considerable degree of family cohesion among slaves on the plantations. A plantation owner often encouraged his slaves to marry. He gained any offspring as slaves and a family provided a more secure social unit on a plantation. If an illegitimate child was born, this too became the property of the master. Thus slavery offered a form of insurance to the child, be he legitimate or illegitimate. In both cases he was fed and housed in return for his potential as a future source of income and social prestige for the owner.

Free coloured people did not benefit from this rather dubious form of protection. They were more at the mercy of external economic factors. They were not so subject to social prejudices as their white counterparts in a correspondingly modest position. An illegitimate child did not dishonour the mother to the same extent as a white woman. Whenever financial means would permit, the illegitimate child was brought up as one of the family. A visitor to modern Bahia cannot fail to notice the ease with which coloured families absorb another child, be he illegitimate or the child of a dead neighbour or relation. Somehow there is always room for yet another child. The Negro seems to regard the family as a more flexible social unit than the white man. Financial considerations are not given such prominence, provided that the family can manage to escape starvation. This attitude towards the child cannot have been so different in colonial Brazil and may explain why so few coloured children were placed in the turning wheel.[3]

[3] The turning wheel was a revolving, cylindrical box that was originally used in convents for the transference of messages, food, and medicine from the outside world into the cloistered community. Poor women, however, put it to another use—they placed their unwanted babies in it, abandoning them to the nuns' care.—Ed.

13

CHARLES R. BOXER

BLACK'S GOLD, BRAZILIAN DIAMONDS–EIGHTEENTH-CENTURY MINING CAMPS

When gold replaced sugar as Brazil's main economic support, both slaves and freedmen migrated from the plantations and cities into new mining areas. In the following selection, Charles Boxer describes the conditions of black and mulatto miners in the boom towns of Minas Gerais. Boxer is Professor of History at Yale University and also holds a special appointment in history at the Lilly Library at the University of Indiana. He is the author of numerous books and articles on the subject of Portuguese imperial history.

Efforts to limit the number of Negro slaves entering Minas Gerais were . . . futile. In January, 1701, the Crown decreed that only two hundred Negro slaves could be imported annually from West Africa via Rio de Janeiro

From Charles R. Boxer, *The Golden Age of Brazil, 1695–1750* (Berkeley and Los Angeles, 1969), pp. 45, 174–175, 184–186, 212, 216–218. Originally published by the University of California Press; reprinted by permission of The Regents of the University of California.

to the mines, and the other slave markets in Brazil were expressly forbidden to sell slaves to the miners. This restriction was relaxed by another decree of March, 1709, but owing to the outcry from the planters, the Crown went into reverse again two year later. The decree of February, 1711 ordained that Negro slaves who were engaged in agricultural labor could not be sold for service in the mines, with the sole exception of those "who by the perversity of their character are congenitally unfitted for work in the sugar mills and fields." The obvious loophole which this concession provided was exploited to the full by the slaveowners, despite the threat of severe punishment for transgressors of the letter and spirit of this law. In 1703 the Crown had instituted an annual import quota of 1,200 African slaves for Rio de Janeiro, 1,300 for Pernambuco, and the balance for Bahia, while maintaining the existing limit of 200 on re-export for Minas Gerais. This law likewise remained largely a dead letter and the quota system was finally abolished in 1715.

Given the hard work and the short commons which were usually his lot, a slave's working life was likely to be nasty, brutish, and short. . . . [O]wners did not normally expect to get more than twelve years work out of the slaves they bought as young men. . . . [T]heir reproduction rate was very low, "owing to the small fecundity of the women who are commonly prostitutes, and to the infirmities and diseases among Negro children in their infancy." . . .

A good idea of the number of able-bodied slaves in Minas Gerais can be ascertained from the figures of the capitation tax returns for adult slaves of both sexes between 1735 and 1750. The first return of 1735 gave a total of 100,141 slaves and the last return of 1749 a figure of 86,797. . . . Other estimates range between 80,000 and 150,000 slaves. . . . [I]t would appear that the wealthier proprietors in Minas Gerais possessed between thirty and fifty able-bodied slaves; but the majority of people seem to have had about half a dozen, and many owners had only one or two.

Since their death rate was so high and their reproduction rate so low, a rapid turnover of slaves resulted. This in turn made great demands on the resources of the slave trade with West Africa. . . . [T]he Mineiros preferred "Minas," exported principally from Whydah, both because they were stronger and more vigorous than the Bantu, as because they were believed to have almost magical powers of discovering gold. . . . The demand for "Minas" is also reflected in the taxation rolls for slaves, whether for payment of the fifths or for capitation, which are still preserved in considerable numbers in the archives of Minas Gerais. In those for the years 1714–1740 . . . "Minas" appeared to be the most numerous, closely followed by slaves from Angola and Benguela.

. . . Some of the mining techniques were apparently of West African origin, for the Portuguese evidently knew less about mining than did some of their slaves from the Western Sudan.

Most of the mining was done by Negro slaves, but many "poor whites" engaged in prospecting and mining on their own. These were the so-called *faiscadores*, who are still found in Minas Gerais today. . . . As regards the more substantial miners, few of them owned more than a dozen slaves; but they were continually petitioning the Crown to grant them similar immunities from distraint for debt as those enjoyed by the large-scale sugar and tobacco planters. After much hesitation, the Crown decreed in 1752 that miners who had thirty or more slaves working for them, would be exempted from having these slaves or their mining equipment distrained for debt. This measure was opposed on the grounds that since virtually all business was done on credit in Minas Gerais, merchants and shopkeepers would be reluctant to extend credit facilities to customers on whom they could not foreclose. Nevertheless, this law remained on the statute book for many years, and in 1813 was extended to all miners without qualification.

Whether working in gold-washings or in subterranean galleries, the miners' toil was often long, arduous, and conducive to disease. . . . "There they work, there they eat, and often there they have to sleep; and since when they work they are bathed in sweat, with their feet always in the cold earth, on stones, or in water, when they rest or eat, their pores close and they become so chilled that they are susceptible to many dangerous illnesses, such as very severe pleurisies, apoplectic, and paralytic fits, convulsions, pneumonia, and many other diseases." The resultant mortality was particularly heavy among the Negro slaves, who . . . were mostly badly treated, poorly housed, and worse clothed. . . .

Among the common illnesses which afflicted both Black and White in Minas Gerais, as elsewhere in Brazil, were bacillary dysentery, intestinal worms, and venereal diseases. . . .

Luís Gomes Ferreira was a skillful surgeon as well as a qualified physician, and the unruly population of Minas Gerais gave him plenty of practice in blood staunching and bonesetting. He records some astonishing cures of severe gunshot, sword and knife wounds, many of his patients being clearly as tough as they come, even in an age when pain killers were unknown. He was often called upon to treat Negro slaves in mining accidents, . . .

. . . Understandably enough, chronic alcoholism was widespread among the Negro slaves, who found that they could best endure their work and forget their misery when fortified by the "white girl (*moça branca*), as *cachaça* was commonly called. . . .

[During the period from January 1, 1740 to December 31, 1743, a search for diamonds was undertaken in the vicinity of the Jequitinhonha River.] Not more than 600 slaves were to be employed by the contractors in the actual mining, for each of whom an annual capitation tax of 230 *milreis* was paid to the Crown. Any of the contractors' slaves found washing or digging for diamonds outside the allotted area would be confiscated to the Crown, as would any slaves over and above the permitted 600 who were found in them. All diamonds mined by the slaves were kept in the Intendant's safe, and were only handed over to the contractor for remission to headquarters at Lisbon. . . .

Although the Negro slaves were closely watched while mining or washing for diamonds, and rigorously searched when the day's work was over, they still contrived to steal many of the best gems. "Ten whites are not enough to watch one Negro," wrote [an] anonymous eyewitness of 1735. "For this reason," he explained, "the Negroes give very few large diamonds to their masters, for they all prefer to give them to the Negresses, who then sell them in the taverns to whites who buy them secretly. The Negroes only give the small diamonds to their owners, and this is one of the reasons—and not the least of them—why it is not much use employing Negroes in this work." As in the gold fields, the authorities were—rightly or wrongly—convinced that the mulatas and Negresses who sold food and drinks to the miners were the chief intermediaries in the smuggling game. This accounts for the severely worded edicts forbidding these colored women to hawk their wares—or their persons—in places where mining was in progress.

The writer of 1735 alleged that when diamond mining was still open to all who could afford to pay the capitation tax, as many as 18,000 Negro slaves were employed mining for diamonds in the Serro do Frio. This was certainly a gross exaggeration, the real number being between eight and nine thousand, . . . One of the objects in limiting the number of working slaves to 600 under the contract system was to reduce the risk of their stealing or smuggling diamonds. Thenceforward there was usually one white (or mulatto) factor to supervise every eight

Negro slaves, but the latter still found means of cheating their employers, though only allowed to wear the equivalent of a loincloth or G string when they were actually working.

The slaves had to work in a stooping position facing their overseer, so as to sift the *cascalho* in the troughs and throw away the gravel while picking out the diamonds. They frequently had to change places with each other so as to prevent them from finding again some diamonds they might have concealed in a heap of stones or earth. Even so, they could sometimes identify the exact spot where they had hidden a diamond, and return under cover of night to secure it. The first thing that old hands among the slaves taught the *moleques* or new arrivals was how to steal diamonds. "For this purpose they practice on them with beans, or grains of maize, which they throw from a distance into the mouth, and in this way they teach them to catch them in the mouth and swallow them." They also practiced sleight of hand and other tricks which enabled them to hide a diamond between their fingers, or in the palm of the hand, and convey it to the mouth unseen. By dint of practice, they could even pick up a diamond with their toes, "concealing it between them for hours on end, and walking with it in this way to the slave quarters." Another favorite trick was to push the diamond up a nostril when taking snuff, or when pretending to do so. The slaves also let their nails grow long, so as to conceal small diamonds behind them, and they had recourse to many other ingenious methods, too complicated to describe here. Swallowing the diamond seems to have been their favorite device. When a slave was suspected of this practice, he was locked in a strongroom and given a violent purge of Malagueta pepper.

When a Negro found a diamond which he saw no chance of concealing, he stood upright, clapped his hands, and then extended his arms upwards and sideways, holding the gem between the forefinger and thumb. The overseer then took it from him and put it in a bowl which was kept ready to hold all the diamonds found in the course of a day's work. In Mawe's [John Mawe, famous for his accounts of his travels in Brazil] time, the slaves received a bonus according to the size of the diamonds which they turned in. Thus, the lucky finder of a diamond which weighed an *oitava* (17½ carats) was "crowned with a wreath of flowers and carried in procession to the administrator, who gives him his freedom, by paying his owner for it. He also receives a grant of new clothes, and is permitted to work on his own account. When a stone of 8 or 10 carats is found, the Negro receives two new shirts, a complete new suit, with a hat and a handsome knife. For smaller stones of trivial amount, proportional premiums are given." Despite these incentives, Mawe noted that the Negro slaves' fare was poor and scanty, "and in other respects they are more hardly dealt with than those of any other establishment which I have visited." Their masters, on the contrary, lived high, . . .

14

MARY KARASCH

RIO'S BLACK *BRASILEIRAS*

Until recently women have been neglected in historical writings. Indeed, the only mention of women is usually found in travel accounts. In this selection Mary Karasch, using a variety of sources, describes conditions of life among African and Afro-Brazilian women in Rio de Janeiro between 1807 and 1849. She concludes that African slave women generally enjoyed more opportunities and fewer restrictions than did their Afro-Brazilian counterparts, and she explains why both groups of women enjoyed a definite advantage over their male contemporaries in a nineteenth-century urban society.

Mary Karasch is Assistant Professor of Latin American History at Oakland University.

More African women bought their freedom than African men, both at the beginning of the period and in 1849. But even for all categories of manumission in 1849, 4,150 African women outnumbered the 3,439 African men who were freedmen. The difference is even more outstanding, when compared to Brazilian born freedwomen—4,150

From Mary Karasch, "Slave Life in Rio de Janeiro, 1808–1850" (Ph.D. diss., University of Wisconsin at Madison, 1972). Editorial arrangement of material from pp. 421–426 by permission of Mary Karasch. Reprinted by permission of the author.

African to 1,892 Brazilian freedwomen. There are a number of reasons to explain these discrepancies. First, more African women than men received their freedom because they had more opportunities than African men to live in a close relationship with the masters. In a city, they generally served as domestic servants, prostitutes, and mistresses. If a master lived with his female slave, the act made her free; also slave women were seldom disposed to testify against their masters. Due to the shortage of white women in that period, slave women easily formed liaisons with white men, who could help them obtain their freedom, if they were not their slaves, or who could free them themselves. Such relationships were almost completely closed to African men, since society disapproved of white women living with black men, although there were exceptions.

Second, African women may have more easily freed themselves because of more opportunities to earn money with which they could buy their freedom. The obvious case is prostitution, which was particularly common among slave women. Black prostitutes were described as freedwomen. But many slave women worked in the streets selling fruits, vegetables, pastries, and assorted goods; but many used their freedom of movement to arrange . . . alliances or to obtain extra money. In addition, slave women formed more permanent arrangements —such as, common-law marriages; in which case, the husbands evidently helped them buy their freedom.

Many of these women earned enough simply by selling goods in the streets to buy their freedom and maintain their own shops. Their ability or inclination to buy and sell goods may have been a characteristic they brought from Africa, since many African women engaged in marketplace activities. . . . Their African background possibly explains the great discrepancy in numbers between Brazilian and African freedwomen. Brazilian women, both slave and free, were generally raised in and confined to the home; but African slave women were not as cloistered. Moreover, they had undergone the trauma of the slave ship. Whereas a Brazilian slave woman could live a confined but possibly comfortable existence within the master's home and perhaps expect to be freed after years of service, an African slave woman had more motivation to improve her position. She did not have this security. Coming from another society, she would not know the Brazilian way of obtaining one's freedom. She would tend to use an African approach, going out into the market and making enough money to buy herself. She would perhaps apply African techniques or innovations that would make her more efficient and thus more capable of earning more money than a Brazilian slave woman.

The maintenance of African patterns of economic behavior may also partly explain the African woman's greater success in becoming free than the African man's. In many African societies, the woman was the one who did the domestic chores, grew the crops, raised the children, and marketed the vegetables and fruits. All of these skills were easily transferred to Rio and often turned into profit. In those societies where the man's function was to hunt and fight, he did not learn to cook, to sell, or to make shoes, all skills that a master might require of him in Rio. Consequently, men in general seem to have had more difficulty in adjusting to slavery, especially in the cities, where they had to do domestic work. This may in turn be reflected in a lower rate of freedmen because of the number of forms of freeing slaves that required a master's consent. Also, African men may have chosen to liberate their wives or mistresses first so that their children would be free. A couple may have worked together to buy first her freedom, then that of the children, and finally that of the husband. Unfortunately, clear-cut cases of this do not enter the records. Maria Graham narrates the case of a mulatto boatman who bought his wife; but his master would not allow him to buy himself because he was too valuable as a slave. . . . In 1807 Maria Mina, a freedwoman, bought her two sons for 230$400 reis, a considerable sum of money; but there is no way of knowing how she did it.

African women were proportionately more successful than African men; in figures, women numbered 6,042 or 56.3% versus 4,690 men or 43.7%. It is even more significant because of the sexual imbalance among the slave population, which ran 40% women and 60% men. There are a number of explanations for this discrepancy, in addition to those for the success of African women. One of the major ones was economic. Women simply cost less, especially older women, and they had to save less money to buy themselves. Whereas Maria Mina had to pay 230$400 reis for her two sons, if she were past the prime age, she might have bought herself for about 80$000. Moreover, women had the advantage in that they were not valued so much for their labor but for their services, which a master could obtain whether a woman was free or enslaved. Unless children were involved, it often made no difference whether the woman was legally free or not, since she was tied to the man in any case. Therefore if masters freed women, they did not feel threatened that they would lose their labor.

The history of one slave woman . . . is among the most complete pictures of an African freedwoman in the historical record. Her name was Manuela do Bom Jesus. Described as a Mina, she and her father had been imported into Brazil when she was about fourteen years of age, which would have been about 1850. She was twenty-five years of age in 1861. While her father was sold to a plantation owner in Pernambuco, she went to the plantation of a rich Senhor Madrinhão in Mata-Porcos. He had bought her to serve as his wife's *mucama* [Brazilian female household servant or slave]; but she was too rebellious and did not make a good house slave. He then allowed her to take the fruits from his plantation and sell them as a *quitandeira* [female street vendor] in the streets of the city.

Given her freedom and the opportunity to save money —she worked on an *ao ganho* basis [by hiring herself out to earn money]—she soon became quite successful. Because of her beauty, she was also popular with her male customers. She rejected their offers, however, because she had fallen in love with a young Frenchman. When he avoided her at first, she went to the *Igreja dos Militares* [a church in Rio de Janeiro], where charms and amulets were sold. Besides praying in the Church, she bought the most powerful charms she could to win his love. When she did approach him and declare her love, he was flattered and accepted her attention. Eventually he did fall in love with her and began to try and find a method of buying her freedom. Because he was then poor, he could not buy her himself. Finally, he had an idea for a benefit play to be put on at a theater. He advertised in the newspapers that the benefit would be held to free a beautiful young slave woman. The benefit was a success; and he went to Senhor Madrinhão to purchase Manuela. At first, her master refused to sell her because she was a good slave; but the notary public and the director of the theater pressured him into selling her for 4,000 francs. Manuela went with Fruchot, left the *quitandeira* business, and lived with him as his mistress, or common-law wife. Eventually, as Fruchot prospered in his businesses, he took her to the Northeast to be reunited with her father. Her story, while unique for the way in which she won her freedom, was typical of many black women who lived with immigrants. Moreover, it was quite acceptable for a white man to live with a black woman; and for these women such liaisons were one major way in which they could obtain their freedom.

15

STANLEY J. STEIN

A NINETEENTH-CENTURY PLANTATION

In his classic study of a coffee plantation in south-central Brazil's Parahyba Valley, Stanley Stein analyzes a community whose entire existence depended on the labor of African slaves. Between 1850 and 1900 the Parahyba Valley was the greatest coffee-producing region in the world. Yet the plantations functioning in Brazil after the abolition of the slave trade in 1850 faced a dwindling labor supply. This fact is crucial to an understanding of the utilization and treatment of African labor during the latter half of the nineteenth century. A detailed discussion of the situation is presented in the following selection.

Stein, author of several books and articles concerning Brazilian history, is Professor of Latin American History at Princeton University.

"My property consists of land and slaves." With these words innumerable testaments throughout the nineteenth

Reprinted by permission of the publishers from Stanley Stein, Vassouras, a Brazilian Coffee County: 1800–1900, pp. 55–56, 70, 75, 78, 132, 135–137, 139, 141–143, 150–151, 155–156, 161–166, 168–171, *Cambridge, Mass.: Harvard University Press,* Copyright, 1957, by the President and Fellows of Harvard College.

century down to 1888 began the statement and distribution of what Vassouras planters had inherited, purchased, and mortgaged, and ordered built or cultivated in their lifetimes. . . .

At the end of the eighteenth century and in the early decades of the nineteenth, many of the large grants were growing sugar cane with the use of slave labor. Thus the sugar engenho of the area contributed to the establishment of the slave-operated plantations. . . . Within the município of Vassouras the sugar plantation worked by slaves had been started even sooner. . . . To serve up-country planters . . . a host of middlemen developed. . . . [These] dealers maintained a dispassionate attitude toward their trade: one retailer bought slaves landed on the coast and sold them to planters of the province of Rio in the same way he "used to retail mules" in the southern provinces. With the dealer interested solely in disposing of his lot of slaves as quickly and profitably as possible (often "selling them loaded with incurable diseases"), planters had to know and recognize the signs of a good slave capable of withstanding hard labor, poor feeding, and poor clothing in a climate of variable temperature. For plantation conditions were such that it was common for a planter to have twenty-five acclimated and trained slaves left three years after buying a lot of one hundred. . . .

A final source of slave labor—one which was common in the large urban centers of the coast—was found in the renting of slaves, both in the town of Vassouras and on surrounding plantations. Construction and maintenance of public works required slave labor, and the município rented slaves for this purpose. So-called "Free Africans" —slaves confiscated in the suppression of the slave trade— were rented to public authorities and private contractors. Moreover, as a scarcity of labor developed on the plantations after 1850, planters proceeded to hire neighbors' slaves or even to rent out their own. Interfamily renting became common as evidenced by the following executor's report: "The growing disproportion between needs of the fields and the number of field hands available for cultivation obliged the executor to hire the slaves of several of the estate's heirs and even the labor of the estate's slaves on Sundays and saints' days." And equally frequent were advertisements such as: "For rent. One young girl suitable as wetnurse. Healthy." . . .

Until the end of the slave trade forced planters to look more carefully to the physical needs of their slaves to prolong their working existence, planters sought field hands whom they could work out efficiently and replace with new levies. Under such circumstances planters preferred males to females for, during the latter stages of gestation and in the months after parturition, female labor in the fields and on the coffee hillsides was not dependable. Consequently, among Africans in Vassouras, the proportion of male to female approximated roughly seven to three, and it was undoubtedly the normal birth ratio that caused any change in the proportion of the whole slave population. Change it did, however, from 77 per cent males and 23 per cent females in the decade 1820–1829, to 56 per cent and 44 per cent respectively in 1880–1888. So gradual was the change that it may be concluded that Vassouras slave society remained predominantly male during the município's growth and decline. . . .

. . . Constant supervision and thorough control through discipline joined to swift, often brutal punishment were considered an absolute necessity on coffee plantations. Proper functioning of a fazenda varied directly with the steady application of the working force; in an epoch of little machinery, slave labor or what Brazilians termed "organized labor," had to be guided carefully and supervised closely.

It seemed that apparently slow-witted slaves had to be driven to produce. In a day's work conscientious planters had to "look for a fugitive slave, consider punishing a second, decide to send a third to help a neighbor—check the weeding . . . complain about the escolha . . . explain each morning in detail to a flock of slaves the nature of extremely simple tasks they were to accomplish, check each evening to see if they have been barely achieved." In their reasoning, the needs of production dovetailed with concepts of slave character. "Only with constantly exercised vigilance under military-like discipline" would slaves work hard and earnestly, was a widespread opinion. The Negro slave was "by nature the enemy of all regular work," the "passive partner" in the transaction that entrusted him to his owner at the time of purchase. His salary? The purchase price and food and clothing provided by his master. . . .

Most visible symbol of the master's authority over the slave [was] the whip. . . .

Whipping was not done by the senhor himself, who "ordered his overseer to beat the slaves." The whipping over, overseers rubbed on the open wounds a "mixture of pepper, salt and vinegar," probably as a cauterizer but interpreted by slaves as "to make it hurt more." An ingenious labor-saving variation . . . was reported by ex-slaves. This was a water-driven "codfish" by which a whip secured to a revolving water-wheel lashed slaves tied to a bench. . . . Typical is an eye-witness account of a beating told by an ex-slave. On orders from the master, two drivers bound and beat a slave while the slave folk stood in line, free folk watching from further back. The slave died that night and his corpse, dumped into a wicker basket, was borne by night to the slave cemetery of the plantation and dropped into a hastily dug grave. "Slaves could not complain to the police, only another fazendeiro could do that," explained the eyewitness. . . .

Only slightly less brutal than the whippings were the hours spent by male and female slaves alike in the *tronco,* a form of heavy iron stock common on plantations. Arms and legs were imprisoned together forcing the victim to sit hunched forward with arms next to ankles, or to lie on one side. . . . Another variation was the long wooden stock . . . into which were locked the feet of four or five slaves. For inveterate offenders an iron hook or collar . . . was used to encircle the neck. For less important offenses the slave's open palm was slapped with a hardwood palm-slapper . . . Inveterate runaways were chained to each other and put into field gangs, or forced to wear a heavy iron weight on one foot. . . .

In a society half free and half slave, many Vassouras planters maintained harmonious relations with the individual members of their labor force. Strong attachments based upon affection and mutual respect often obscured the harsh reality of slavery. A notable difference developed between the affluent planters and the proprietors of small holdings with regard to this relationship. While the large planter had to employ intermediaries to direct the activities of his labor force, the *sitiante* directed his few field hands personally, resided in unpretentious quarters hardly better than those of his slaves, even "maintained his slaves as part of his family and fed them on the same fare."

It appears, however, that slaves bore perennial animosity toward planters as a group. While slaves in general accommodated themselves to the conditions of their existence, few were ever reconciled to them. Range of reaction was wide—from merely verbal acquiescence to masters' orders to violent, organized insurrection. . . .

Where slaves could not bring themselves to react by passive resistance or violence, many committed suicide. . . . Many slaves escaped to the woods until accidentally discovered or rounded up by local police and planters helped by *agregados* and [other] slaves. . . . Once in the woods, the fugitive built a shelter and might prepare a small patch for growing corn and beans. It was probably more common to obtain supplies by stealing from nearby plantations. . . .

Frequently slave runaways lived in organized communities or *quilombos*, . . . When thefts of cornmeal, sugar, or other foodstuffs became too frequent, planters called in the local authorities.

In a society where manumitted slaves were common, apprehension of fugitives was not easy. Recapturing fugitives gathered in quilombos was one thing, finding them after they had fled to other coffee growing towns, another. . . .

The Negro slave child . . . learned that he had few rights, that he could be ordered by the master's children, that he —not they—was expected to be saddled, ridden, and switched in play. His reaction to inferior status was expressed mainly in the form of impassivity; if he failed to do so, he "caught it." . . .

The role of free and slave women on the nineteenth-century plantation differed markedly. At the level of the planter, merchant, and professional groups, free married women were usually molded into passive creatures. . . .

On the slave level, women were far more independent economically. They performed the work of men—weeding, hoeing and harvesting—on the coffee slopes. They raised foodstuffs on their patches of land for sale; in this fashion, a few, sometimes aided by outsiders, purchased their freedom. Of the latter, many were seamstresses. In many respects, Negro women, both before and after emancipation, enjoyed an independence denied their upper-class sisters. . . .

Married slaves, according to one early manual, were to live apart, meeting briefly at night in the slave quarters. "As for the passing unions, these must remain completely secret and unknown . . ." [P]lanters permitted their slaves to be together two or three hours each evening with the result that "most of the slave children have only one parent, the mother."

These conditions helped foster among Brazilian Negroes the passing union or *amazia* that replaced the African tradition of polygyny. The pattern of temporary union was reinforced by economic equality between male and female slaves, by the importance of the mother in African polygymous society and by the disproportion between male and female slaves in Vassouras until the closing decades of slavery. Fights over women were a constant source of friction among male slaves, and undoubtedly were more frequent until the normal reproductive ratio equated the number of female to male slaves. Nor were planters perturbed by the problem of paternity. Drawing an analogy between the slave mothers and cows, one ex-planter explained that if another man's bull inseminated his cow, the cow and calf were his. . . .

Slave life on the average Vassouras plantation of approximately eighty to one hundred slaves was regulated by the needs of coffee agriculture, . . . Since the supply of slaves was never adequate for the needs of the plantation either in its period of growth, prosperity, or decline, the slaves' work day was a long one begun before dawn and often ending many hours after the abrupt sunset of the Parahyba plateau.

. . . The sun had not yet appeared when . . . the cast-iron bell, or sometimes a blast from a cowhorn or the beat of a drum, reverberated across the terreiro and entered the tiny cubicles of slave couples and the separated, crowded tarimbas, or dormitories, of unmarried slaves. Awakening from their five- to eight-hour slumber, they dragged themselves from beds of planks softened with woven fiber mats; field hands reached for hoes and bill-hooks lying under the eaves. At the large faucet near the senzallas, they splashed water over their heads and faces, moistening and rubbing arms, legs, and ankles. . . . Now, as the terreiro slowly filled with slaves, some standing in line and others squatting, awaiting the morning . . . prayer, the senhor appeared on the veranda of the main house. "One slave recited the reza which the others repeated," recalled an ex-slave. Hats were removed and there was heard a "Praised-be-Our-Master-Jesus-Christ" to which some slaves repeated a blurred "Our-Master-Jesus-Christ," others an abbreviated "Kist." From the master on the veranda came the reply: "May-He-always-be-praised." The overseer called the roll; if a slave did not respond after two calls, the overseer hustled into the senzallas to get him or her. When orders for the day had been given, directing the various gangs to work on certain coffee-covered hills, slaves and drivers shuffled to the nearby slave kitchen for coffee and corn bread.

The first signs of dawn brightened the sky as slaves separated to their work. A few went into the main house; most merely placed the long hoe handles on their shoulders and, old and young, men and women, moved off to the almost year-round job of weeding with drivers following to check stragglers. Mothers bore nursing youngsters in small woven baskets . . . on their backs or carried them astraddle one hip. Those from four to seven trudged with their mothers, those from nine to fifteen close by. If coffee hills to be worked were far from the main buildings, food for the two meals furnished in the field went along— either in a two-team ox-cart . . . or in iron kettles swinging on long sticks, or in wicker baskets or two-eared wooden pans . . . on long boards carried on male slaves' shoulders. A few slaves carried their own supplementary articles of food in small cloth bags.

Scattered throughout the field were shelters of four posts and a grass roof. Here, at the foot of the hills where coffee trees marched up steep slopes, the field slaves split into smaller gangs. Old men and women formed a gang working close to the rancho; women formed another; the men or young bucks . . . a third. Leaving the moleques and little girls to play near the cook and assistants in the rancho, they began the day's work. As the sun grew stronger, men removed their shirts; hoes rose and fell slowly as slaves inched up the steep slopes. Under the gang labor system . . . used in weeding, the best hands were spread out on the flanks, . . . There four lead-row men were faster working pacesetters, serving as examples for slower workers sandwiched between them. When a coffee row . . . ended abruptly due to a fold in the slope, the slave now without a row shouted to his overseer "Throw another row for the middle" or "We need another row"; a feitor passed on the information to the flanking lead-row man who moved into the next row giving the slave who had first shouted a new row to hoe. Thus lead-row men always boxed-in the weeding gang.

Slave gangs often worked within singing distance of each other and to give rhythm to their hoe strokes and pass comment on the circumscribed world in which they lived and worked—their own foibles, and those of their master, overseers, and slave drivers—the master-singer . . . of one gang would break into the first "verse" of a song in riddle form, a *jongo*. His gang would chorus the second line of the verse, then weed rhythmically while the master-singer of the nearby gang tried to decipher . . . the riddle presented. . . . [I]f the singing was not good the day's work went badly. . . . Stopping here and there to "give a lick" . . . of the lash to slow slaves, two slave drivers usually supervised the gangs by criss-crossing the vertical coffee rows on the slope and shouting "Come on, come on"; but if surveillance slackened, gang laborers seized the chance to slow down while men and women slaves lighted pipes or leaned on their hoes momentarily to wipe sweat away. To rationalize their desire to resist the slave drivers' whips and shouts, a story developed that an older, slower slave should never be passed in his coffee row. For the aged slave could throw his belt ahead into the younger man's row and the youngster would be bitten by a snake when he reached the belt. . . .

To shouts of "lunch, lunch" [at] ten A.M., slave *par-céiros* [companions] and drivers descended. At the shaded rancho they filed past the cook and his assistants, extending bowls or . . . gourds split in two. On more prosperous fazendas, slaves might have tin plates. Into these food was piled; drivers and a respected or favored slave would eat to one side while the rest sat or sprawled on the ground. Mothers used the rest to nurse their babies. A half hour later the turma was ordered back to the sun-baked hillsides. At one P.M. came a short break for coffee to which slaves often added the second half of the corn meal cake served at lunch. On cold or wet days, small cups of cachaça distilled from the plantation's sugar cane replaced coffee. Some ex-slaves reported that fazendeiros often ordered drivers to deliver the cachaça to the slaves in a cup while they worked, to eliminate a break. . . . [S]upper came at four P.M. and work was resumed until nightfall when to drivers' shouts of "Let's quit" . . . the slave gangs tramped back to the sede. . . . Once more the slaves lined up for roll call on the terreiro where the field hands encountered their slave companions who worked at the plantation center . . .

. . . [A] high percentage of plantation slave labor, which some estimated at fully two-thirds, others at one-half of the labor force, was not engaged directly in field work. "On the plantation," . . . "everything or almost everything is the product of the Black man: it is he who has built the houses; he has made the bricks, sawed the boards, channeled the water, etc.; the roads and most of the machines in the engenho are, along with the lands cultivated, the products of his industry. He also has raised cattle, pigs and other animals needed on the fazenda." Many were employed in relatively unproductive tasks . . . as waiters and waitresses, stableboys and cooks, and body servants for the free men, women, and children.

Throughout the day in front of the house could be seen the activity of the terreiro. From his shaded veranda or from a window the fazendeiro watched his slaves clean the terreiro of sprouting weeds, or at harvest time revolve the drying coffee beans with wooden hoes. Until the hot sun of midday drove them to the shade, bare-bottomed black and mulatto youngsters played under the eye of an elderly "aunt" and often with them a small white child in the care of his male body servant . . . or female "dry nurse." In a corner slaves might butcher a pig for the day's consumption while some moleques threw stones at the black turkey buzzards which hovered nearby. Outside the senzella a decrepit slave usually performed some minor task or merely warmed himself in the sun. . . . In the shade of the engenho an old slave wove strips of bamboo into mats and screens. Washerwomen, beating and spreading clothes to bleach in the sun, worked rhythmically "to the tune of mournful songs." . . .

At evening roll call . . . slaves were checked and sent to evening tasks to begin . . . the "brutal system of night tasks" . . . sometimes lasting to ten or eleven P.M. During winter months the principal evening task—the sorting of coffee beans on the floor of the engenho or on special tables—was continued in the light of castor-oil lamps or woven taquara torches. Preparation of food for humans and animals was the next most important job: manioc was skinned by hand, scraped on a huge grating wheel, dried, and then toasted for manioc flour. Corn cobs were thrown to pigs, while slaves beat other ears on tables . . . with rods to remove kernels to be ground into corn meal. Women pounded rice in mortar and pestle to hull it. Coffee for the following day's consumption was toasted in wide pans, then ground. Slaves were sent out to gather firewood, and moleques walked to nearby abandoned groves to drive in the few foraging cows, oxen, mules, and goats. A light supper ended the serão.

In the dwelling house slaves cleared the supper table and lit castor-oil lamps or candles. The planter's family retired soon to their rooms, followed by the mucama "whose job was to carry water to wash the feet of the person retiring." She departed immediately to return after a short wait, received a "God-bless-you" and blew out the light.

And now field hands straggled from the engenho to slave senzallas where they were locked for the night.

Household help too was locked in tiny rooms located in rear of the house near the kitchen. For the slaves it was the end of a long day—unless a sudden storm blew up during the night while coffee was drying on the terreiros; then they were routed out once more by the jangling bell to pile and cover hurriedly the brown beans. Except for the patrollers, . . . moving in groups on the roads and through the coffee groves to pick up slaves out without passes . . . to visit nearby plantations or taverns, activity ceased.

With the arrival of Saturday evening and Sunday . . . came the only interruption of the work routine of plantation life. On Saturday the evening stint was usually omitted to give the labor force an opportunity to live without close supervision. Near a fire on the drying terrace, to the beating of two or three drums, slaves—men, women, and children—led by one of their master-singers, danced and sang until the early morning hours.

Even Sunday too was partially devoted to work. In morning chores, lasting until nine or ten, field hands attended to the auxiliary tasks of the plantation: hauling firewood from clearings, preparing pasture by burning the grass cover, clearing brush from boundary ditches, repairing dams and roads, and killing ever-present saúva ants with fire and bellows. Sunday was the day for distribution of tobacco cut from a huge roll of twisted leaf smeared with honey, and of clean clothing for the following week's use. Chores completed, the master "gave permission"— permitted slaves to dispose of the remainder of the day until the line-up at nightfall. It was also common for planters to "give permission" on days other than Sunday to stagger the weekly day off and prevent slaves from meeting with friends from nearby plantations.

Many now scattered to small roças near the plantation center, where they raised coffee, corn, and beans. Planters gave them these plots for various reasons: they gave the slave cultivators a sense of property which, known or unknown to Brazilian masters, continued an African tradition and softened the harsh life of slavery; they provided subsistence foodstuffs which planters failed to raise in their emphasis on one-crop agriculture; and, by offering cash for the produce, planters put into slaves' hands small change for supplementary articles not provided by the plantation. Often planters insisted that slaves sell only to them the coffee they raised. Slaves obtained cash too when the custom became widespread among planters to pay for Sunday or saints'-day labor.

Where male and female slaves cohabited, men often were accompanied to the roças by their children, while women washed, mended, and cooked, bringing the noon meal to their mates in the field. The single men brought firewood for the cook to prepare their meal, returning at eating hours. Other slaves used the free time to weave sleeping mats or cut and sew clothing for sale. With cash or corn or beans, slaves went on Sundays to trade at nearby saloons . . . or small country stores.

16

MAHOMMAH G. BAQUAQUA

RECOLLECTIONS OF
A SLAVE'S LIFE

In one of the most vividly detailed accounts of slavery in Brazil, Mahommah Baquaqua, an ex-slave, describes his experiences as a slave in Pernambuco (a state in northeastern Brazil). This document is particularly valuable in that it includes a comparison of the living conditions among slaves in northern and southern Brazil in the 1830s and 1840s.

After his Brazilian experience, Baquaqua traveled to New York as a slave sailor on a merchant vessel. There he was freed and, later, went to Haiti and then to Canada.

We arrived at Pernambuco, South America, early in the morning, and the vessel played about during the day, without coming to anchor. All that day we neither ate or drank anything, and we were given to understand that we were to remain perfectly silent, and not make any out-cry, otherwise our lives were in danger. But when "night

---

From Mahommah G. Baquaqua, *Biography of Mahommah G. Baquaqua, A Native of Zoogao, in the Interior of Africa.* Edited by Samuel Moore, Esq. (Detroit: George E. Pomeroy and Co., Tribune Office, 1854), pp. 41–50.

threw her sable mantle on the earth and sea," the anchor dropped, and we were permitted to go on deck to be viewed and handled by our future masters, who had come aboard from the city. We landed a few miles from the city, at a farmer's house, which was used as a kind of slave market. The farmer had a great many slaves, and I had not been there very long before I saw him use the lash pretty freely on a boy, which made a deep impression on my mind, as of course I imagined that would be my fate ere long, and oh! too soon, alas! were my fears realized.

When I reached the shore, I felt thankful to Providence that I was once more permitted to breathe pure air, the thought of which almost absorbed every other. I cared but little then that I was a slave, having escaped the ship was all I thought about. Some of the slaves on board could talk Portuguese. They had been living on the coast with Portuguese families, and they used to interpret to us. They were not placed in the hold with the rest of us, but came down occasionally to tell us something or other.

These slaves never knew they were to be sent away, until they were placed on board the ship. I remained in this slave market but a day or two, before I was again sold to a slave dealer in the city, who again sold me to a man in the country, who was a baker, and resided not a great distance from Pernambuco.

When a slaver comes in, the news spreads like wild-fire, and down come all those that are interested in the arrival of the vessel with its cargo of living merchandize, who select from the stock those most suited to their different purposes, and purchase the slaves precisely in the same way that oxen or horses would be purchased in a market; but if there are not the kind of slaves in the one cargo, suited to the wants and wishes of the slave buyers, an order is given to the Captain for the particular sorts required, which are furnished to order the next time the ship comes into port. Great numbers make quite a business of this buying and selling human flesh, and do nothing else for a living, depending entirely upon this kind of traffic.

I had contrived whilst on my passage in the slave ship, to gather up a little knowledge of the Portuguese language, from the men before spoken of, and as my master was a Portuguese I could comprehend what he wanted very well, and gave him to understand that I would do all he needed as well as I was able, upon which he appeared quite satisfied.

His family consisted of himself, wife, two children and a woman who was related to them. He had four other slaves as well as myself. He was a Roman Catholic, and had family worship regularly twice a day, which was something after the following: He had a large clock standing in the entry of the house in which were some images made of clay, which were used in worship. We all had to kneel before them; the family in front, and the slaves behind. We were taught to chant some words which we did not know the meaning of. We also had to make the sign of the cross several times. Whilst worshiping, my master held a whip in his hand, and those who showed signs of inattention or drowsiness, were immediately brought to consciousness by a smart application of the whip. This mostly fell to the lot of the female slave, who would often fall asleep in spite of the images, crossings, and other like pieces of amusement.

I was soon placed at hard labor, such as none but slaves and horses are put to. At the time of this man's purchasing me, he was building a house, and had to fetch building stone from across the river, a considerable distance, and I was compelled to carry them that were so heavy it took three men to raise them upon my head, which burden I was obliged to bear for a quarter of a mile at least, down to where the boat lay. Sometimes the stone would press so hard upon my head that I was obliged to throw it down upon the ground, and then my master would be very angry indeed, and would say the cassoori (dog) had thrown down the stone, when I thought in my heart that he was the worst dog; but it was only a thought, as I dared not give utterance in words.

I soon improved in my knowledge of the Portuguese language whilst here, and was able very shortly to count a hundred. I was then sent out to sell bread for my master, first going round through the town, and then out into the country, and in the evening, after coming home again, sold in the market till nine at night. Being pretty honest and persevering, I generally sold out, but sometimes was not quite so successful, and then the lash was my portion.

My companions in slavery were not quite so steady as I was, being much given to drink, so that they were not so profitable to my master. I took advantage of this, to raise myself in his opinion, by being very attentive and obedient; but it was all the same, do what I would, I found I had a tyrant to serve, nothing seemed to satisfy him, so I took to drinking likewise, then we were all of a sort, bad master, bad slaves.

Things went on worse and worse, and I was very anxious to change masters, so I tried running away, but was soon caught, tied and carried back. I next tried what it would do for me by being unfaithful and indolent; so one day when I was sent out to sell bread as usual, I only sold a small quantity, and the money I took and spent for whiskey, which I drank pretty freely, and went home well drunk, when my master went to count the days, taking in my basket and discovering the state of things, I was beaten very severely. I told him he must not whip me any more, and got quite angry, for the thought came into my head that I would kill him, and afterwards destroy myself. I at last made up my mind to drown myself; I would rather die than live to be a slave. I then ran down to the river and threw myself in, but being seen by some persons who were in a boat, I was rescued from drowning. The tide was low at the time, or their efforts would most likely have been unavailing, and notwithstanding my predetermination, I thanked God that my life had been preserved, and that so wicked a deed had not been consummated. It led me seriously to reflect that "God moves in a mysterious way," and that all his acts are acts of kindness and mercy.

I was then but a poor heathen, almost as ignorant as a Hottentot, and had not learned the true God, nor any of his divine commandments. Yet ignorant and slave as I was, slavery I loathed, principally as I suppose, because I was its victim. After this sad attempt upon my life, I was taken to my master's house, who tied my hands behind me, and placed my feet together and whipped me most unmercifully, and beat me about the head and face with a heavy stick, then shook me by the neck, and struck my head against the door posts, which cut and bruised me about the temples, the scars from which savage treatment are visible at this time, and will remain so as long as I live.

After all this cruelty he took me to the city, and sold me to a dealer, where he had taken me once before, but his friends advised him then not to part with me, as they considered it more to his advantage to keep me as I was a profitable slave. I have not related a tithe of the cruel suffering which I endured whilst in the service of this wretch in human form. The limits of the present work will not allow more than a hasty glance at the different scenes which took place in my brief career. I could tell more than would be pleasant for "ears polite," and could not possibly do any good. I could relate occurrences which would "freeze thy young blood, harrow up thy soul, and make each particular hair to stand on end like quills upon the fretful porcupine;" and yet it would be but a repetition of the thousand and one oft told tales of the horrors of the cruel system of slavery.

The man to whom I was again sold was very cruel indeed. He bought two females at the time he bought me; one of them was a very beautiful girl, and he treated her with shocking barbarity.

After a few weeks he shipped me off to Rio Janeiro, where I remained two weeks previous to being again sold. There was a colored man there who wanted to buy me, but for some reason or other he did not complete the purchase. I merely mention this fact to illustrate that slaveholding is generated in power, and any one having the means of buying his fellow creature with the paltry dross, can become a slave owner, no matter his color, his creed or country, and that the colored man would as soon enslave his fellow man as the white man, had he the power.

I was at length sold to a Captain of a vessel who was what may be termed "a hard case." He invited me to go and see his Senora, (wife). I made my best bow to her, and was soon installed into my new office, that of scouring the brass work about the ship, cleaning the knives and forks, and doing other little matters necessary to be done about the cabin. I did not at first like my situation; but as I got acquainted with the crew and the rest of the slaves, I got along pretty well. In a short time I was promoted to the office of under-steward. The steward provided for the table, and I carried the provisions to the cook and waited at table; being pretty smart, they gave me plenty to do. A short time after, the captain and steward disagreed, and he gave up his stewardship, when the keys of his office were entrusted to me. I did all in my power to please my master, the captain, and he in return placed confidence in me. The captain's lady was anything but a good woman; she had a most wretched temper. The captain had carried her off from St. Catharine's, just as she was on the point of getting married, and I believe was never married to her. She often got me into disgrace with my master, and then a whipping was sure to follow. She would at one time do all she could to get me a flogging, and at other times she would interfere and prevent it, just as she was in the humor. She was a strange compound of humanity and brutality. She always went to sea with the captain.

Our first voyage was to Rio Grande; the voyage itself
was pleasant enough had I not suffered with sea sickness.
The harbor at Rio Grande is rather shallow, and on entering we struck the ground, as it happened at low water,
and we had great difficulty in getting her to float again.
We finally succeeded, and exchanged our cargo for dried
meat. We then went to Rio Janeiro and soon succeeded in
disposing of the cargo. We then steered for St. Catharines
to obtain Farina, a kind of breadstuff used mostly by the
slaves. From thence, returned again to Rio Grande and
exchanged our cargo for whale oil and put out again to
sea, and stood for Rio Janeiro. The vessel being very
heavily laden, we had a very bad time of it; we all expected that we should be lost, but by lightening the ship
of part of her cargo, which we did by throwing overboard
a quantity, the ship and all hands were once more saved
from the devouring jaws of the destructive element. Head
winds were prevalent, and although within sight of port
for several days, we could not make the harbor, do all
we could.

Whilst in the doubtful position of whether we should
be lost or not, it occurred to me that death would be but
a release from my slavery, and on that account rather
welcome than otherwise. Indeed I hardly dared to care
either way. I was but a slave, and I felt myself to be one
without hope or prospects of freedom, without friends or
liberty. I had no hopes in this world and knew nothing of
the next; all was gloom, all was fear. The present and the
future were as one, no dividing mark, all Toil! Toil!!
Cruelty! Cruelty!! No end but death to all my woes. I
was not a Christian then; I knew not of a Savior's love,
I knew nothing of his saving grace, of his love for poor
lost sinners, of his mission of peace and good will to all
men, nor had I heard of that good land so beautifully
spoken of by the poet, "a land of pure delight where
saints immortal dwell," and to which land of promise the
Christian is daily shortening the journey. No! These "tid-

ings of great joy" had not then been imparted to my gloomy mind, and all was black despair. But when I heard the Savior's words "come unto me all ye that are heavy laden and I will give you rest," I sought and found him, which came as a balm to my wounds, as consolation to my afflicted soul. When think of all this and consider the past, I am content to struggle on in this world to fulfil my mission here and to do the work that is given me to do. Oh! Christianity thou soother of man's sufferings, thou guide to the blind, and strength to the weak, go thou on thy mission, speak the peaceful tidings of salvation all around and make glad the heart of man, "then shall the wilderness be glad and blossom as the rose." Then will slavery with all its horrors ultimately come to an end, for none possessing thy power and under thy influence can perpetuate a calling so utterly at variance with, and repugnant to all thy doctrines.

After great labor and toil we were landed in perfect safety. During this voyage I endured more corporeal punishment than ever I did my life. The mate, a perfect brute of a fellow, ordered me one day to wash down the vessel, and after I had finished, he pointed to a place where he said was a spot, and with an oath ordered me to scrub it over again, and I did so, but not being in the best of humor he required it to be done a third time, and so on again.

When finding it was only out of caprice and there being no spot to clean, I in the end refused to scrub any more, when he took a broom stick to me, and having a scrubbing brush in my hand I lifted it to him. The master saw all that was going on, and was very angry at me for attempting to strike the mate.—He ordered one of the hands to cut a piece of rope for him; he told me I was to be whipped, and I answered "very well," but kept on with my work with an eye continually turned towards him, watching his movements. When I had set the breakfast ready, he came behind me before I could get out of his way, and struck me with the rope over my shoulders, and being rather long, the end of it swung down and struck my stomach very violently, which caused me some pain and sickness; the force with which the blow was struck completely knocked me down and afterwards he beat me whilst on deck in a most brutal manner.—My mistress interfered at this time and saved me from further violence.

V

Responses to Slavery: Rebels and Runaways

A POEM OF A FREE MAN

"*In the days of captivity, I endured many an insult*
I got up early in the morning, the leather whip beat
me for no reason.
But now I want to see the fellow who shouts to me
from the hilltop
"*Say, God bless you, master*"—*no sir, your Negro*
is a freedman today."—*Anonymous**

Any study of slavery must also consider the divers avenues to freedom. Some means were legal, allowed for by the system; others were illegal and often violent. The major prenineteenth-century form of overt resistance was running away, with a concomitant establishment of maroon or escapee communities.[1] Active rebellion often preceded the escape to freedom. And during the nineteenth century rebellion superseded flight as the prevalent form of slave resistance.

Brazil was plagued with resistance throughout her history with understandable cause. Economic policy on her northern plantations was to extract maximum labor at minimum cost. Living conditions among slaves were miserable, and a deliberate policy of punishment and terror was utilized as a means of control. Intervention by manumission societies, brotherhoods, and—occasionally—the crown alleviated conditions, but, generally, the slave's situation was so unbearable that "runaway communities flourished in almost all areas of the captaincy (Bahia)."[2] Naturally, once the slave became a fugitive he had no way to support himself and was forced to steal from the white community he had fled. As a result, the majority of Bahian slave communities sprang up close to population centers or surrounding plantations.[3]

Spain's desire to protect her conquered Indian populations in Mexico resulted in the importation of Africans to labor in Mexican mines, on plantations, and at a variety of other tasks in rural and urban areas. David Davidson has argued that the Iberian concern for "Spanish subjects and Catholic souls," although expressed through conciliatory legislation, was tempered by the necessity for a stable, dependable labor supply. Decrees to make slave life more palatable and measures to hispanize Africans appear to have had only limited effects. Efforts by crown and Church to protect the stability of the slave family

[1] These runaway communities were known variously as *quilombos, ladeiras, mocambos, palenques, cumbes,* or *mambises.* An important source book is Richard Price, ed., *Maroon Societies: Rebel Slave Communities in the Americas* (New York: Anchor Books, 1973).

[2] Stuart Schwartz, "The *Mocambo*: Slave Resistance in Colonial Bahia," *Journal of Social History,* 3 (Summer 1970), 319.

[3] *Ibid.,* pp. 321–322.

were constantly being thwarted by slave traders and owners. Thus the frustrated efforts of slaves to achieve freedom, as well as maltreatment by their owners, gave impetus to rebellion and escape.

Motivations for resisting slavery were varied, however, and not always a matter of dissatisfaction: for example, the flight of urban slaves was as much a result of in-group problems as it was a reaction to slavery per se. An important point is raised by Bowser concerning fugitive slaves in colonial Spanish America: "However widespread and serious the runaway problem was, its importance has obviously been exaggerated, otherwise the institution of slavery would have collapsed under the strain."[4] Using the same logic, we can also question the "serious danger" of slave rebellions in nineteenth-century Latin America.

[4] Frederick P. Bowser, "The African in Colonial America," *Latin American Research Review*, 7 (Spring 1972), 84.

17

R. K. KENT

PALMARES

The quilombo, *a pre-nineteenth-century phenom-enon, constituted the closest re-creation of African society in the new environment of Latin America. Ten major* quilombos *existed in colonial Brazil, but seven were destroyed within two years of their for-mation.[1] Perhaps the most famous* quilombo *in all Latin America was Palmares, in Brazil's Pernam-buco-Alagoas area. R. K. Kent, Professor of African History at the University of California, Berkeley, has applied historicolinguistic evidence to the study of this African "state" within a state. He demon-strates that in Palmares were reflected many of the complexities of African culture, that it was an "African political system which came to govern a plural society and thus give continuity to what could have been at best a group of scattered hide-outs."[2]*

From R. K. Kent, "Palmares: An African State in Brazil," *Journal of African History*, 6 (1965), 161–175 *passim*. Reprinted by per-mission of the Cambridge University Press.

[1] All sources concerning Palmares and other *quilombos* are noted in Kent's original article.

[2] Kent, "Palmares: An African State in Brazil," p. 169.

The foundation of Palmares appears to have taken place in 1605/06, possibly earlier, but certainly not later. As [a] report of 1612 indicates, the first Portuguese expedition against Palmares attained little by way of military victory. Nothing else, however, is heard of Palmares until the mid-1630s. . . . Increasing *palmarista* militancy after 1630 can safely be associated with slaves who took advantage of the Dutch presence to escape and who eventually found their way into Palmares. It is also certain that Palmares antedates the Dutch in Brazil by at least a quarter of a century. Given an earlier origin, and the absence of *quilombo* from the contemporary vocabulary, it is even less probable that Jagas were the founders of Palmares. . . .

'Negroes from Guiné' were mentioned long before 1597 in connexion with attempted rebellion. . . . But the 'Guiné' of early Portuguese sources is not a fruitful geographical expression. It stood for nearly anything between a limited section of West Africa and the entire continent. . . . With Loanda as the undisputed slave funnel from the 1580s until well into the seventeenth century, it is quite unlikely that more than a handful of *palmaristas* originated outside the Angola–Congo perimeter. *Crioulos*—in Pernambuco of 1605—could not have been numerous either. All of this leads to the only plausible hypothesis about the founders of Palmares. They must have been Bantu-speaking and could not have belonged exclusively to any sub-group. Palmares was a reaction to a slave-holding society entirely out of step with forms of bondage familiar to Africa. As such, it had to cut across ethnic lines and draw upon all those who managed to escape from various plantations and at different times. The Palmares which emerged out of this amalgam may be glimpsed in a little more detail during the second half of the seventeenth century.

. . . Dutch activities concerning Palmares, from 1640 until . . . 1645, begin with a reconnaissance mission by Bartholomeus Lintz, . . . Lintz discovered that Palmares was not a single enclave, but a combination of many *kleine* and two *groote* units. The smaller ones were clustered on the left bank of the Gurungumba, six leagues from its confluence with the larger Paraiba and twenty leagues from Alagoas. They contained 'about 6,000 Negroes living in numerous huts'. The two large *palamars* were deeper inland, thirty leagues from Santo Amaro, in the mountain region of Barriga, and 'harboured some 5,000 Negroes'. . . .

A second Dutch expedition left Selgado for Palmares on 26 February 1645. . . . It was headed by Jürgens Reijmbach, . . . His task was to destroy the two *groote* Palmares. On 18 March. Reijmbach reached the first and found that it had been abandoned months earlier. . . . Three days later, his men located the second one. . . . This Palmares, . . .

> is equally half a mile long, its street six feet wide and running along a large swamp, tall trees alongside. . . . There are 220 *casas*, amid them a church, four smithies and a huge *casa de conselho*; all kinds of artifacts are to be seen. . . . (The) king rules . . . with iron justice, without permitting any *feticeiros* among the inhabitants; when some Negroes attempt to flee, he sends *crioulos* after them and once retaken their death is swift and of the kind to instill fear, especially among the Angolan Negroes; the king also has another *casa*, some two miles away, with its own rich fields. . . . We asked the Negroes how many of them live (here) and were told some 500, and from what we saw around us as well we presumed that there were 1,500 inhabitants all told. . . . This is the Palmares *grandes* of which so much is heard in Brazil, with its well-kept lands, all kinds of cereals, beautifully irrigated with streamlets.[1]

[1] Edison Carneiro, *O Quilombo dos Palmares*, 2d ed. (n.p., 1958), pp. 255–258.

. . . An undestroyed Palmares . . . remained free of further interference by Pernambucan authorities until 1672. The ensuing two decades can best be described as a period of sustained war which ended in the complete destruction of Palmares in 1694. . . .

. . . Of the eight expeditions between 1672 and 1680, two did hurt Palmares. . . . The Palmares of 1677 encompassed over sixty leagues:

> In the northeast, mocambo of *Zambi*, located 16 leagues from Porto Calvo; north of it, at 5 leagues' distance, mocambo of *Arotirene*; along it two others called *Tabocas*; northeast of these, at 14 leagues, the one of *Dombabanga*; 8 leagues north another, called *Subupuira*; another 6 leagues north, the royal enclave of *Macoco*; west of it, at 5 leagues, the mocambo of *Osenga*; at 9 leagues from our Serin-haem, northwest, the enclave of *Amaro*; at 25 leagues from Alagoas, northwest, the palamar of *Andalaquituche*, brother of *Zambi*; and between all these, which are the largest and most fortified, there are others of lesser importance and with less people in them.[2]

There was no doubt . . . that Palmares maintained its 'real strength' by providing 'food as well as security' for the inhabitants—largely tillers of land who planted 'every kind of vegetables' and knew how to store them against 'wartime and winter'. All the inhabitants of Palmares considered themselves:

> subjects of a king who is called *Ganga-Zumba*, which means Great Lord, and he is recognized as such both by those born in Palmares and by those who join them from outside; he has a palatial residence, *casas* for members of his family, and is as-

[2] Edison Carneiro, "Relacão das Guerras," *Revista do Instituto Historico e Geographico Brasileiro*, 22 (1959), 303–329.

sisted by guards and officials who have, by custom, *casas* which approach those of royalty. He is treated with all respect due a Monarch and all the honours due a Lord. Those who are in his presence kneel on the ground and strike palm leaves with their hands as sign of appreciation of His excellence. They address him as Majesty and obey him with reverence. He lives in the royal enclave, called *Macoco*, a name which was begotten from the death of an animal on the site. This is the capital of Palmares; it is fortified with parapets full of caltrops, a big danger even when detected. The enclave itself consists of some 1,500 *casas*. There are keepers of law (and) their office is duplicated elsewhere. And although these barbarians have all but forgotten their subjugation, they have not completely lost allegiance to the Church. There is a *capela*, to which they flock whenever time allows, and *imagens* to which they direct their worship. . . . One of the most crafty, whom they venerate as *paroco*, baptizes and marries them. Baptismals are, however, not identical with the form determined by the Church and the marriage is singularly close to laws of nature. . . . The king has three (women), a *mulata* and two *crioulas*. The first has given him many sons, the other two none. All the foregoing applies to the *cidade principal* of Palmares and it is the king who rules it directly; other *cidades* are in the charge of potentates and major chiefs who govern in his name. The second *cidade* in importance is called *Subupuira* and is ruled by king's brother (Gana) *Zona*. . . . It has 800 *casas* and occupies a site one square league in size, right along the river *Cachingi*. It is here that Negroes are trained to fight our assaults (and weapons are forged there).[3]

Nearly three decades of peace had a number of important results in the internal evolution of Palmares.

Instead of the two major *palmars* of 1645, there were now ten. There was a very substantial element in the Macoco of those native to Palmares, people unfamiliar with *engenho* slavery. Afro-Brazilians continued to enjoy preferential status, but the distinction between *crioulos* and Angolas does not appear to have been as sharp as it was in 1645. There was a greater degree of religious acculturation. The reference to a population composed mainly of those born in Palmares and those who joined from outside suggests that slaves had become less numerous than free commoners. . . . [T]he only slaves in Palmares were those captured in razzias. But they had the option of going out on raids to secure freedom by returning with a substitute. [T]he main 'business' of *palmaristas* 'is to rob the Portugueses of their slaves, who remain in slavery among them, until they have redeemed themselves by stealing another; but such slaves as run over to them, are as free as the rest.'

The almost equally long years of peace and war between 1645–94 point to Palmares as a fluctuating 'peril'. While not necessarily unfair to the merits of a particular event, the Portuguese took it for an article of faith that Palmares was an aggressor state. No written document originating within Palmares has come to light. It probably does not exist. . . .

Pernambucan authorities did not view Palmares from the perspective of the *moradores* who were in contact with it. They were too far removed from the general area of Palmares. . . . The governors did, however, respond to *morador* pressure. . . . Among the complaints most frequently heard were loss of field hands and domestic servants, loss of settler lives, kidnapping and rape of white women. Two of the common grievances do not stand up too well. Women were a rarity in Palmares and were actively sought during razzias. But female relatives of the *morador* did not constitute the main target, and those occasionally taken were returned unmolested for ransom. . . . [C]lose examination of documents . . . failed to reveal a single substantiated case of a *morador* killed in *palmarista* raids. Settler lives appear to have been lost in the numerous and forever unrecorded 'little' *entradas* into Palmares. They were carried out by small private armies of plantation owners who sought to recapture lost hands or to acquire new ones without paying for them. Some of the *moradores* had secret commercial compacts with Palmares, usually exchanging firearms for gold and silver taken in the razzias. . . .

Loss of plantation slaves, through raids as well as escape, emerges as the one solid reason behind the *morador-palmarista* conflict. The price of slaves is known to have increased considerably by the late 1660s. The very growth of Palmares served to increase its fame among the plantation slaves, 'More and more Negroes from Angola' . . . have now for some years fled on their own from the . . . mills and plantations of this Captaincy.' But this growth was not one-sided. . . .

The native-newcomer ratio was not identical in every *mocambo* of Palmares. The Macoco, at forty-five leagues from Porto Calvo, must have had a far greater number of the native-born than did the *mocambos* of Zumbi, at sixteen leagues from Porto Calvo, and Amaro, at nine leagues from Serinhaem. Socio-cultural differences, moreover, between *crioulos* and recent arrivals from Africa were not sufficiently great to challenge the unity of Palmares, which stood against the Portuguese economic and political order. The diplomacy of Ganga-Zumba, an elected ruler, might have worked had the promise to return those who found refuge in Palmares been observed. It might have worked if Palmares had been contiguous to other similar states facing an intrusive minority. Again, it might have worked if Palmares had been a homogeneous society with hereditary rulers. None of these conditions were present. In its time and place, Palmares had only two choices. It could continue to hold its ground as an independent state or suffer complete extinction. Zambi's palace revolt finally brought the unyielding *palmarista* and *morador* elements to full agreement. . . .

The story of Palmares' final destruction has been told in great detail. . . . The Paulistas had to fight for two years to reduce Palmares to a single fortified site. After twenty days of siege by the Paulistas, the state of Pernambuco had to provide an additional 3,000 men to keep it going for another twenty-two days. The breakthrough occurred during the night of 5–6 February 1694. Some 200 *palmaristas* fell or hurled themselves—the point has been long debated—'from a rock so high that they were broken to pieces'. Hand-to-hand combat took another 200 *palmarista* lives and over 500 'of both sexes and all ages' were captured and sold outside Pernambuco. Zambi, taken alive and wounded, was decapitated on 20 November 1695. The head was exhibited in public 'to kill the legend of his immortality'.

. . . In spite of hundreds of *mocambos* which tried to come together, Palmares was never duplicated on Brazilian soil. This is ample testimony of its impact on the Portuguese settler and official. They organized special units, under *capitães-do-mato* or bush-captains, to hunt for *mocambos* and nip them in the bud. And they sought to prevent, at ports of entry, an over-concentration of African slaves from the same ethnic group or ship. This policy was abandoned in the wake of the Napoleonic wars, and the immediate repercussion came by way of the nine Bahian revolts after 1807. The well-established thesis that uninhibited miscegenation and the corporate nature of the Portuguese society in Brazil produced a successful example of social engineering must also take into account the historical role of Palmares.

Palmares was a centralized kingdom with an elected ruler. Ganga-Zumba delegated territorial power and appointed to office. The most important ones went to his relatives. His nephew, Zambi, was the war chief. Ganga-

Zona, the king's brother, was in charge of the arsenal. Interregnum problems do not seem to have troubled Palmares, the history of which spans about five generations of rulers. Zambi's palace revolt did not displace the ruling family. Assuming that Loanda was the main embarkation point for Pernambucan slaves, which is confirmed by the linguistic evidence, the model for Palmares could have come from nowhere else but central Africa. Can it be pinpointed? Internal attitude toward slavery, prostrations before the king, site initiation with animal blood, the placing of the *casa de conselho* in the 'main square', or the use of a high rock as part of man-made fortress lead in no particular direction. The names of *mocambo* chiefs suggest a number of possible candidates. The most likely answer is that the political system did not derive from a particular central African model, but from several. Only a far more detailed study of Palmares through additional sources in the archives of Angola and Torre do Tombo could refine the answer. None the less, the most apparent significance of Palmares to African history is that an African political system could be transferred to a different continent; that it could come to govern not only individuals from a variety of ethnic groups in Africa but also those born in Brazil, pitch black or almost white, latinized or close to Amerindian roots; and that it could endure for almost a full century against two European powers, Holland and Portugal. And this is no small tribute to the vitality of traditional African art in governing men.

18

DAVID M. DAVIDSON

PROTEST AND *PALENQUES:* BLACK RESISTANCE AND CONTROL IN COLONIAL MEXICO

In the following selection, David Davidson offers a vivid account of slave resistance in colonial Mexico that challenges typical notions about black docility and passive submission to slavery. It is a view of slave resistance set against a backdrop of social change and illustrates the interplay of diverse races and cultures.

Negro resistance to enslavement was an integral feature of the history of African slavery in the Americas. . . . Repeated evidence of more subtle forms of resistance—for example, suicide and voluntary abortion and infanticide—

From David M. Davidson, "Negro Slave Control and Resistance in Colonial Mexico, 1519–1650," *Hispanic American Historical Review,* 46 (August 1966), 235–237, 242–253 *passim.* Reprinted by permission of the Publisher. Copyright 1966, Duke University Press, Durham, North Carolina.

reveals further the determined refusal of many slaves to accept their position, and their reluctance to bear children in slavery. Such resistance occurred in varying degrees wherever Europeans established Negro slavery in the New World, primarily in the southern United States, the Antilles, the Pacific and Caribbean coasts of Central and South America, and northeastern Brazil. . . . Negro slave resistance was also present in colonial Mexico. . . .

It is now fairly certain that in the period 1519–1650 the area received at least 120,000 slaves, or two-thirds of all the Africans imported into the Spanish possessions in America. The early development of Negro slavery in colonial Mexico was a direct response to the serious labor shortage resulting from the startling decline of the Indian population. . . . Royal decrees throughout the late sixteenth century prohibited the use of Indians in certain industries considered detrimental to their health, especially sugar processing and cloth production, and ordered their replacement by Negro slaves. African labor was also encouraged for the mines.

The response to these conditions was a constant demand for Negroes, a flourishing slave trade, and a rising Negro population throughout the sixteenth and early seventeenth centuries. As a result, by 1570 Mexico contained over 20,000 Negroes, and by 1650 there were more than 35,000 Negroes and over 100,000 Afromestizos (mulattoes and zambos). Slaves were found throughout the colony, serving in the mines, plantations and ranches, as well as in the urban areas as peddlers, muleteers, craftsmen, day laborers, and domestics.

Concentrations of Negro population appeared in four distinct areas. In the eastern region, from the coastal lowlands between Veracruz and Pánuco to the slopes of the Sierra Madre Oriental, there were some 8,000–10,000 Africans. The port of Veracruz alone contained about 5,000 Negroes and Afromestizos in 1646, most of whom served as carriers and dock hands, while in the rural areas over 3,000 slaves worked on the sugar plantations and cattle ranches that spread inland to the mountains. In the region north and west of Mexico City were at least 15,000 slaves in silver mines and on cattle, sheep, and mule ranches. In the broad belt extending southwestward from Puebla to the Pacific coast were another 3,000–5,000 slaves on sugar plantations and ranches, in mines, and on the docks of Acapulco. Finally, the largest Negro concentration of all was in Mexico City and the valley of Mexico, where 20,000–50,000 Africans, slave and free, were employed in urban occupations. . . .

Unfortunately conciliatory legislation and hispanization failed to eliminate the general causes of slave resistance in Mexico. Unstable familial and marital life, mistreatment, overwork, and the scarcity of effective channels to freedom undoubtedly contributed heavily to slave discontent. Although these conditions certainly varied from one region, master, and economic activity to another, the worst treatment and the most brutal revolts occurred in the mines and sugar plantations of the colony. Here the deplorable circumstances intensified that common factor behind all slave resistance, the wholly human desire for freedom. . . .

Although individual Negroes fled in the early years, the first alleged effort by slaves to organize a large-scale uprising occurred in 1537. . . .

Whether reality or fantasy . . . the conspiracy struck fear into the Spanish population and created a serious concern for Negro slave activity. . . .

Continued tension in Mexico City and the occurrence of at least two more revolts in the 1540s prompted Spanish officials to issue a number of decrees restricting Mexico's Negro population. Mendoza's ordinances of 1548 prohibited the sale of arms to Negroes and forbade public gatherings of three or more Negroes when not with their masters. The viceroy also declared a night curfew on Negroes in the capital city. . . .

With restrictive measures barely under way, Mexico experienced its first widespread wave of slave insurrections in the period 1560–1580 as a result of the increased use of Negroes in mines and estates. By the 1560s fugitive slaves from the mines of the north were terrorizing the regions from Guadalajara to Zacatecas, allying with the Indians and raiding ranches. In one case maroons from the mines of Guanajuato joined with unpacified Chichimec Indians in a brutal war with the settlers. . . . To the east, slaves from the Pachuca mines took refuge in an inaccessible cave from which they sallied forth periodically to harass the countryside. Negroes from the Atotonilco and Tonavista mines joined them with arms, and created an impregnable *palenque* [runaway community]. Local reports revealed that the uprisings were spreading eastward, and that much of the area in the quadrangle between Mexico City, Zacatecas, Pánuco, and Veracruz faced similar revolts. . . .

A series of royal decrees from 1571 to 1574, forming a fugitive slave code, consolidated previous restrictive legislation and articulated a complex system of slave control and surveillance. Slaves absent from their masters for more than four days were to receive fifty lashes; those absent for more than eight days were to receive one hundred lashes "with iron fetters tied to their feet with rope, which they shall wear for two months and shall not take off under pain of two hundred lashes." The death sentence was to be applied to all those missing for six months, although this penalty was reduced at times to castration. In other circumstances the leaders of revolts were condemned to summary hanging, while the other maroons were to be returned to slavery. Local governments aided by rural police units were to provide a vigilance system in the countryside, and overseers were to make nightly checks on plantations and ranches. The decrees established rewards for the capture of runaways and encouraged fellow slaves and returned fugitives to join or aid the posses. The crown hoped to prevent any assistance for fugitives by placing heavy fines on those caught aiding slaves. . . .

During the last decades of the sixteenth century the focus of slave revolts shifted to the eastern sugar regions of the viceroyalty. Isolated uprisings had occurred there since the 1560s, but by the turn of the century the slopes and lowlands between Mt. Orizaba and Veracruz teemed with small maroon settlements and roaming bands of slaves who raided the many plantations and towns in the area.

The geography of the region so favored maroon guerrila activities that local authorities proved incapable of thwarting their raids or pursuing them to the palenques. . . .

In one attack of 1609 "the Negro maroons robbed and destroyed some wagons which carry from Veracruz to Mexico City the clothing that comes from Spain, routing the carriers and breaking to pieces the Spaniard who led them." In 1609 such activities prompted Viceroy Luis de Velasco to commission Captain Pedro Gonzalo de Herrera to lead a pacifying force to the distraught area. The story of this expedition is perhaps the only surviving detailed account of an armed encounter between Spanish troops and ex-slaves in the colony. . . .

. . . The Negroes knew of Herrera's departure but continued their raiding in the hinterland. In one attack they captured a Spaniard and brought him to their main setlement at the Cofre de Perote in the mountains near Mt. Orizaba.

The ruler of the Negro settlement was an aging first generation African referred to as Ñaga, Ñanga, or Yanga. . . . "This Yanga was a Negro of the Bron [sic] nation, of whom it is said that if they had not captured him, he would have been king in his own land. . . . He had been the first maroon to flee his master and for thirty years had gone free in the mountains, and he has united others who held him as chief, who are called Yanguicos." In

Yanga's settlement were some sixty huts housing about eighty adult males, twenty-four Negro and Indian women, and an undetermined number of children. Although the settlement had existed in that location for only nine months, "they had already planted many seedlings and other trees, cotton, sweet potatoes, chile, tobacco, squash, corn, beans, sugar cane, and other vegetables." The settlement was by necessity a war camp with its internal structure oriented to the needs of self-defense and retaliation. [There existed] a distinct division of labor within the palenque, with half the population tending the crops and cattle and the remaining men comprising a constant military guard and forming the guerrilla troops which periodically raided the countryside. The command of the army was in the hands of a Negro from Angola, while Yanga reserved to himself the civil administration. Most of the Negroes had received some religious instruction before escaping, and, like many other maroons in the Americas, they retained at least a limited form of Catholicism. The town had a small chapel with an altar, candles, and images.

. . . Herrera found the palenque deserted. Earlier Yanga had sent his people to another location, and he and the remaining inhabitants fled just before the army arrived, leaving most of their possessions behind. . . . "The spoils that were found in the town and huts of these Negroes were considerable. A variety of clothing that they had gathered, cutlasses, swords, axes, some harquebuses and coins, salt, butter, corn, and other similar things without which, although the enemy was not left totally helpless, he was very much weakened." . . .

. . . Yanga and Herrera soon came to terms, . . . Judging from the terms of the negotiation, however, the two leaders arrived at a mutual accommodation, which was not a surrender for the slaves. The terms of the truce, as preserved in the archives, included eleven conditions stipulated by Yanga upon which he and his people would cease their raiding. The African demanded that all of his people who had fled before September of the past year (1608) be freed and promised that those who had escaped slavery after that date would be returned to their masters. He further stipulated that the palenque be given the status of a free town and that it have its own cabildo and a *justicia mayor* who was to be a Spanish layman. No other Spaniards were to live in the town, although they could visit on market days. Yanga asked that he be named governor of the town and that his descendants succeed him in office. He also required that only Franciscan friars minister to his people and that the crown finance the ornamentation of the church. In return Yanga promised that for a fee the town would aid the viceroy in capturing fugitive slaves. The Negroes, he said, would aid the crown in case of an external attack on Mexico.

. . . [T]he viceroy accepted these terms. Besides being unable to conquer Yanga, the authorities needed the aid of his guerrillas to capture other fugitive slaves in the area. Thus, shortly after the negotiations, the new town of San Lorenzo de los Negros was established as a free Negro settlement not far from the old palenque. How long it existed is unknown, but the Italian traveler Gemelli Careri, who traversed the region in 1698, testified to its prosperity and industry.

Yanga's maroon movement is a notable incident in the history of Negroes in Mexico—the only known example of a fully successful attempt by slaves to secure their freedom *en masse* by revolt and negotiation and to have it sanctioned and guaranteed in law. This experience demonstrates that, under capable leadership, slaves could maintain an active guerrilla campaign, negotiate a truce, and win recognition of their freedom. In view of the tenacity displayed by other maroons as well, it is likely that similar incidents occurred which have not been recorded.

The violence of slave insurrections in the eastern slopes and northern mining regions kept Mexico City in a prolonged state of anxiety. By the first decade of the seventeenth century the Negro population of the capital had grown enormously, and there was a general fear that the urban slaves would unite to take the city. The tensions in the metropolis exploded in 1609 and 1612 when rumors circulated that the Negroes had chosen leaders and planned massive uprisings. In both cases elaborate defensive preparations followed brief periods of panic and confusion. Negroes were apprehended and punished, and the plots, if indeed they existed at all, never materialized. Yet whether or not these conspiracies actually existed, the terror which they caused was a reflection of the tensions inherent in multiracial Mexico where insecurity plagued the Spanish and creole population well into the seventeenth century.

. . . Countless minor revolts and escapes occurred in the sheep ranching regions of the north in 1620s and 1630s. . . . [I]t was so easy to flee the ranches that it was almost a daily happening. . . . [S]ome ranchers were near bankruptcy, not merely because of the loss of their slaves, but also because of the exorbitant fees charged by local officials for capturing fugitives. Constables and corregidores held a monopoly of slave-capturing in the ranching regions and made lucrative profits by reselling runaways, not always to their original owners. The frequent complaints of ranchers and viceroys indicate that slaves continued to flee, local officials continued to capture them and charge high fees, and ranchers continued to suffer throughout the first half of the seventeenth century.

It is apparent that officials and slaveowners found it extremely difficult to prevent or contain slave resistance. Few in numbers, they were forced to rely on the scarce royal troops in Mexico aided by untrained and undisciplined bands of mestizos and Indians. These haphazard military operations faced serious strategic and tactical problems, especially in campaigns against distant hideaways in the frontier regions. Mexico's rugged terrain compounded the difficulties, for fugitives could establish settlements in the mountains and isolated barrancas which afforded excellent defensive sites. Moreover, Indian cooperation seems to have been instrumental to the success of various revolts and made the job of repression all the more difficult. With such a weak system of control, the flight and insurrection of slaves continued into the eighteenth century, and it was only the abolition of slavery in the early nineteenth century that put an end to slave resistance in Mexico.

In conclusion, some implications of slave control and resistance in colonial Mexico are evident. In the first place, it appears that flight and revolt constituted the most effective avenue to liberty for the slave population, despite the existence of an elaborate (if often ineffective) machinery of control and conciliation. Thus a major consequence of resistance was the development of the free Negro and Afromestizo population of the colony. Second, slave resistance, real or imagined, had a notably disturbing effect on the society of the conquerors. In this respect the anxiety of colonial society differed more in degree than in kind from that of the fear-ridden slavocracies of the Caribbean and southern United States. The same restrictive and precautionary measures, the same false alarms, and similar bands of roaming vigilantes characterized Mexico as well. Moreover, preventive legislation and Spanish fears extended to the free Negro population, and the status of freedmen in the colony suffered regardless of their role in slave resistance. Finally, the study of Negro slave activity reveals an area of social life barely perceived by many students of colonial Mexico—the relations within the nonwhite and mixed peoples in the multiracial societies that developed throughout tropical America.

19

ANN M. PESCATELLO

PRÊTO POWER,
BRAZILIAN STYLE

*In Latin America, and especially Brazil, revolts and
attempts to seize power were the prevalent forms
of slave protest during the first half of the nineteenth century. This was due, in part, to the general
instability caused by political and social upheavals,
as well as to intensification of the slave trade. In
the following selection, Ann Pescatello discusses several famous slave revolts in nineteenth-century Bahia.*

*Ann M. Pescatello is the author of several articles
and books on women, families, slaves, immigrants,
and land and labor systems in Latin America.*

Of the various nineteenth-century armed insurrections,
attempts at seizure of power, or other similar movements,
nine occurred in Bahia between 1807 and 1835. . . .

The nine major Bahian "reactions" to slavery had their
roots in a long tradition of Afro-Brazilian dissatisfaction
and their immediate prelude in a conspiracy of 1806. We
know little of this incipient "revolt" because a raid on a

"conspirator's" house resulted in its defusing and in government orders to arrest every slave in the streets after the 9 P.M. curfew if he or she did not have a letter from his or her master or was not accompanied by same.

The first of the reactions commonly referred to as the "nine Bahian revolts" was to occur on May 28, 1807; the uprising had been elaborately planned, with each section of the city under the charge of an emissary, or agent, of the conspirators whose functions were to direct black slaves from the plantations into rebel quarters in the city of Salvador and to perform the diversionary tactic of harassing the whites. Correspondence between African conspirators in Bahia and Santa Amaro in the Recôncavo (a sugar area in the state of Bahia) was intercepted on May 27 and the governor of Bahia informed; the leaders were captured, tried, and later executed. At the same time two troublesome *quilombos* on the outskirts of Salvador city, Cabula and Nossa Senhora dos Mares, that the Governor had, in March, ordered destroyed, were finally eliminated. The confiscated evidence, as well as the betrayal of blacks by blacks, indicated a polarization of the racial groups in the conspiracy that does much to negate the theory that the blacks' singular avowed purpose was to destroy all in their path for the sake of Allah.

On September 26, 1808 in the town of Jaguaripe, and again on January 4, 1809, groups of Hausas and members of Yoruban and Dahomean slave groups from the plantations and the cities revolted. In the latter movement they wreaked destruction in Salvador, especially within a twelve-mile distance from the city, until they were forced into retreat in the countryside and were finally defeated by government troops. Nonetheless, plots for other revolts were planned and organizational tasks performed by such secret Hausa, Yoruban, and Dahomean societies as the Ogboni, powerful associations utilized as defense groups by the migrant Africans in America. Their activities and the preceding uprisings were preludes to the "large-scale" revolt that occurred on February 26, 1814, when Hausas moved on the city of Salvador, burned homes, and killed every white who resisted; while in the suburb of Itapoan, plantation slaves burned the houses and *senzalas* of their masters. In 1816 (February 12) a relatively widespread revolt occurred in the areas of Crauassu, Guaiba, Itatinga, and Legoa that was ended through betrayals by Africans and military expeditions sent by the then governor, Conde dos Arcos.

No other major reactions followed until 1826 when a cluster of uprisings occurred. A group of Yorubas fled Salvador and established a *quilombo* in Urubú, not too far interior from the city. The leader of this movement was a black woman named Zeferina, who directed the Yoruba in numerous assaults on plantations and towns in that area of Bahia. The confessions of captured Yorubas indicated that these Afro-Brazilians had planned numerous insurrections against the government and their slave masters for the purpose of emancipation and eventual abolition of the institution of slavery. Elsewhere, the Yoruba and other groups attempted to carry out those plans in various sections of the Recôncavo, including Cachoeira, where Zeferina had been chosen as queen of the Africans, replete with monarchical paraphernalia. In areas closer to Salvador City, such as Pirajá, a *quilombo* of fugitive slaves successfully resisted the attacks of small government military forces.

The Yorubas continued in opposition to the Brazilian regime's slavocracy, raising the standard of insurrection in 1827, 1828, and 1830. In 1827 a group of Yoruba slaves fled their plantations, sacked and burned houses in the suburbs of Salvador, and fled into the bush country outside of the limits of the city. The resistance lasted only a few days but was a prelude to three separate "revolts" in the Recôncavo the following year . . . that continued into 1829. So easily did they seem to occur that slaveholders finally appealed to the Bahian governor for more substantial and effective police protection. On April 1, 1830, in Salvador, a small band of Yorubas armed themselves and one hundred other blacks, attacked the police station at Soledad in a Salvador suburb, and swept through the city before losing a significant percentage of their contingent.

But the final and most severe of the Bahian "revolts" occurred on January 24 and 25, 1835. Plans included the participation of slaves from the entire Recôncavo area, many of whom had in the nights before the uprising fled the plantations for Salvador. . . . During the revolt of 1835 in Bahia, it was revealed that plans called for the rising of the Africans under Chief Arrumá (or Alumá), the taking over of the lands, and the massacring of whites, Creole Negroes, and African blacks who refused to join the jihad [holy war]. Mulattoes were to be spared but forced into servitude. Precisely because Islam had *not* been successful with the generations of mulattoes and Creole blacks the Hausa Muslims moved against them, planning conspiracies in Moslem temples and establishing their movements under *alufás* or *marabús*, who exercised absolute authority over the blacks.

The 1835 revolt was quickly countered due to warnings by two free Africans to the authorities; police squads and military units, alerted in city and countryside, encountered numerous rebellious groups, and forced the insurrectionists into retreat and then surrender. Thereafter, intensive searches were conducted throughout the city with the certainty that the "religious rebels" would reopen the fighting. It has been suggested that many of the leaders were Muslim blacks who wore *patuás* (charms) to protect them from death, that Bahia was the seat of the Imam in Brazil, and that a banner and the robes worn at Muslim ceremonies were designated as war costumes. But it has also been suggested that the plan was instigated solely against whites and for the purpose of eliminating slavery, that the conspirators planned to establish a queen after exterminating all of the Europeans, and, further, that they enlisted the support of all blacks and mulattoes without concern for their religious affiliations.

In all of these reactions it has been difficult to determine whether they were merely a series of separate uprisings, a core of related urban revolts, or . . . part of the broader historical cycle; whether, in either case, they were concerned with achieving emancipation for their own groups or abolition of slavery for all Afro-Brazilians; whether they were religious or secular in nature.

VI

Pathways to Freedom: Manumission, Emancipation, and Abolition

If thousands of black and mulatto slaves rebelled or ran away, thousands of others obtained freedom legally. Manumission—the voluntary freeing of a slave by his or her master—and *coartación*—the purchase by a slave of his or her own freedom—were the two acceptable avenues to freedom. Evidence indicates that manumission occurred frequently and was encouraged by Church and government. The ways in which it was accomplished and how it affected society are examined in the following selections on Mexico and Cuba.

Manumission and *coartación* notwithstanding, the ultimate end of slavery could only come when the slave trade was eliminated and all the slaves were freed. One of the European nations that supported the abolition of slavery was Great Britain, which pushed doggedly for the development of free trade, free labor, and expanded markets. However, this should not be construed as altruism. The primary reasons behind British pressures for abolition were economic; her increasingly industrialized economy called for additional markets in which to sell her products. These markets were, in turn, predicated upon the growth of a paid labor force with wages to purchase goods. In addition, such economic developments could not be realized without free trade, in general understood in terms of laissez-faire commerce.

Thus Great Britain embarked on a course of preventive diplomacy with the newly independent Spanish American republics, binding her commercial treaties to agreements for abolition. By 1851 she had achieved her end almost everywhere in the Americas. The last two countries to capitulate were Cuba and Brazil. Economic pressures and the force of world opinion finally forced Cuba to abolish slavery in 1886. Two years later Brazil followed suit, thereby ending a system of oppression and exploitation that had plagued Latin America since the first colonies were established in the New World.

20

EMANCIPATION DEED FOR AN AFRO-MEXICAN SLAVE WOMAN, 1585

*The following document is one of the earliest rec-
ords we have concerning manumission. It represents part of the proceedings in a suit instituted by
the Marqués del Valle[1] against Doña Inéz de Léon,
for the recovery of the slave Juana and her two
children. The marqués claimed that Juana had been
born of slave parents on his sugar plantation in
Cuernavaca and that Doña Inéz's husband, Diego
Pérez, who had been factor and major-domo on the
marqués's estate, had simply taken Juana and kept
her in his service. Doña Inéz claimed, however, that
Juana was part of her husband's estate, insisting that
he had purchased Juana from the marqués's brother,
Martín Cortés, and that Juana's children had been
born while she belonged to Pérez.*

*The case was in litigation for nine months, the
provincial judge (or oidor of the audiencia) finally
ruling in the marqués's favor. When the case was
appealed to the audiencia of Mexico, Juana appeared in court with her emancipation decree.*

From a sixteenth-century collection of Mexican manuscripts, in the
Harkness collection, the Library of Congress, Washington, D.C.
Translated by Ann M. Pescatello. Reprinted by permission of the
Library of Congress.

[1] See Ward Barrett (Selection 5).

Papers indicating the outcome of the trial are miss-
ing, but it is likely that the case was again decided in
the favor of the marqués, since the Cortés family
was one of the most powerful in Mexico.

Know all men who see this letter that I, Doña Inéz de
Léon, former wife of Diego Pérez de Algaba, deceased,
and a resident of this great city of Mexico in New Spain,
so far as what concerns me and, as the person in possession of the negro woman, my slave Juana, so far as what
concerns my dowry and *arras*; declare that inasmuch as I
have held and hold as my slave, obtained by fair and lawful means, the said my slave Juana, a negro woman born in
this country; who to the end that I liberate her, has given
and paid me [the sum of] two hundred pesos *de oro de*
minas in *reales* in the following way: two hundred and
thirty pesos *de oro común* in silver *reales*, and to complete
the aforementioned sum a box of gold alloy with a slender
chain of seven strands, another box of gold alloy, and two
gold medals weighing eight ounces, these articles being
valued at a hundred pesos [*do oro común*] and seven
tomines over; all which was given and paid me by the
said negro woman Juana and Andrés Moreno, her husband, in presence of the notary of this present instrument,
whom I ask to bear witness thereof: Wherefore in consideration of the payment which she has made me and
for the further consideration of the good service which the
negro woman, my slave Juana, has rendered me and the
good will that I bear her and the said her husband; in
the best legal manner and form, and of my own free and
gracious will, without constraint or compulsion, I do
declare and acknowledge by this present letter that I
emancipate, set free, and release from all captivity, subjection, and servitude the said my slave Juana, creole
negro woman. And it is my will that she shall be free
now and for all time, and not subject to servitude. And as
such person she may and shall go in whatever parts and

places she desires; and may appear in judgment and collect and receive her property and manage and administer her estate; and may make wills and codicils and name heirs and executors; and may act and dispose of her person in whatsoever a free person born of free parents may and must do. And I bind myself to regard this instrument as valid, and that it shall be kept and fulfilled, and this freedom held and considered inviolate; and that neither I, nor any other in my behalf, shall speak against her; and that her going and coming shall be a matter of indifference to me. And more, if I fail in this and it be proved and confirmed, I will give and pay and return to her the two hundred *pesos de oro* that she has herewith given and paid me for her liberty. For the aforesaid, I pledge my person and the property which I now possess or shall possess. And I give full authority to his majesty's justices and judges in any place whatsoever within the jurisdiction of any and all of them and especially to the justices of this city of Mexico and to the royal *audiencia* and the court justices who reside therein, wherein I submit myself, renouncing my own [jurisdiction] and the law . . . to the end that these judges may constrain me to what is herein contained, as if decreed by them in court. And I renounce the laws in my favor, and my right, and the general right, and as a woman I renounce the laws of the emperors Justinian and Valerian, and the new constitution and the laws of Toro and Partidas, and any others in my favor. Dated in Mexico, the fourteenth day of the month of September, fifteen hundred and eighty-five.

21

HUBERT H. S. AIMES

COARTADOS:

THE HALF-LIFE OF HALF-SLAVES

*Slaves could obtain money to purchase their free-
dom in various ways: they could work as* negros
de aluguel *or* negros de ganho *in urban areas or
labor overtime in the mines; they could cultivate
tree and garden crops; or they might receive dona-
tions from brotherhoods or loans from relatives or
benefactors. Marriage to a free citizen was another
alternative. Partners of free citizens could sometimes acquire freedom by making a nominal contribution to officials.*

*Coartación[1] achieved its most refined state in
Cuba. By the seventeenth century it was a well-
established custom, and by the eighteenth century it
had been codified by royal decrees. Essentially,
Cuban* coartación *gave slaves the right to demand
that their price be publicly announced in a law
court, and that they be entitled to pay the price in
installments.*

[C]oartación consisted in fixing the value, by agreement
between master and slave, of a slave definitely, so that at

From Hubert H. S. Aimes, "Coartación: A Spanish Institution for
the Advancement of Slaves into Freedmen," *Yale Review,* 17 (Old
Series, 1909), 412–431 *passim.*

[1] The process of *coartación* has its basis in the peculium, or
private fund, of Roman law. The peculium gave slaves absolute
rights to property of their own—including themselves. This became
part of Iberian tradition and was passed on in Latin America.

no time thereafter could a larger sum be exacted for his or her liberty. The essential point was the definite limitation of value. The practice grew up in Cuba previous to the middle of the eighteenth century; for we find it in full operation in the year 1766, . . .

. . . [E]*nteros*, or slaves in entirety, . . . could not change masters without the consent of their owners except in the cases established by law, to wit: when he is ill-treated. . . . [A] slave *coartado* was different from a slave *entero*.

By equity and immemorial custom the slaves of Cuba were allowed to acquire a *peculium*, or private fund, through their own labor and industry, after they had satisfied the claims of their owners upon their services and wages, and to use it for the purchase of their freedom, which was accomplished by paying installments upon their value in sums of one hundred dollars, more or less. When such a sum had been paid, the slave *entero* became a slave *coartado* (limited) in the remainder existing between the sum, or sums, paid and his value. For example, if the price, or value, of a slave be three hundred dollars and the slave pay his master one hunderd dollars toward his freedom, his price remains limited to two hundred dollars. Thereafter he could not be sold or otherwise alienated for a higher price than that fixed at the time of the transaction; and, moreover, they then had the "free and uncontrolled privilege of changing masters whenever they can do so, with or without a cause,"—a thing prohibited to the *enteros*, except in the three cases of inhumanity, false spiritual teaching, or insufficient food. . . .

Coartación, as a bargain concerning the master and the slave, involved the disposal of the slave's services. Technically, the usufruct alone was affected; not the proprietory title. That is to say, there was no transfer of property. Hence, no tax was collected.

In Venezuela there was in use a fixed tariff of prices at which sales for freedom should take place. This was to oppose the interests of the master and slave, unconditionally, which could only result to the prejudice of the slave, either keeping him always at field and rough labor, or causing a resort to fraud and force to prevent the slaves from availing themselves of a situation so obviously to their advantage. Imperial orders affected the Cuban *régime* very slightly and the Venezuelan practice appears not to have prevailed at the Habana. . . .

There were several methods by which the slave could become *coartado*: by purchase out by his own *peculium*; by stipulating for it at the time of his sale by his master to a second person and paying a part of the purchase price himself; by legacy; at the volition of his master; by the act of a third party; and by stipulation at the time of transfer for ill-treatment, a rather hazardous matter.

When the value of the slave had been agreed upon, or fixed by the court, or umpires, the master gave a certificate (*escritura de coartación*) expressing that he was *coartado* in the difference between the appraised value and the sum paid on it, binding himself never to demand more than that amount for him. The appraised value had no relation to the price originally paid for him; thereafter the slave could pay installments, by custom not less than fifty dollars, and force his master to admit the fact.

The *coartado* could increase his earning capacity to his utmost without at the same time making it harder to gain his freedom. Skillful slaves worked out at a daily hire, and it was customary for the slave to pay his master one *real* per day for each hundred dollars remaining unpaid on his valuation; . . . Sundays and holidays belonged to the slave by law. If a master wished to use the *coartado* for a short time, it was customary to allow him the difference between his daily hire and the quota due to his master. Masters did indeed pay their slaves for extra work on the plantation on Sundays and holidays, but that was on a different principle. The practice of hiring slaves was very old, being mentioned in the ordinances of Alonso de Cáceres, 1574.

It sometimes happened that slaves redeemed themselves

by means of these partial payments until the remainder reached the small sum of fifty or one hundred dollars, and declined to pay any more, preferring to remain a technical slave and continue to pay a few cents daily to the master; . . .

The master was as fully bound to maintain his *coartado* negro in sickness, to feed and shelter him, as his slave *entero*. When once he had become *coartado* he could in no way be reduced to his former status; . . .

There was plenty of opportunity for slaves to earn and save money. Day labor was so dear early in the century that a *bocal* negro could gain from fifty to sixty-two and a half cents per day . . . and a negro with a handicraft from sixty-two and one-half to seventy-five cents. . . . In the last days of slavery, the tendency was to find in the *coartado* a readier means of revenue than in the slave *entero*. . . .

The tendency to interpret *coartación* more and more liberally became more pronounced as the end of slavery drew nearer. . . .

. . . In 1880 there were 3,526 *coartados*, 196,359 slaves and 269,547 free colored, and more slaves were gaining freedom directly by means of *coartación*.

The *coartado*, like the freedmen and the *emancipado* (slave captured during illegal importation), passed into the condition of *liberto*, where he remained under the supervision of the State during a period of probation. This, however, was only during the period of rapid emancipation brought on by the abolition laws, 1880–87. . . . [T]he principles of *coartación* and of the patronage system were identical . . . to allow a slave to become free as soon as he had given evidence of his fitness to be free.

ROBERT CONRAD

THE DESTRUCTION OF BRAZILIAN SLAVERY

Brazil clung to her slave system as tenaciously as she adhered to other outmoded economic and political institutions. In the following selection Robert Conrad, Associate Professor of History at the University of Illinois, Chicago Circle, refutes recent interpretations of abolition and offers, instead, a revisionist theory of slavery in Brazil, based on the nature of her economy and the force of traditionalism in the country.[1]

From its beginnings in the sixteenth century until its final decades, slavery was an extraordinarily vital and deeply rooted institution in most of the settled parts of Brazil. As a result of its great importance, during the first sixty-five years of the nineteenth century Brazil, in contrast to the United States, failed to develop a vigorous anti-

From Robert Conrad, *The Destruction of Brazilian Slavery, 1850–1888* (Berkeley and Los Angeles, 1972), pp. xiii–xvi, 277. Originally published by the University of California Press; reprinted by permission of The Regents of the University of California.

[1] For opposing interpretations, see Graham and Toplin, as cited in the Bibliographic Essay.

slavery movement. Even during the 1860's and the following decade, opposition to the institution was weak, sporadic, emancipationist (as opposed to abolitionist), and generally inspired from abroad. Why, then, did a true abolitionist movement finally appear in 1880 to emerge triumphantly from the struggle against slavery only eight years later?

. . . [A]lthough the work of the abolitionists was important in the destruction of slavery, economic and demographic developments in various regions of the country also worked strongly against the survival of the institution.

Without powerful opposition from abroad and the moral example of other countries, felt in the highest circles of Brazilian government, Brazil would hardly have acted to deprive herself of her two sources of slaves. The suppression of the African slave trade in the early 1850's and the freeing of the newborn children of slave women in 1871 were decisions which effectively condemned the slave system to extinction, despite its enormous importance to the Brazilian economy and society. The abolition of the slave trade, accomplished after more than forty years of titanic British pressure, by itself condemned Brazilian slavery to eventual extinction. Slaves in Brazil were not capable of maintaining their numbers through natural reproduction; the system was dependent for its replenishment upon a permanent source of new African workers. The decision of 1871 to free the newborn (made palatable by then by the decline of slavery in much of the country) hastened the conversion to a free-labor system. Yet it was not until the beginning of the 1880's that this conversion had proceeded to the point that a powerful, popular, and widespread abolitionist movement could at last appear.

The reasons for this lack of opposition to slavery are not difficult to find. They are related to the survival long after independence of an essentially colonial society. In Brazil slavery was still regarded as necessary to the functioning of the most respected and profitable segment of the economy, even when this was no longer true. A planter class dominated the land and the very lives of a large part of the active population, both slave and free. That same class controlled political institutions and most economic opportunities, including those of merchants, magistrates, bureaucrats, and a small and dependent intelligentsia, the very groups who might have been expected to oppose slavery most strongly.

A comparison of the situation in the United States with that of Brazil reveals the Brazilian situation in bold relief. Unlike the United States, Brazil lacked a large and politicized middle class. Effective popular education was never instituted in Brazil during the period of the Empire (1822–1889), and as late as the 1870's more than eighty-six percent of the population, including slaves, were classified as illiterate. Most of these unschooled people were undoubtedly without any political voice or influence, and therefore made poor candidates for the ranks of an effective protest movement. Protest, when it came, was almost always the individual act of the slave, which took the form of flight, rebellion, or personal assault upon the visible representatives of the system, the overseer or the master.

Until slavery was almost defeated, Brazil, unlike the United States, provided no havens where slaves could find refuge on free soil or where abolitionism could flourish unhampered by local economic interests. Until the appearance of Castro Alves, the poet of the slaves, in the mid-1860's, there was no developed Brazilian school of abolitionist writers, only individual voices expressing personal sentiments. Before 1880 even the press seldom took advantage of its unfettered state under the benign rule of Emperor Pedro II to attack the nation's dominant economic institution, except for brief periods when the issues of the slave trade and free birth were under debate. In the United States Protestant clergymen were among the most fearless and persistent leaders of abolitionism, but in Brazil, where the Catholic Church was the supreme moral and spiritual force, organized religion never developed an anti-slavery mission, and individual clergymen who opposed the institution were exceptional.

In the United States a literate and independent public reacted strongly against slavery a hundred years before this occurred in Brazil, and opponents of slavery in the United States continued to harass the system until they helped to bring on a major war. Again, by contrast, widespread and prolonged violence were avoided in Brazil during the final conversion to a free-labor system. In the United States slavery was struck down in its prime by that section of the country which had given it up, while in Brazil the institution collapsed in a late stage of disintegration. When slavery at last came under attack during the 1880's most of Brazil had advanced far toward a free-labor system. Nevertheless, a small but powerful group of planters and their representatives defended their "legal" rights until the end, fully aware that slavery could no longer be sustained for a long period of time but determined to derive profit from their remaining workers until the processes of aging and death reduced their economic importance to insignificance.

Sectional differences on the slavery issue were not as clear-cut in Brazil as in the United States, but they were important. As stressed throughout this study, a significant factor in the abolitionist process was the differing degree of commitment to slavery in the various regions of the country. Though Brazilian slavery was subjected to little organized opposition until its last years, regional cracks in the façade of the national pro-slavery consensus were apparent in the 1860's and 1870's, and they rapidly widened during the 1880's to threaten the stability of the entire structure. The most avid supporters of the institution, certainly during the last thirty years of its existence, were concentrated in the coffee-producing provinces—Rio de Janeiro, Minas Gerais, and São Paulo—while in the northeastern sugar and cotton regions and in other less prosperous sections, the interest in slavery was rapidly dissipated during the same period as a result of relative poverty and the consequential shift of tens of thousands of slaves into the coffee zones.

A large body of evidence derived from a study of Brazil as a whole and not merely the coffee provinces, where slavery was strongest and its collapse most dramatic, negates the theory that, as a group, the coffee planters of western and northern São Paulo were in the vanguard of opposition to slavery. Although the planters of that part of Brazil showed signs of a greater willingness than planters elsewhere to adopt modern solutions to their economic problems, in part as a result of their greater affluence, few of them displayed much of a tendency to adopt a free-labor system until only months before the abolition of slavery. The coffee planters of São Paulo, in fact, were one of the most powerful and adamant pro-slavery groups in Brazil until the second half of 1887, when a rapidly changing local and national situation forced them to accomplish at once that conversion to a free-labor system which had been under way for decades in other parts of the country. The elucidation of the role of São Paulo in the process of abolition is a major aim of this work, for it was indeed an important one. As the leading abolitionist, Joaquim Nabuco, put it years after the slaves had been freed, "the last of the apostles can become the first, like St. Paul (São Paulo), in services and proselytism." . . .

The aims of the abolitionists . . . varied greatly, from ardent and consistent commitment to justice and social change to late and reluctant surrender to the unavoidable. As the struggle neared its culmination in 1887 and 1888, most informed Brazilians probably felt a strong desire to rid their country of an unjust and humiliating institution, but far fewer persons were conscious of a need for collateral reforms, which the leaders of the movement had been urging for years: the establishment of a system of popular education, broader political representation, and alterations in the landholding system. Abolitionism, however, meant more than liberation, as Joaquim Nabuco and other prominent leaders claimed. Abolition, they hoped, was to be the first of a series of national reforms intended to end the domination of the traditional slaveholding class over the nation's institutions. . . . [T]he reformers of the era envisioned not only freedom for the slaves but the transformation of Brazil into a social and political democracy in which ex-slaves and the impoverished rural population would be prepared to participate more fully in national life. . . .

. . . Freeing the slaves, however, had been the easiest of the goals that the reformers had set for themselves, for slavery was destroyed in fact by forces that had undermined it during most of the nineteenth century. The abolitionists had hastened the collapse of slavery, but were stopped short in their pursuit of further reforms. The traditional elite maintained their power and authority and swept the democratic movement aside in the military coup d'état that overthrew the Empire of Pedro II in 1889 and established a conservative republic.

In the last years of the nineteenth century, after chaos, dictatorship, and even a senseless civil war, Brazilian society reverted to the norms that had been threatened by the brief abolitionist experience, and millions of Brazilians, particularly those whose dark skins marked them as descendants of slaves, remained much as they had been under slavery—legally free now, but unable to compete in freedom because of their class and color, with few alternatives beyond working another man's land in poverty and servility or migrating to a precarious urban environment, where opportunities were normally limited to the humblest and hardest of work. Although it was a great victory for Brazilians, though it gave them a measure of pride and a brief sense of greatness, the abolition of slavery did not create an environment in which former slaves could expect to rise up to the level of prosperous participants in national life. Nearly a century later—a hundred years in fact since the liberation of the newborn—millions of their descendants are still denied the equality of opportunity envisioned for them by anti-slavery leaders.

EPILOGUE: THE AFRICAN HERITAGE AND THE AFRICAN EXPERIENCE IN RETROSPECT

In a sense this epilogue could serve as a prologue to another book—on the present and future of Afro-Latin Americans. In anticipation of that possibility, I offer some final reflections on our rich African heritage and a sober indictment of those "born free."

One of the dimensions of the African experience that should be mentioned is an earlier prototype of the "back to Africa" movement, which occurred before abolition of the Atlantic slave trade and of the American slave system in general. Some freedmen returned to Africa and themselves became slave merchants.[1] Other freedmen, such as Olaudah (Selection 4), became involved with abolition movements or Sierra Leone recaptive programs.[2]

---

[1] See David Ross, "The Career of Domingo Martinez in the Bight of Benin, 1833–1864," *Journal of African History*, 6 (1965), 79–90, in which is discussed the career of a Brazilian mulatto, who attained great wealth and influence as a slave dealer in Africa; and Pierre Verger, *Flux et Reflux de la Traite des Nègres Entre le Golfe de Bénin et Bahia de Todos os Santos* (Paris: Mouton and Co., 1968).

[2] After the British had abolished their own slave trade in 1807, they made it a practice to capture slave ships at sea and then to land the slaves at England's only territorial holding on the western coast of Africa, Sierra Leone. These liberated slaves were called recaptives.

Some individuals even decided to return to slavery:

> . . . [H]e had left secretly for Le Havre in order to
> return to his chains in Rio de Janeiro, having given
> way to his affection for his old master, promises of
> good treatment, and above all to the memory of the
> smiling climate of Brazil and a son he had left there.
>
> He was old enough to have gained an accurate
> and thoughtful knowledge of his environment, and
> in the slave country where he had already spent
> seventeen years of his life, he had found enough of
> his fellow countrymen to make it possible for them
> to recall their homeland, which they often talked of
> together, in all its force and clarity—though no
> doubt it was already deeply engraved on his
> memory.[3]

In the twentieth century new generations of blacks and
mulattoes have also returned to the land of their ancestors.
So many have settled on the western coast of Africa that
there is, in fact, an identifiable community of Latin American blacks, especially Brazilians, that flourishes in parts
of Nigeria and Dahomey.[4]

In cultural terms the plastic arts, sculpture, architec-
ture, and literature all bear the imprint of black skill and
imagination. One of Brazil's greatest artists and architects,
Alejadinho, was of African ancestry, as was her great
writer Machado de Assis. Music, too, has been strongly
influenced by African styles and instruments. This is particularly evident in the music of coastal Ecuador, Vene-

---

[3] From a slave narrative in Philip D. Curtin, ed., *Africa Remembered: Narratives by West Africans from the Era of the Slave
Trade* (Madison: University of Wisconsin Press, 1968), pp. 217–
288.

[4] Verger, *Flux et Reflux de la Traite,* discusses Brazilian communities in Lagos and Dahomey and includes an excellent selection
of photographs demonstrating the similarities between Brazilian and
African cultures.

zuela, Cuba, and Brazil.[5] Cultural enthusiasts have a rather romantic—though perhaps not unjustified—view of the Afro-American influence in Latin America. One writer noted that black contributions to Brazilian society "run from the culinary art to the manner of making love and suffering. We owe more to the Negro than to the Portuguese."[6]

Catholicism in Latin America has been modified by African religions. In addition, there have developed several Afro-Catholic syncretic cults, which many Latin Americans patronize while still adhering to the more traditional forms of Christianity. Most familiar to non-Latins is the Afro-Catholic spirit cult of *vodû* (voodoo) that flourishes in Haiti Cuba, and the Caribbean. No less important, however, .re the *Santería* of Cuba and the Central American–Caribbean region; the *Candombé* in continental Spanish America; and the *Candomblé*, the *Macumba*, and the *Umbanda* in Brazil. All have large followings, black and white, and all reflect the blending of African religious forms with Catholicism.[7]

[5] See Richard A. Waterman, "African Influence on the Music of the Americas," in *Acculturation in the Americas*, ed. Sol Tax (Chicago: University of Chicago Press, 1952); and Richard A. Waterman, "Music de Culto Afrobahiana," *Revista de Estudios Musicales*, 1 (December 1949), 65–127. Numerous useful ᵔrks on Afro-Latin American art forms, particularly musiᵣ ᵤᵣᵤ listed in the bibliography in Norman Whitten and John Szwed, eds., *Afro-American Anthropology: Contemporary Perspectives* (New York: Free Press, 1970).

[6] João Dornas Filho, *A Escravidão no Brasil* (Rio de Janeiro: n.p., 1939), p. 211.

[7] See Russell G. Hamilton, "The Present State of African Cults in Bahia," *Journal of Social History*, 3 (Summer 1970), 357–373; Pierre Verger, *Notes sur les Cultes des Orisa et Vodun à Bahia, la Baie de Tous les Saints au Brésil et à l'Ancienne Côte des Esclaves en Afrique* (Dakar: IFAN, 1957); Roger Bastide, *Le Candomblé de Bahia, Rite Nagô* (The Hague: Mouton, 1958), *The African Religions in Brazil During the Industrial Era* (Paris: Flammarion, 1974), and *Religions Africaines au Brésil* (Paris: Presses Universitaires de France, 1960); and Seth Leacock and Ruth Leacock, *Spirits of the Deep* (New York: American Museum of Natural History, 1971).

Peoples of African ancestry have contributed substantially to South American cuisine, dress, folklore, language, economic development, and social organization.[8] Ironically, while so much of what the black has given is positive, much that he has received is negative, the agonizing result of racial conflict, prejudice, and discrimination.

The readings in this book have been chosen especially for the light they might shed on contemporary racial problems. The experiences of freedmen and women during slavery are particularly revealing in this context. In the case of manumission, differences in the age and sex of the slave and the time, place, and manner of his manumitting seem to have influenced emerging patterns of racial and sexual relations. Changes in attitudes toward manumission are also important. Prior to the eighteenth century manumission was commonplace, and freedmen enjoyed reasonable economic and social mobility. However, during the eighteenth century campaigns to curb manumission and a steady decline in economic opportunities through which slaves might purchase their freedom limited the free-colored community's growth and consequently its influence. Increasingly strident and often brutally enforced antimanumission laws created a gulf between free and enslaved coloreds, for it behooved those already free to cooperate with whites. It appears that by the time of abolition little cooperation existed anywhere between free and enslaved Afro-Latin Americans. This lack of alliance between men of color, between already free and newly freed, suggests why freedmen in South America were forced into self-centered concerns. Free coloreds solidified their status as a group with certain special privileges, inter-

[8] Contributions are referred to in anthropological terms as retentions, reinterpretations, and/or syncretisms. See Whitten and Szwed, *Afro-American Anthropology;* Renato Mendoza, *A Influencia Africana Portuguesa do Brasil* (Rio de Janeiro: n.p., 1934); Fernando Ortíz, *Hampa Afrocubana: Los Negros Brujos* (Madrid: Editorial-America, 1906); and Roger Bastide, *Les Ameriques Noires* (Paris: Payot, 1967).

mediary between free white and slave. After abolition such distinctions helped perpetuate racial cleavages in Latin American societies.[9]

Another factor that contributed to the uncomfortable relationship between different groups of Afro-Americans was the dependency structure of the Latin American colonies. In Spanish America the colonial system had been able to gradually assimilate small numbers of freedmen into the limited work force. But when mass emancipation was decreed during the early nineteenth century, the socioeconomic infrastructures of the new nations proved inadequate to absorb large numbers of free blacks. Consequently, a sizable percentage of those newly freed could be integrated only at the lowest levels of society, thus further aggravating social tensions. In Brazil the marginal existence into which many newly freed men were forced definitely helped to aggravate prejudice.

As a result of these variations in living conditions among blacks and mulattoes, several patterns of race relations have evolved in contemporary Latin America. In Spanish American countries such as Argentina and Uruguay, where only a small percentage of the population is of African ancestry, race prejudice manifests itself in a somewhat less overt form than it does in areas with large populations of African descent. Northern Brazil, an area of early-capitalistic slave systems, is described by Donald Pierson as "a freely competitive order in which individuals compete for position largely on the basis of personal merit and favorable family circumstance. Individual competence tends to overbalance ethnic origin as a determinant of social status."[10] Herbert Klein finds in Cuba that an "open quality of color definition has led

[9] The preceding discussion owes much to Jack P. Greene and David W. Cohen, *Neither Slave Nor Free* (Baltimore: Johns Hopkins Press, 1972).

[10] Donald Pierson, *Negroes in Brazil* (Carbondale, Ill.: Southern Illinois University Press, 1967), p. 177.

to heavy miscegenation and to a massive movement between color categories."[11] Furthermore, he claims that since 1943 Cuba "has experienced a total social revolution that resulted in rapid upward mobility of the lowest classes and the deliberate breakdown of the last vestiges of color impediments."[12]

On the other hand, in the coastal areas of Ecuador, Peru, Colombia, and Venezuela, where there are heavy concentrations of blacks, limited economic opportunities and a fixed social structure relegate blacks to marginal positions in society. As a result racial conflicts are strong. This is also the case in southern Brazil, an area of capital-intensive slavery in the nineteenth century. In São Paulo, for example, a wave of immigrant labor prevented the freed Afro-Brazilian from participating in industrial production and thrust him or her into an antagonistic position in a white-dominated social structure. Only in this area of Brazil have there developed incipient black power movements and civil rights organizations—although, until now, these have not materialized into anything remotely resembling their relatively successful counterparts in the United States.[13]

It seems that wherever opportunities for social and economic mobility are few, competition heightens conflict, and the degree of racial anxiety is maximized. Since Latin America clearly does not display the simple, monolithic model of a phlegmatic Ibero-Catholic culture, it seems likely that it is not so much differences in religion or law that are responsible for variations in race relations as it is differences in socioeconomic systems.

The presence of the black man in Latin America is

[11] Herbert S. Klein, *Slavery in the Americas: A Comparative Study of Cuba and Virginia* (Chicago: University of Chicago Press, 1967), p. 259.
[12] *Ibid.*, p. 264.
[13] See Florestan Fernandes, *The Negro in Brazilian Society* (New York: Columbia University Press, 1969).

manifested in ways both beautiful and ugly. Despite their travails blacks in slavery contributed much that was good to Latin American civilization. For descendents of these slaves, however, the past is still painfully alive. And the question remains: Although they are now freeeborn, are they really free? Or is life for them expressed in these poignant words by a Brazilian black woman:

> I sent my thoughts toward the sky. . . . I wonder if the favela exists there? And if up there a favela does exist, can it be that when I die I'm going to live in a favela?[14]

[14] Carolina Maria de Jesus, *Child of the Dark* (New York: Dutton, 1962), p. 50. A *favela* is a slum or shantytown.

GLOSSARY*

alufás: name used by blacks in Brazil, who had come under Islamic influence, for socioreligious leaders who exercised considerable, in some cases absolute, authority over their followers.

amazia, amásia: concubinage; in Afro-Brazilian usage the term meant cohabitation without legal or religious sanction.

arboledillas: small groves of trees; stands of woods.

arras: at nuptials, the sum promised by the husband to the wife to pay for her dowry, virginity, or nobility; the sum could not exceed one-tenth the value of the husband's property.

asiento, assiento: a contract or license; used here to refer to a system of permissions for hauling slaves as cargo.

assientista: the recipient of an *assiento*.

audiencia: the Spanish word for a high court and its jurisdiction.

bangüê: in Brazil, a stretcher-litter for dead slaves.

barracoon, barração: a warehouse or large shed; in Brazil, also a trading post.

Glossary sources: *Appleton's Revised Cuyas Spanish Dictionary* (New York: Appleton-Century-Crofts, 1956); Antonio Houaiss and Catherine Avery, eds., *The New Appleton Dictionary of the American and Portuguese Languages* (New York: Appleton-Century-Crofts, 1964).

* Where there are two words for an entry, for example, *blanco, branco,* the first is Spanish, the latter Portuguese.

blanco, branco: white; a white person.

bodega: a tavern; also a wine vault and cellar storeroom; in Cuba and Mexico, a retail grocery.

bozales, boçales: coarse, stupid; used to identify slaves recruited directly from Africa.

brasileiro (a): a Brazilian man (woman).

brazos, braços: laborers; literally "arms."

cabildo, câmara: a council or city hall; a chamber or house of a legislative body; also a town or municipal council.

cachaça: a potent cane alcohol; in Brazil, white rum or any drink made from rum or brandy.

Candombé, Candomblé: the name by which Afro-Brazilian or Afro-Hispanic cults (in Argentina and Uruguay) are known; the word also means place or form of worship.

capela: chapel or shrine.

capitão do mato: in Brazil, the term for a slave-catcher, a man whose official occupation was to capture runaway slaves.

cascalho: gravel or crushed rock; a dirt hump (in the road).

castas: from a medieval Iberian word that designated any kind of animal or human group; the Portuguese used the term to describe groups in India, but it has acquired a different usage in other parts of the Iberian world (see *Régimen de Castas*).

caxambú: in parts of Brazil, refers to an African slave festival incorporating verse, music, drumming, and dance.

cédula: an order, decree, bill, or permit; a *cédula real* was a royal letter of patent.

chácaras: a small agricultural holding.

cimarrones: fugitive blacks; runaway slaves; literally "wild" or "unruly."

coartación: the right of a slave to purchase his or her freedom at a set price; for a full definition, see the Aimes reading (Selection 21) in this book.

coartado: a slave who had entered into an agreement with his or her master enabling the slave to gain, through *coartación*, his or her freedom; the *coartado* was, therefore, no longer totally enslaved.

coffilas: slave coffles or chain gangs.

cofradía: a religious brotherhood.

criollo, crioulo: a word of varied meaning. In general usage, it has come to pertain to a white person of European descent born in the Americas; however, in Brazil it also refers to Brazilian-born blacks, mulattoes, or mestiços and is sometimes used to refer to blacks in general. In Spanish-American usage, it may also refer to blacks native to America and to Europeans naturalized in America; in addition, it is the name for the dialect spoken by white persons in the Americas.

caudrilla: a meeting of four or more persons; a gang, party, or herd; a band of armed men.

cumbé: a Negro dance.

de oro común: a sum of money in the latter part of the sixteenth century in New Spain, one *peso de oro común* equaled 300 *maravedis* (an old Spanish coin).

de oro de minas: a sum of money equaling 450 *maravedis*.

emancipado: used here to refer to groups of nineteenth century Africans, imported into Latin America, who were legally free but were held in de facto slavery.

engenho: a sugar plantation or mill.

entero: a slave in entirety, who belonged totally to his or her master and had none of the privileges of the slave *coartado*.

entrada: a type of expedition or exploration; an opening.

escritura de coartación: a certificate of *coartación*.

esquife: a litter; a casket or coffin.

estancia: a dwelling; in Spanish America, a type of ranch.

faiscador: a poor-white gold miner; in Brazil, a gold panner or gold gleaner.

favela: in Brazil, a slum, usually on a hill; a shantytown.

fazenda: a farm, plantation, ranch, homestead, or estate; a hacienda.

fazendeiro: a farmer, planter, rancher; in Spanish *hacendado.*

feticeiro: a witch doctor or medicine man; a black healer or diviner.

fugido: a fugitive.

groot(e): Dutch word for large; used in reference to *quilombos* in Brazil.

hacendado: landholder, farmer, rancher (see *fazendeiro*).

hacienda: property, plantation, ranch, estate (see *fazenda*).

haciendilla: little hacienda.

hermandad, irmandade: a brotherhood or fraternity.

horro: an enfranchised freedman; the term can be synonymous with servant.

jihad .nmonly used to refer to the proselytizing wars of Muslim religious fanatics. Jihads were actually a complex phenomenon, provoked by such diverse factors as political disputes, conflicts between sacred and secular spheres of influence, and controversies over the interpretation and authority of Islamic law; the term is also applied loosely to similar movements in nineteenth-century Brazil that superficially resembled African jihads.

justicia mayor: chief justice or judge.

klein(e): Dutch word for small or petty; used to describe *quilombos.*

ladeira: see *palenque, quilombo,* et cetera.

ladino: refers to people of African descent brought from the Iberian peninsula to America.

Las Siete Partidas: see *Siete Partidas.*

liberto(a): a freedman or freedwoman.

libre: a free black.

limpieza de sangre: literally "purity of blood"; the term has been used in an ethnic sense, although it originally defined a lineage of pure orthodoxy in religion.

major-domo: in Spanish America, a steward who acted as overseer of labor forces and collector of tribute.

mandingueiro: a sorcerer or witch.

manumismos: in Gran Colombia, slave children born after 1821.

marabús: Muslim hermits.

mayoral: a steward, overseer, or foreman.

mestizo, mestiço: a half-breed; usually refers to a person of mixed white and Indian ancestry.

milreis: Brazilian and Portuguese monetary unit.

Misericórdia: a charitable institution in Brazil and throughout the Portuguese Empire; similar to the *Obra Pia*, which was in Spanish America.

moça: a girl or young woman; in Brazil, a virgin or maiden.

mocambo: from the Umbunda word *mu-kambo*, meaning hideout; a term that preceded usage of *quilombo* to describe hideouts or hideaway huts for runaway slaves in Brazil.

molecas, moleques: boys and girls up to ten or twelve years of age; also means small black boys or street urchins; pickaninnies; literally "scampish."

morador: a resident or inhabitant.

moreno: a light mulatto; in Cuba, a darky or a black; literally "tawny" or "swarthy."

mucama: a Brazilian household slave or servant girl; a mammy.

mulato(a): dark-skinned; a person who is a mixture of black and white.

muleque: in Cuba, a newly arrived black boy.

município: a municipality or city; city council.

negro de aluguel, prêto de aluguel: a slave who was hired out by his or her owner for the latter's profit.

negro de ganho, prêto de ganho: a slave who was able to hire himself or herself out to earn money, giving a fixed amount to his or her owner.

Obra Pia: an institution in Spanish America dedicated to charitable works.

oidor: a provincial judge; member of an *audiencia*.

oitava: in eighteenth century Brazil, a unit of weight equivalent to 17½ carats.

palanqueros: occupiers of *palenques*.

palenques: palisade hideouts for runaway slaves.

Palmares: at the beginning of the seventeenth century, the name given to an area covered by palm trees; later it became the name of the most famous *quilombo* in the Alagoas-Pernambuco territory in Brazil.

pardo: brown, dark gray; in Cuba the term was used to refer to mulattoes, in Paraguay to blacks.

patuás: charms; amulets.

pieza (de India): used in the slave trade to mean a measure of potential labor. One full *pieza* meant a young adult male meeting certain specifications of size, physical condition, and health; all other slaves were measured in fractions relative to this ideal.

prêto: in Brazil, black or dark.

quilombo: from the Jaga (an African tribal group) word *ki-lombo*, meaning "war camp"; in Brazil, a hideout for runaway slaves.

quitandeira: a street vendor or greengrocer; Afro-Brazilian women, particularly in the Northeast, still perform these services. Also, slang for ill-bred woman, fishwife.

razzìa: Italian word meaning raid or foray; to comb out.

reales, reálaes: monetary units.

Régimen de Castas: a term applied to the overall society of colonial Spanish America to describe its class structure; it was a *sui generis* type of multiracial society, imbued with the notions of *limpieza de sangre* and reminiscent of the hierarchic, estate-based corporate structure of medieval Castile. (For a fuller description see Mörner, *Race Mixture*, pp. 53ff.)

repartimiento: distribution or allotment of labor or goods.

Labor *repartimiento* represented a type of corvée in which each laborer owed a certain amount of work time to a landowner; it was not a condition of formal servitude. The goods *repartimiento* resembled the company store system: laborers had no choice but to purchase goods at prices they could not afford, thereby putting themselves into debt.

senzalas: slave quarters.

Siete Partidas: laws of medieval Castile, codified under Alfonso the Wise, that summarized the Mediterranean legal mores of many centuries. The code maintained an inherent belief in the equality of man under natural law and, consequently, a belief that slavery was against both nature and reason. This legal system promoted the belief that slavery under the Iberians was less harsh than it was under the English or French.

tamberos: people in charge of roadside inns in Inca territory.

tambos: roadside inns of the Incas.

tronco: heavy iron stock.

tumba de arco: a covered funeral bier.

vegas: in Cuba, tobacco farms or plantations; in Chile, damp or swampy ground; otherwise, flat lowlands.

zafra, safra: a sugar harvest.

zambo, sambo: offspring of an Indian and African couple.

BIBLIOGRAPHIC ESSAY

Space dictates that bibliographic materials be limited, so in the following essay I have attempted to direct the reader to references that are themselves rich in sources. I have also included discography, films, and other special source materials.

For the purpose of comparison, one may consult three valuable bibliographic works detailing research that has been done on the Afro-American: Elizabeth W. Miller and Mary L. Fisher, comps., *The Negro in America: A Bibliography* (Cambridge, Mass.: Harvard University Press, 1970); Dwight L. Smith, ed., *Afro-American History: A Bibliography* (Santa Barbara: American Bibliographical Center, 1974); and Lambros Comitas, *Caribbeana, 1900–1965* (Seattle: University of Washington Press, 1968).

No comparable collections exist for Latin America. There are, however, several excellent historiographical essays on the Afro-Latin American, beginning with James Ferguson King, "The Negro in Continental Spanish America: A Select Bibliography," *Hispanic American Historical Review*, 24 (August 1944), 547–559. Eventually, this was supplemented by Miguel Acosta Saignes, "Introducción al Estudio de los Repositorios Documentales Sobre los Africanos y sus Descendientes en América," *América Indígena*, 29 (1969), 727–786; and Frederick P. Bowser, "The African in Colonial Spanish America: Reflections on Research Achievements and Priorities," *Latin American Research Review*, 7 (Spring 1972), 77–94.

Much more work has been done on the African in Brazil. Excellent bibliographies exist in the monographs and surveys included here. In addition, a valuable source essay is Richard Graham, "Brazilian Slavery Re-examined: A Review Article," *Journal of Social History*, 3 (Summer 1970), 431–453.

Excellent discussions of race relations in Latin America are available in Magnus Mörner, "The History of Race Relations in Latin America: Some Comments on the State of Research," *Latin American Research Review*, 1 (Summer 1966), 17–44; and Mörner, *Race Mixture in the History of Latin America* (Boston: Little, Brown, 1967). Other sources include the following periodicals: *Hispanic American Historical Review* (HAHR), *Latin American Research Review*, *Journal of Inter-American Studies and World Affairs*, *The Americas*, *Journal of Social History*, *Luso-Brazilian Review*, *Caribbean Studies*, *Social and Economic Studies*, and *The Journal of Negro History*. Important Latin American periodicals to be consulted are: *Revista do Instituto Historico e Geographico Brasileiro*, *Cuadernos Americanos*, *América Indigena*, *Etnología y Folklore*, *Boletin de la Academia Nacional de Quito*, *Annuario Colombiano de Historia Social y de la Cultura*, *Historia Mexicana*, and *Revista de Historia* (São Paulo). An all-encompassing annual guide is the *Handbook of Latin American Studies*.

One cannot really study Africans in Latin America without attempting to understand the milieus from which they came. African history has been the subject of many books and articles over the past two decades. Some of the best surveys available are Monica Wilson and Leonard Thompson, eds., *Oxford History of South Africa*, 2 vols. (New York and Oxford: Oxford University Press, 1969, 1971); Roland Oliver, et al., eds., *History of East Africa*, 3 vols. (Oxford: Clarendon Press, 1963, 1965, 1968); A. J. Wills, *An Introduction to the History of Central Africa* (London: Oxford University Press, 1973); J. D. Fage,

A History of West Africa, 4th ed. (New York: Cambridge University Press, 1969); Basil Davidson, *A History of West Africa* (New York: Anchor Books, 1966); A. G. Hopkins, *An Economic History of West Africa* (New York: Columbia University Press, 1973); T. A. Osae, S. N. Nwabara, and A. T. O. Odunsi, *A Short History of West Africa: A.D. 1000 to the Present* (New York: Hill and Wang, 1974); and Creighton Gabel and Norman R. Bennett, eds., *Reconstructing African Culture History* (Boston: Boston University Press, 1967). Other useful works are Robin Hallett, *Africa to 1875: A Modern History* (Ann Arbor: University of Michigan Press, 1970); Michael Crowder, *Short History of Nigeria* (New York: Praeger, 1966); Daniel McCall, *Africa in Time Perspective* (New York: Oxford University Press, 1970); Robert W. July, *A History of the African People* (New York: Scribners, 1974); Paul Bohannan and Philip Curtin, *Africa and Africans* (Garden City, N.Y.: Natural History Press, 1971); and the works of Roland Oliver and John Fage. Scholarly aids include the *Journal of African History, Race, Bulletin IFAN* (Institut Français d'Afrique Noire), *Journal of the Historical Society of Nigeria, The Journal of Modern African Studies,* and *Tarikh.*

More specialized, but uniformly excellent, studies on various periods and events in African history are listed here chronologically and roughly according to the areas from which Africans were taken. For the fifteenth century and earlier see: Maurice Delafosse, *Haut-Sénégal-Niger* (Paris: n.p., 1912); Raymond Mauny, *Tableau Geographique de l'Ouest Africain au Moyen Age* (Dakar: IFAN, 1961); Joseph Greenberg, "The Negro Kingdoms of the Sudan," *Transactions of the New York Academy of Sciences,* no. 11 (1949); Gomes Eanes de Zurara, *The Chronicle of the Discovery and Conquest of Guinea,* trans. Charles R. Beazley and Edgar Prestage (London: n.p., 1896); and John William Blake, *Europeans in West Africa, 1450–1560,* 2 vols. (London: Hakluyt Society,

1942). A more comprehensive study is Alan F. C. Ryder, *Benin and the Europeans, 1485–1897* (Cambridge: Cambridge University Press, 1967).

Material on the sixteenth century, especially Angola, and on areas further into Central Africa in the seventeenth century can be found in D. P. Gamble. *The Wolof of Senegambia* (London: International African Institute, 1957); Jan Vansina, *Kingdoms of the Savanna* (Madison: University of Wisconsin Press, 1968); and G. Balandier, *Daily Life in the Kingdom of the Kongo* (New York: Pantheon Books, 1968). Portuguese influence in the Congo, Angola, and Moçambique from 1500 to the present is thoroughly examined in James Duffy, *Portuguese Africa* (Cambridge, Mass.: Harvard University Press, 1961); and David Birmingham, *Trade and Conflict in Angola: The Mbundu and Their Neighbors Under the Influence of the Portuguese, 1483–1790* (Oxford: Oxford University Press, 1966).

Valuable studies on various African ethnic groups and their societies and polities in the eighteenth century include: Colin W. Newbury, *The Western Slave Coast and Its Rulers* (Oxford: Oxford University Press, 1961); I. A. Akinjogbin, "The Oyo Empire in the Eighteenth Century—A Reassessment," *Journal of the Historical Society of Nigeria*, 5 (1966), 449–460; Peter Morton-Williams, "The Oyo Yoruba and the Atlantic Trade, 1670–1830," *Journal of the Historical Society of Nigeria*, 3 (1964), 24–45; G. I. Jones, *The Trading States of the Oil Rivers* (London: Oxford University Press, 1963); D. Forde, ed., *Peoples of the Niger-Benue Confluence* (London: International African Institute, 1955); and D. Forde, ed., *Efik Traders of Old Calabar* (London: Oxford University Press, 1956). The Ashanti and, in general, the Akan-speaking areas are represented in extensive studies by R. S. Rattray, *Ashanti* (London: Oxford University Press, 1927); Ivor Wilks, *The Northern Factor in Ashanti His-*

tory (Accra: n.p., 1961); and Meyer Fortes, *The Ashanti Social Survey*, Human Problems in British Central Africa, no. 6 (London: n.p., 1948). See also Karl Polanyi, *Dahomey and the Slave Trade* (Seattle: University of Washington Press, 1966); I. A. Akinjogbin, *Dahomey and Its Neighbors, 1708–1818* (Cambridge: Cambridge University Press, 1967); Walter Rodney, *A History of the Upper Guinea Coast, 1534–1800* (Oxford: Oxford University Press, 1970); and E. J. Alagoa, *A History of the Niger Delta* (London: Holmes and Meier, 1972).

Significant works on nineteenth-century slaving and Afro-European contact include K. Onwuke Dike, *Trade and Politics in the Niger Delta, 1830–1885* (Oxford: Oxford University Press, 1956); Daryll Forde and P. M. Kaberry, eds., *West African Kingdoms in the Nineteenth Century* (London: Oxford University Press, 1969); Obaro Ikime, *Merchant Prince of the Niger Delta* (New York: Africana Publishing Corp., 1968); Robert Smith, *Kingdoms of the Yoruba* (London: Methuen, 1969); J. F. Ade Ajayi and Robert Smith, *Yoruba Warfare in the Nineteenth Century* (Cambridge: Cambridge University Press, 1964); E. J. Alagoa, *The Small Brave City-State—A History of Brass-Nembe in the Niger Delta* (Madison: University of Wisconsin Press, 1964); S. O. Biobaku, *The Egba and Their Neighbors, 1832–1872* (London: Oxford University Press, 1957); and Edward A. Alpers, "Trade, State and Society Among the Yao in the Nineteenth Century," *Journal of African History*, 10 (1969), 405–420.

Some of the latest research, combining historical and anthropological techniques, may be extremely valuable for the student of Afro-Latin America. Of particular interest is Alan Isaacman, *Moçambique: The Africanization of a European Institution: The Zambesi Prazos, 1750–1902* (Madison: University of Wisconsin Press, 1972).

For comprehensive discussions of Muslim influence on West African history, see the works of J. S. Trimingham, including his *A History of Islam in West Africa* (Oxford: Oxford University Press, 1970). For literature on eighteenth- and nineteenth-century jihads in West Africa, see Marilyn Robinson Waldman, "The Fulani Jihād: A Reassessment," *Journal of African History*, 6 (1965), 333–355.

Personal narratives are also of great value in understanding the African experience. Of particular excellence are Philip D. Curtin, ed., *Africa Remembered: Narratives by West Africans from the Era of the Slave Trade* (Madison: University of Wisconsin Press, 1968); and Margaret Priestley, *West African Trade and Coast Society: A Family Study* (London: Oxford University Press, 1969). Jan Vansina's *Oral Traditions: A Study in Historical Methodology* (Chicago: Aldine, 1965) is a classic manual on oral traditions in Africa.

Among the best materials on linguistics are Joseph Greenberg's *Studies in African Linguistic Classification* (New Haven: Yale Univeresity Press, 1955), *The Languages of Africa* (Bloomington, Ind.: Indiana University Research Center, 1966), and his numerous excellent articles. Philip Curtin's "The Archives of Tropical Africa: A Reconnaissance," *Journal of African History*, 1 (1960), 129–147 is immensely helpful to the researcher, as is his pamphlet, *Pre-Colonial African History* (n.p.: American Historical Association, 1974).

Increased contact between Spanish, Portuguese, and Africans produced a literature on Iberian attitudes toward their African cohorts in slaving. Thanks to Frank Tannenbaum and Lewis Hanke we have numerous bibliographies that apprise us of Iberian legal and social codes. In addition, sources in Ruth Pike, *Enterprise and Adventure: The Genoese in Seville and the Opening of the New World* (Ithaca: Cornell University Press, 1966) are of substantial help in providing a backdrop for understanding European attitudes regarding slavery. Toward this end, see also Frédéric Mauro, *L'Expansion Européene*

(1600–1870) (Paris: Presses Universitaires de France, 1964), his *Le Portugal et l'Atlantique au XVIIᵉ Siècle (1570–1670): Étude Economique* (Paris: S.E.V.P.E.N., 1960); and Anthony Luttrell, "Slavery and Slaving in the Portuguese Atlantic (to about 1500)," in *The Transatlantic Slave Trade from West Africa*, ed. C. Fyfe (Edinburgh: Centre of African Studies, University of Edinburgh, 1965). Mauro's works, as well as Huguette Chaunu and Pierre Chaunu's *Seville et l'Atlantique (1504–1650)*, 8 vols. (Paris: A. Colin, 1955–1960) and Charles Verlinden's *L'Esclavage dans l'Europe Médiévale*, vol. 1 (Brussels: Tempelhof, 1955) demonstrate the excellence of French scholarship on slavery.

On the Atlantic slave trade itself, all previous work—including much of excellent quality by such as Verger, Deere, Scheuss, Studer, Mellafe, and Scelle—is cited in and superseded by Philip Curtin's *The Atlantic Slave Trade*. In addition to the first-rate bibliography, Chapter 1, a historiographical review of the literature and numerical calculations on the trade, is especially useful. A study that addresses itself to a major problem raised by Curtin is Herbert S. Klein's "The Trade in African Slaves to Rio de Janeiro, 1795–1811: Estimates of Mortality and Patterns of Voyages," *Journal of African History*, 10 (1969), 533–549.

The multi-volume, thirteenth-century compilation of laws known as *Las Siete Partidas* has been important to scholars since Tannenbaum and has been utilized by them in their examinations of the juridical and the theological debates on slavery. The *Recopilación de Leyes* covers decrees through the year 1680, when the *Recopilación* was completed. Much of the Spanish imperial legislation dealing with her American slaves is contained in Richard Konetzke, ed., *Colección de Documentos para la Historia de la Formación Social de Hispanoamérica, (1493–1810)*, 5 vols. (Madrid: Consejo Superior de Investigaciones Científicas, 1953–1962). For the most part, however, laws, opinions, notarial records, parish registers, personal letters, and official and nonofficial correspondence repose untouched in archives and libraries. So, too, do plantation records, bills of sale, *cabildo* and *câmara* documents, and the like. These are the bases for as yet unwritten studies. Finding them will require enormous energy and painstaking research, but the documents are essential to an understanding of the experience of the Latin American black.

Documentary sources on Brazilian slavery abound in Charles R. Boxer, *The Portuguese Seaborne Empire* (New York: Knopf, 1970) and *Race Relations in the Portuguese Colonial Empire, 1415–1825* (Oxford: Oxford University Press, 1963); Edison Carneiro, *Antologias de Negro Brasileiro* (Rio de Janeiro: Editôra Globo, 1950); and Pedro Calmon, *Historia do Brasil, 1500–1800*, 3d ed., 3 vols. (São Paulo: n.p., 1939–1943). Other extensive materials on colonial Brazilian attitudes toward, and treatment of, the African are found in Jesuit works and travel accounts, as cited in Serafim Leite's comprehensively documented *Historia da Companhia de Jesus no Brasil*, 10 vols. (Rio de Janeiro: Civilizacão Brasileira, 1938–1950) and his *Artes e Ofícos dos Jesuitas no Brasil, 1549–1760* (Lisbon: n.p., 1953), the latter containing much material on the colored brotherhoods. An eighteenth-century treatise by a Lisbon-born parish priest, Manuel Ribeiro Rocha, *Ethiope Resgatado, Empenhado, Sustenado, Corregido, Instruido e Libertado* (Lisbon: n.p., 1758), includes a section on punishment and abuse of slaves, infringements of Portuguese law on the part of Brazilian slave owners, and calls for the substitution of African slavery by white indentured labor.

Among the best surveys of the Brazilian slave trade are Affonso de Escragnolle Taunay, *Subsidios para a Historia do Trafico Africano* (São Paulo: n.p., 1941); and José Antônio Gonçalves de Melho, *Tempo dos Flamengos: Influência da Occupação Holendesa na Vida e Cultura do Norte do Brasil* (São Paulo: n.p., 1951). Other valuable sources include Mauricio Goulart, *Escravidão Africana no Brail* (São Paulo: Livraria Martins, 1949); the compendium of Brazilian slave law in Agostino Marques Perdigão Malheiro, *A Escravidão no Brasil: Ensaio Historico-Juridico-Social*, 2 vols. (São Paulo: n.p., 1857, 1944); and Maurilio de Gouveia, *História da Escravidão* (Rio de Janeiro: Gráfica Tupy, 1955).

Students of Brazilian history also have at their disposal numerous travel accounts that discuss slavery. A listing of many of these accounts can be found in Manuel Cardozo, "Slavery in Brazil as Described by Americans," *The Americas*, 17 (1961), 241–260; and Charles G. Hamilton, "English-Speaking Travelers in Brazil, 1851–1887," *Hispanic American Historical Review*, 40 (November 1960), 533–547.

On ethnic origins of African slaves and how they preserved their ethnic identities, Bowser, "The African in Colonial Spanish America," cites several excellent sources for colonial Spanish America. See also his discussion (pp. 81–87) and notes 29 to 67 for listings of both recent and classic studies on such subjects as urban life among slaves and freedmen, blacks and mulattoes; living and working conditions for mining, plantation, and cowboy slaves; resistance, rebellion, and runaways; manumission and abolition; the lot of the free black and mulatto populations; and the process of assimilation into white society. A useful model for one of these categories is Edgar F. Love's analysis of "Marriage Patterns of Persons of African Descent in a Colonial Mexican City Parish," *Hispanic American Historical Review*, 51 (February 1971), 79–91. One of the most comprehensive studies in this area is Miguel Acosta Saigne's *Vida de los Esclavos Negros en Venezuela* (Caracas: n.p., 1967).

For nineteenth- and twentieth-century Spanish America, the following works contain excellent source material: L. M. Díaz Soler, *Historia de la Esclavitud Negra en Puerto Rico, 1493–1890* (Madrid: Ediciones de la Universidad

de Puerto Rico, 1953); Guillermo Feliu Cruz, *La Aboli-
tión de la Esclavitud en Chile* (Santiago: Ediciones de la
Universidad de Chile, 1942); the studies of Uruguay by
Paulo de Carvalho Neto, especially *El Negro Uruguayano
(Hasta la Abolicion)* (Quito: Editorial Universitaria,
1965); Ildefonso Pereda Valdes, *Negros Esclavos y Negros
Libres* (Montevideo: n.p., 1941); Carlos Martinez Duran
and Daniel Contreras, "La Abolición de la Esclavitud en
Centro-America," *Journal of Inter-American Studies*, 4
(1962), 223–232; the several excellent studies by Sidney
Mintz on Puerto Rico, among them "The Culture History
of a Puerto Rican Sugar Cane Plantation, 1876–1949,"
Hispanic American Historical Review, 33 (1953), 224–
251; Ernesto Posada and Carlos Restrepo Canal, *La
Esclavitud en Colombia: Leyes de Manumisión* (Bogotá:
n.p., 1933); Restrepo Canal, *La Libertad de los Esclavos
en Colombia o Leyes de Manumisión* (Bogota: n.p., 1938);
Julio Tobar Donoso, "La Abolición de la Esclavitud en
el Ecuador," *Boletin de la Academia National de Historia*
(Quito), 39 (1959), 5–30; Ricardo Rodriguez Molas, "Ne-
gros Libres Rioplatenses," *Revista de Humanidades*
(Buenos Aires), 1 (1961), 99–126; John Lombardi,
"Manumission, *Manumismos,* and *Aprendizaje* in Republi-
can Venezuela," *Hispanic American Historical Review*,
49 (November 1969), 656–678, and *The Decline and
Abolition of Negro Slavery in Venezuela, 1820–1854*
(Westport, Conn.: Greenwood Press, 1971); Robert Con-
rad, *The Destruction of Brazilian Slavery* (Berkeley and
Los Angeles: University of California Press, 1972); and
Robert Brent Toplin, *The Abolition of Brazilian Slavery*
(New York: Atheneum, 1972). For Ecuador, Peru, and
Colombia see works by Robert West and, especially, the
numerous excellent books and articles by Norman Whit-
ten, such as *Class, Kinship, and Power in an Ecuadorian
Town: The Negroes of San Lorenzo* (Stanford: Stanford
University Press, 1965), and *Black Frontiersmen: A South
American Case* (New York: Schenkman, 1972).

Many of the best sources on the Spanish Caribbean are

found in Herbert Klein, *Slavery in the Americas* (Chicago: University of Chicago Press, 1967); and in the superb study of Cuba by Franklin Knight (see Selection 9). For a comparative study see Gwendolyn Midlo Hall, *Social Control in Slave Plantation Societies: A Comparison of St. Domingue and Cuba* (Baltimore: Johns Hopkins Press, 1971).

The best major source of information on abolition of the slave trade to Spanish America is Arthur Corwin's *Spain and the Abolition of Slavery in Cuba, 1817–1886* (Austin: University of Texas Press, 1967). A recent analysis of postabolition racial problems in the Spanish Caribbean is found in Franklin J. Franco's *Los Negros, los Mulatos y la Nación Dominicana* (Santo Domingo: Editora Nacional, 1969).

We still possess only two excellent monographs on Brazilian plantation life in the southern regions: Emilia Viotti da Costa, *Da Senzala à Colonìa* (São Paulo: Corpo e Alma do Brasil Difusão Européia do Livro, 1966); and Stanley Stein, *Vassouras: A Brazilian Coffee County, 1850–1900* (Cambridge, Mass.: Harvard University Press, 1957). (See Selection 15 in this book.) The most recent study of Brazilian slaves and freedmen is Peter Eisenberg's *The Sugar Industry of Pernambuco, 1840–1910* (Berkeley and Los Angeles: University of California Press, 1973). Besides the Eisenberg work, no comparable studies of the North and Northeast supplant the numerous impressionistic works, dealing with domestic slavery, by Gilberto Freyre. See, for example, *Masters and Slaves* (New York: Knopf, 1964), and *Mansions and the Shanties* (New York: Knopf, 1963). We have little information about slavery on the cotton and rice plantations in the Maranhão, and studies are negligible for mining and other forms of servitude in Minas Gerais.

Fernando Henrique Cardoso's *Capitalismo e Escravidão no Brasil Meridional: O Negro na Sociedade Escravocrata do Rio Grande do Sul*, no. 8 (São Paulo: Corpo e Alma do Brasil, 1962) discusses the violence and inequities of life in the cattle-raising areas of southern Brazil. Cardoso joined Octavio Ianni in a rigorous case study of color and social mobility in Florianópolis, Brazil, which has been published as *Côr e Mobilidade Social em Florianópolis: Aspectos da Relações Entre Negros e Brancos numa Comunidade do Brasil Meridional* (São Paulo: Brasiliana, 1960). Ianni himself analyzed the southern state of Paraná in *As Metamorphoses do Escravo: Apogeu e Crise da Escravatura do Brasil Meridional*, no. 7 (São Paulo: Corpo e Alma do Brasil, 1962). A major drawback to these studies is that Ianni and Cardoso focused on areas that possessed relatively few slaves and in which African influence had been relatively negligible.

Almost all pre-1966 sources on manumission and the abolition of Brazilian slavery are discussed in Richard Graham, "Causes for the Abolition of Negro Slavery in Brazil: An Interpretive Essay," *Hispanic American Historical Review*, 46 (May 1966), 123–137. Also useful is Leslie Bethell, *The Abolition of the Brazilian Slave Trade* (Cambridge: Cambridge University Press, 1970). Various pathways to freedom are noted in R. K. Kent, "Palmares: An African State in Brazil," *Journal of African History*, 6 (1965), 161–175 (Selection 18 in this book); and Stuart B. Schwartz, "The *Mocambo*: Slave Resistance in Colonial Bahia," *Journal of Social History*, 3 (Summer 1970), 313–333, and sources cited therein. In the same issue appears an analysis of a specific revolt, R. K. Kent's "African Revolt in Bahia: 24–25 January 1835," pp. 161–175. A revisionist analysis is offered in Ann M. Pescatello's *"Prêto Power, Brazilian-Style: Modes of Resistance in the Nineteenth Century,"* in *The African Diaspora: Historical and Anthropological Essays on Black Experiences in the Americas*, ed. Ann M. Pescatello (Pittsburgh: University of Pittsburgh Press, forthcoming). (See Selection 19 in this book.)

Recent studies on the Afro-Brazilian include Robert Conrad's assessment of how custom and economic pressure rendered legislation ineffectual, "The Contraband Slave Trade to Brazil, 1831–1845," *Hispanic American Historical Review*, 49 (November 1969), 617–638. The same issue includes Robert Brent Toplin's case study of Brazilian society in the 1880s, "Upheaval, Violence, and the Abolition of Slavery in Brazil: The Case of São Paulo," pp. 639–655. Complementing Conrad's study is Herbert S. Klein's specific analysis, "The Internal Slave Trade in Nineteenth-Century Brazil: A Study of Slave Importations in Rio de Janeiro in 1852," *Hispanic American Historical Review*, 51 (November 1971), 567–585. Geographer J. H. Galloway examines the persistence of slavery in the North in "The Last Years of Slavery on the Sugar Plantations of Northeastern Brazil," *Hispanic American Historical Review*, 51 (November 1971), 586–605. Peter Eisenberg analyzes modes of employment in "Abolishing Slavery: The Process on Pernambuco's Sugar Plantations," *Hispanic American Historical Review*, 52 (November 1972), 580–597. Robert Brent Toplin examines the reasons why *fazendeiros* were reluctant to exchange their African slaves for African freedmen in "From Slavery to Fettered Freedom: Attitudes Toward the Negro in Brazil," *Luso-Brazilian Review*, 7 (Summer 1970), 3–12. Herbert Klein has focused on the condition of the free-colored class in "The Colored Freedmen in Brazilian Slave Society," *Journal of Social History*, 3 (Fall 1969), 30–52. Also see Robert Conrad's perceptive essay, "Neither Slave Nor Free: The *Emancipados* of Brazil, 1818–1868," *Hispanic American Historical Review*, 53 (February 1973), 50–70.

In the past two decades several excellent anthropological studies have redefined and reexamined the problem of contemporary race relations in rural and urban Brazil. See particularly Charles Wagley, *Race and Class in Rural Brazil* (Paris: UNESCO, 1952); Marvin Harris, *Town and Country in Brazil* (New York: Columbia University Press, 1969); Harry Hutchinson, *Village and Plantation*

Life in Northeastern Brazil (Seattle: University of Washington Press, 1957); and L. A. da Costa Pinto, *O Negro ao Rio de Janeiro* (Rio de Janeiro: Companhia Editoria Nacional, 1953). Frenchmen and Brazilians have provided us with several excellent analytical studies of Brazil's race relations. French sociologist Roger Bastide's studies, for example, *African Civilizations in the New World* (New York: Harper & Row, 1972), those he coauthored with his student Florestan Fernandes, and the works of Oracy Nogueira and Fernandes are gems of insight into Brazilian racial attitudes. See Florestan Fernandes and Roger Bastide, eds., *Relações Racais Entre Negros e Brancos en São Paulo* (São Paulo: Anhembi, 1955).

Among the most authoritative studies of the religious heritage of Africans in Brazil is Pierre Verger's *Notes sur les Cultes des Orisa et Vodun à Bahia, la Baie de Tous les Saints au Brésil et a l'Ancienne Côte des Esclaves en Afrique* (Dakar: IFAN, 1957). For the most recent assessment of religion and the Afro-Latin American, see Roger Bastide's "Afro-American Research in Latin America," *Daedalus* (Spring 1974), 111–123.

For excellent refutations of the Tannenbaum-Elkins thesis, see Marvin Harris, *Patterns of Race in America* (New York: Walker & Co., 1964); Sidney Mintz, "Review of Stanley M. Elkins' *Slavery*," *American Anthropologist,* 63 (June 1961), 579–587; David B. Davis, *The Problem of Slavery in Western Culture* (Ithaca, N.Y.: Cornell University Press, 1969) (see Selection 2); and Carl Degler, *Neither White Nor Black* (New York: Macmillan, 1971). Other recent discussions of merit are contained in the *Journal of Social History* (Summer 1970) and Eugene Genovese and Laura Foner, *Slavery in the New World: A Reader in Comparative History* (Englewood Cliffs, N.J.: Prentice-Hall, 1969).

Some new studies that are methodologically and conceptually useful for the student of the African in Latin America are David W. Cohen and Jack P. Greene's

Neither Slave Nor Free: The Freedmen of African Descent in the Slave Societies of the New World (Baltimore: Johns Hopkins Press, 1972); Robert W. Fogel and Stanley Engerman's superb two-volume cliometric study, *Time on the Cross: The Economics of American Negro Slavery* (Boston: Little, Brown, 1974); and Stanley Engerman and Eugene Genovese's *Race and Slavery in the Western Hemisphere: Quantitative Studies* (Princeton: Princeton University Press, 1974). Also valuable are Robin Winks's *Slavery* (New York: New York University Press, 1972); the sometimes polemical *Slavery and Racism in the Americas*, edited by H. Hoetink (New York: Harper & Row, 1972); the collection of essays entitled "Slavery, Colonialism, and Racism," *Daedalus* (Spring 1974); and Eugene Genovese's *The Slave Economies*, 2 vols. (New York: Wiley, 1973). Genovese's *Roll, Jordan, Roll: The World the Slaves Made* (New York: Pantheon, 1974) is indispensable and may well revolutionize the study of slavery and race relations.

A NOTE ON FILMOGRAPHY AND DISCOGRAPHY

Students and teachers are realizing more and more that the written work is but one of the tools available for analyzing historical events. The rich heritage of Africans, Amerindians, and others is also transmitted through oral tradition and through artifact. Another supplement that can give added dimension to historical study is the audio-visual aid. Most schools, colleges, and universities have some audio-visual materials available. Consonant with my belief that films, records, and tapes deserve a place of reference in any bibliography, I have listed below some suggestions for study.

The Universities of California, Indiana, and Arizona have extensive and inexpensive rental programs for films, as do such well-known companies as Crowell Collier-Macmillan, Audio-Brandon, and Radim. Through them the student can rent films made by the National Educational Television Network (NET), NBC and other commercial networks, theater companies, and the like. Perhaps the most widely known film dealing with the Afro-Latino is *Black Orpheus*, which resets the tragedy of Orpheus and Eurydice in the *favelas* of Brazil. Other films, more specific in nature, that may be useful references include *Shango* and *Yanvallou*, two short pieces about African dances in America, and *Berimbau*, which deals with the importation of an African musical instrument into Brazil. Films on music and art include *African Musicians* and *Under the Black Mask*, both of which deal

with the Congo, Equatorial Africa, and Central Africa.
These might be used in conjunction with Afro-Latino recordings for purposes of tracing cultural continuities.
Another film, this one focusing on Portuguese America
and, in idealistic terms, stressing differences between the
experiences of North and South American blacks, is
Brazil: The Vanishing Negro. All of these films are available through the companies listed earlier.

Also of major importance are the numerous films of
the Brazilian Cinema Nôvo, Latin America's most important cinematic movement. It deals with poverty and social
injustices, focusing on black slums and other Afro-
Brazilian problems. Its films are generally available
through American film distributors.

Films that deal with the black experience are still quite
rare outside of the individual scholar's collection, but recordings are relatively abundant (although admittedly of
varying quality). What follows is a brief survey of selec-
tive recordings of the Afro-Latin American (with occasional mention of guides). Oneyda Alvarenga, directress
of São Paulo's Discoteca Pública Municipal, in 1938
recorded songs and ceremonies of the *Babassûê* rite
(Batuque of St. Barbara) of *Candomblé*. The recording
Babassué, and the 136-page booklet explaining its songs,
can be found in the new audio-visual discography section
of Rio's National Archives. In the United States the songs
are available under the title, *Registors Sonoros de Folclore
Nacional Brasileiro, IV*.

A basic guide to Brazilian music is Luis Heitor Correia
de Azevedo's *Bibliografia Musical Brasileira (1820–1950)*
(Rio de Janeiro: Ministerio da Educação e Saúdé, 1952),
which includes music from outside of Brazil as well.
Azevedo has also provided a commentary, with examples,
of the *Vissungos*, "*Vissungos:* Negro Work Songs of the
Diamond District in Minas Gerais, Brazil," in *Music of
the Americas*, eds. George List and Juan Orrego-Salas
(The Hague: Mouton, 1967).

Melville J. Herskovits and Frances Herskovits have contributed "Drums and Drummers in Afro-Brazilian Cult Life," *Musical Quarterly*, 30 (1944), 477–492; and "Afro-Bahian Religious Songs," album notes on Library of Congress Album XIII, *Folk Music of Brazil*. Melville J. Herskovits and R. A. Waterman wrote "Música de Culto Afrobahiana," *Revista de Estudios Musicales*, 1 (December 1949), 65–127, which also deals with Afro-Bahian cult music.

Ethnic Folkways Records has produced a number of good recordings (usually two sides with notes unless otherwise noted), including *African and Afro-American Drums* (four sides, notes, FP502); Harold Courlander, ed., *Negro Folk Music of Africa and America* (four sides, notes, FE4500); Songs and Dances of Brazil (four sides, notes, FW6953); Norman Whitten, ed., *Afro-Hispanic Music from Western Colombia and Ecuador* (FE4376); *Cult Music of Cuba: Afro-Cuban Cult Music* (FE4410); and *Black Caribs of Honduras: Fiesta and Work Songs of Central America* (FE4435). Supplemental collections are *Drums of Haiti* (FE4403); *Folk Music of Haiti* (FE4407); *Songs and Dances of Haiti* (FE4432); and *Cult Music of Trinidad* (FE4478).

Much music has been recorded in Brazil from such African or African-influenced rites as *Candomblé* (*Candombé* in Spanish America), *Capoeira*, and *Maculele*. The *JS* Company offers *Curso de Capoeira Regional Mestre Bimbo* (two sides, notes, JLP-101). Another good record, issued by Philips, is *Capoeira Angola Mestre Pastinha e Sua Academia* (R765.097L); in addition, several fine records have been produced by Philips for Salvador's folklore academy group, Viva Bahia!: *Viva Bahia! 1* (*Maculelê* and *Puxada da Rêde*, P632.917L); *Viva Bahia! 2* (*Candomblé de Kêto*, one of the types of *Candomblé*, *Samba de Roda*, and *Capoeira*, P632.923L); and songs from each year's Carnival. Philips also distributes a *Coleção Pesquisas da Musica Brasileira*, which includes *Olga de Alakêto Festa no Terreiro/Cantos de Candomblé* (R765.103L) and *Missa do Morro e Cantigas da Boa Terra* (R765.083L). Chantecler, another Brazilian company, offers *Pontos de Terreiro* (CMG-2346), on the religious *Macumba*. In the United States RCA Victor distributes *Saravá Umbanda* (BBL-1387), a recording of another religious ritual.

An excellent series is Documentos Folcloricos Brasileiros. Two of its outstanding records are *Capoeira* (Editora Xaua EX-1.002) and *Candomblé* (Editora Xava, no number). The jacket covers are by Bahia's famous artist Carybé, and the fine recordings are accompanied by extensive notes and detailed photographs. Among United States companies, Nonesuch offers *Black Music of South America* (Colombia, Ecuador, and Brazil) (H-72036).

Ethnomusicologists and folklorists have been contributing increasingly to the recording and filming of Afro-Latin music, lifeways, and rituals. Consult the numerous works of Indiana University's Alan Merriam and George List (and their students) and the University of Illinois's Gerard Behague and Norman Whitten (and their students) for articles, books, records, and films. Two major repositories of audio-visual material, other than the Library of Congress, are the Archives of UCLA's Institute for Ethnomusicology and Indiana University's Archives of Traditional Music. In Europe visit, in particular, the collections of Portugal's Gulbenkian Foundation and France's Musée de l'Homme. My own filmed and taped collection, dealing with the Afro-Brazilian oral tradition and *festas* (fiestas) will soon be available from Florida International University's Media Center, Miami, Florida.

A NOTE ON THE TYPE

The text of this book was set on the Linotype in a face called TIMES ROMAN, designed by Stanley Morison for The Times (London), and first introduced by that newspaper in 1932.

Among typographers and designers of the twentieth century, Stanley Morison has been a strong forming influence, as typographical advisor to the English Monotype Corporation, as a director of two distinguished English publishing houses, and as a writer of sensibility, erudition, and keen practical sense.

Composed by
Cherry Hill Composition,
Pennsauken, N.J.
Printed and bound by
The Colonial Press Inc.,
Clinton, Mass.

BORZOI BOOKS ON LATIN AMERICA

Under the General Editorship of John Womack, Jr.
Harvard University

THE MASTERS AND THE SLAVES (ABRIDGED) *
A STUDY IN THE DEVELOPMENT
OF BRAZILIAN CIVILIZATION
By Gilberto Freyre

DO THE AMERICAS HAVE A COMMON HISTORY?*
A CRITIQUE OF THE BOLTON THEORY
Edited by Lewis Hanke

DICTATORSHIP IN SPANISH AMERICA*
Edited by Hugh M. Hamill, Jr.

THE ORIGINS OF THE LATIN AMERICAN
REVOLUTIONS, 1808–1826*
Edited by R. A. Humphreys *and* John Lynch

BACKGROUND TO REVOLUTION*
THE DEVELOPMENT OF MODERN CUBA
Edited by Robert Freeman Smith

IS THE MEXICAN REVOLUTION DEAD?*
Edited by Stanley R. Ross

FOREIGN INVESTMENT IN LATIN AMERICA*
Edited by Marvin Bernstein

WHY PERON CAME TO POWER*
Edited by Joseph R. Barager

A CENTURY OF BRAZILIAN HISTORY SINCE 1865*
Edited by Richard Graham

REVOLUTION IN MEXICO:
YEARS OF UPHEAVAL, 1910–1940*
Edited by James W. Wilkie *and* Albert L. Michaels

Also available in a hardbound edition